On Course

On Course

A WEEK-BY-WEEK GUIDE
TO YOUR FIRST SEMESTER
OF COLLEGE TEACHING

JAMES M. LANG

HARVARD UNIVERSITY PRESS
CAMBRIDGE, MASSACHUSETTS, AND LONDON, ENGLAND   2008

A Caravan book. For more information, visit *www.caravanbooks.org*

Library of Congress Cataloging-in-Publication Data

Lang, James M.
On course : a week-by-week guide to your first semester of
college teaching / James M. Lang.
    p.   cm.
Includes bibliographical references and index.
ISBN 978-0-674-02806-7 (alk. paper)
1. College teaching—Handbooks, manuals, etc.
2. First year teachers—Handbooks, manuals, etc.
I. Title.

LB2331.L245   2008
378.1´2—dc22   2007043155

Designed by Gwen Nefsky Frankfeldt

Contents

Acknowledgments

Unlike the ideas that redound to our individual credit in academic scholarship, good ideas about teaching seem to circulate much more freely, passed along by word of mouth and observation as much as by research and scholarship. I doubt that I could claim full credit for any technique that I use in the classroom, or that I recommend here. The ideas that came from teachers or researchers who have published books or articles on teaching are credited in the Resources section of each chapter, but in addition, a number of individuals have been extremely helpful in forming my thoughts on teaching over the past dozen years.

First and foremost, the three years I spent working under Ken Bain's tutelage introduced me to excellence in teaching, and convinced me that teaching is a subject worthy of serious study. His ideas and work remain essential to me.

Two colleagues at Assumption College, through hundreds of hallway and office conversations about teaching, have been equally crucial in helping me think about how to translate grand schemes and pedagogical ideas into strategies that work in the classroom, so I am grateful to Rachel Ramsey and Mike Land for a half-dozen great years of conversation, friendship, and advice.

I am equally grateful to another teacher, Matt Robert, for those same three gifts, delivered over many an evening of discussion and music.

Many other people provided me with examples of interesting teaching techniques, or spoke to me about teaching, or gave me information about other fields of study, or inspired me as teachers, and those folks include—but are not limited to—Patty Robert, Lucia Knoles, Owen Sholes, Dave Thoreen, Tony Lang, Peggy Lang, and Maryanne Leone. The members of the Faculty Colloquium Committee at Assumption College, which includes Ann Murphy, Jeanne McNett, Susan Melia, and Kathleen Fisher, were an additional source of information and inspiration. My thanks to all of them.

This book came about partly as a result of my column for *The Chronicle of Higher Education.* I appreciate the *Chronicle*'s continued faith in me as a writer, and the always sharp editing and encouragement of Denise Magner.

Thanks as well to Elizabeth Knoll at Harvard University Press, whose initial interest, and then guidance and timely encouragement, helped bring the project to life.

Of course my favorite teacher for many years now has been Anne, and my favorite students Katie, Madeleine, Jillian, Lucie, and Jack; from them I have learned everything I know that matters.

Preface

Way back at the turn of the millennium, I finished my Ph.D. in English literature in much the same situation as lots of my other fellow Ph.D.'s these days—without the prospect of a tenure-track job in my field. During the time I had been writing my dissertation, though, I had been working part-time at Northwestern University's Searle Center for Teaching Excellence, headed then by the historian Ken Bain. As it happened, the Center had plans to hire a new assistant director around the time I was set to finish my degree, and I was invited to apply. I was very happy to take the job when it was offered to me, and so for the next three years I worked on pedagogical programs for graduate students and new faculty—everything from orientations for new teachers to lecture series on teaching and small discussion groups among folks interested in pedagogy.

As part of my work, I was responsible for familiarizing myself with the research literature on teaching and learning in higher education. The Searle Center had a library of more than a thousand books and articles and videos on this topic, and of course plenty of material was available online as well. I spent some part of almost every day reading or thinking about teaching at the postsecondary level, and many hours each semester listening to lectures or watching instructional videos, observing teachers in the classroom, and talking about teaching with my colleagues at the Center, in graduate school, and on the faculty. I was guided through all of this by Ken Bain, who at that time was working on his book on outstanding teachers in higher education, *What the Best College Teachers Do,* which was published in 2004.

I loved my work, and my interest in teaching came naturally to me—my mother was a teacher, my wife is a teacher, my older brother is a college professor, my sister teaches at the high school level, and my three brothers all married women who have been or still are teachers. If a teaching gene exists, it runs in my family. The irony was that while I was spending so much time reflecting on teaching, and eventually beginning to write about it, I was hardly teaching at all myself. As part of my contract, I was allowed to teach one course a year—but we were on the quarter system, so that meant little more than two months of teaching per year. The more I studied teaching, and counseled others on effective teaching, the more I wanted to take all of those ideas swirling around in my head and test them out in my classes.

After three years at the Searle Center, I left for a tenure-track position in English at a liberal arts college in New England, and boy did I get what I wished for. The teaching load at my college was three courses in the first semester, four in the second—more courses in my first year than I taught in my entire three years at the Center. But I felt prepared and enthusiastic—this was what I had been waiting for, and I was ready to teach.

In my first year, as I recounted in the memoir I wrote about the experience, I found it much more difficult than I had anticipated to jump into such a heavy teaching load. As much as I wanted to revolutionize pedagogy in New England and offer nothing but brilliant and inspiring classes, I found myself mostly just struggling to survive—prepping for several different classes each semester, grading massive amounts of student writing, and getting bowled over by other responsibilities I hadn't anticipated, like advising and office hours and meetings. So while in general the teaching and learning theory I had studied provided a solid foundation for my teaching practices, I also discovered that in the crucible of my first year I had to jettison some of my more extravagant pedagogical ambitions and practice a more modest and realistic teaching plan.

This book came about for three reasons. First, I felt I could offer to new teachers what I would have liked to have in my first year: a modest and realistic approach to teaching, one that has been tested and proven in the classroom as well as being informed by the research on teaching and learning in higher education. My aim in this book isn't to provide a comprehensive overview of teaching and learning theory, or of pedagogical practices, or of anything at all. You will see that I frequently cite such overviews—such as Ken Bain's work, or Wilbert McKeachie's classic *Teaching Tips,* or Barbara Gross Davis's *Tools for Teaching*—but I have targeted this book at teachers who are just embarking on their first pedagogical journeys. As a result, I have limited myself to providing very quick glimpses into the research literature, a handful of concrete strategies in all of the major teaching styles (lecturing, discussion, small group work, and so on), and a review of the issues that I believe will come as a surprise to you in your first year, or that you are most likely to find baffling or disconcerting.

This means, as any experienced teacher or higher education researcher who reads this book will tell you, that I have left out a lot. My focus here will be on helping you to have an effective and satisfying first year of teaching, one that allows you to maintain your sanity and still earns you positive teaching evaluations. I hope this book convinces you that reading and thinking about teaching, as well as practicing it, are worthwhile endeavors. Assuming it does, I have provided lists of references at the end of every chapter that will direct you to further and more comprehensive readings in almost every area of teaching in higher education; and the book concludes with a list of my top ten resources on teaching for college professors. When you are enjoying that first glorious summer after your first year of teaching, pull this book out again and begin exploring some of those references, expanding your horizon of ideas about teaching and reflecting upon your experience.

The second impetus for the book was the inception of "On Course," a monthly column on teaching that I began writing for *The Chronicle of Higher Education* in the summer of 2006. You won't find much overlap between those columns and what you read here, beyond my general teaching philosophy and an occasional description of a great technique or resource. But that column has helped me establish dialogues with faculty members around the country; each new column brings me dozens of e-mails from readers who write to describe interesting or exciting things they are trying in their classrooms, or to inform me about new research and resources in higher education. As a result, though I am only an occasional reader in the literature of higher education these days—I am still teaching those seven courses each year—my own thinking about teaching has been deeply enriched over the past year or two by readers of the column. The relationship between the column and the book also helps explain the fact that I sometimes cite one of my own columns as a resource: I have generally done so because the column describes a technique or idea that I learned about from a reader, and that might not appear anywhere else in print.

Finally, I wanted to provide a specific kind of alternative to many of the overviews and guidebooks about teaching at the college level that are currently available. Most of them are written by senior faculty members whose current positions in deans' offices or faculty development centers have put some distance between themselves and the classroom—or, at the very least, between themselves and the heavy teaching loads that many new faculty members will experience in their first years. That distance, in my opinion, can sometimes skew their perspectives on what actually works and doesn't work in the classroom. Although I am on sabbatical as I write this book, I taught seven classes last year and will do the same next year. Almost everything I recommend here has been tested in the fire, and has helped me survive a relatively heavy teaching load in today's academy—while still allowing me time to write, to perform service responsibilities, and to manage a life with a spouse (who also teaches) and five children. And while I do believe in the value of many of the teaching guidebooks I cite, many of them are written in the sort of objective, abstract, and social science-like prose that can really help cure insomnia. I've tried to make my prose here a little more lively and personal, and to provide specific references to my own experiences as well as different disciplinary examples.

All of this should give you a clear idea of the scope and audience for this book—which includes new faculty on the tenure track, those who are in adjunct positions, and those who are teaching for the first time in their graduate programs. I'll finish with a few words about the book's plan.

The conceit of the book—that each chapter corresponds to a specific week of the semester—is just that: a conceit. Don't take it literally, and expect to read one chapter per week throughout your first semester. You will be best prepared for the semester if you read the book right through at least a month before you begin teaching (among other things, this will give you enough time to think about and plan your syllabus).

But I have tried to stick to the conceit enough that if, during that first semester, you reread the chapter that corresponds to the week in which you find yourself, you will find a fresh idea or perspective on something that you might be facing during that moment in the semester. Donna Killian Duffy and Janet Wright Jones are definitely right when they say, in *Teaching within the Rhythms of the Semester*, that "all classroom experiences are shaped by a rhythm inherent in the progression of a semester, and all professors must work within this time constraint" (35–36). So I expect you will find yourself slumping and exhausted, as we all usually are, around the eleventh week of the semester (give or take a week or two), and thus the Week 11 chapter focuses on how you can revitalize your classroom with experimental teaching techniques. Or you might think it useful to know something about how students learn before the semester starts, but that information will necessarily remain abstract to you until you have been in the classroom for a while. Therefore, I waited to present the information on students as learners until the seventh week of the semester, when you might look back at it and discover some parallels between those ideas and what you've been seeing in your classroom. So you should read the book before you begin teaching, maybe highlighting some techniques or ideas that seem worth trying to you, and then flip back through it as the semester goes along, seeing if you can find timely advice within the chapters.

The resources and references that you will find at the end of each chapter, like the book as a whole, are not meant to be comprehensive. I tried to limit the number of sources to between a half-dozen and a dozen for each chapter, and some of those overlap—especially the comprehensive guidebooks, which I have cited in several different chapters. I also tried to limit the sources I cited to ones that should be easily available in a college or university library, or that are accessible online. So while in the course of my research I occasionally saw interesting article titles in publications like *The Danish Journal for Teaching Archaeology in January,* I mostly restrained myself and stuck to the major journals and publishing houses. The lists of resources in each chapter include any works that I cited or drew an idea from, as well as articles or books that I recommend for further reading on the topic. A brief overview of each reference follows the citation.

I always remain on the lookout for excellent ideas about teaching, so if you come up with something in your first year that really works well, write to me and tell me about it, both so I can try it myself and so that I can share it with readers in my *Chronicle* column or in future editions of this book. I hope you have a great first year of teaching.

Resources

Just so we are all completely clear on this, there is no *Danish Journal for Teaching Archaeology in January.*

The Syllabus

The teaching process starts with the construction of the syllabus, the document that will guide you and your students throughout the course. You'll labor intensely over it, hand it out on the first day, and continue to consult it throughout the semester. And while this may sound like a Zen koan, you begin a syllabus by thinking about the end of the semester.

The syllabus is a required element for most college courses, and an essential tool for helping you stay on track and retain your sanity throughout the semester. It puts the design of the course into concrete form, so syllabus writing really means course planning. The process of drafting the syllabus forces you to think about the learning objectives you want to establish for the students in the course, and those objectives should be formulated by answering a simple question: What should students *know* or *be able to do* as a result of taking this course? Put more broadly, when students walk out of the final exam, or hand you that final paper, in what ways will you have changed them?

This can seem like a daunting question. It's much easier to think about your course according to the coverage model: What material do I need to cover in this course, and in my discipline, between now and the end of the semester? But the coverage model, by which an unfortunate number of college and university faculty still operate, considers only two elements in the teaching process: you (as the coverer) and the course material (the covered).

Raise your hand if you can identify the missing element in the teaching-learning triad.

If your hand is waving wildly, and you're dying to shout "Students, students!" you are ready to begin writing your syllabus. The coverage model constructs teaching as a performative act that involves pulling material out of your head and throwing it on the desks of your students; their job is to figure out the best way to lap it up and hold it down. The model you *should* follow in planning your course, and writing your syllabus, entails your thinking first and foremost about what knowledge or skills students should learn in your course, and then thinking about the best ways for them to learn that knowledge or those skills. This may seem like a subtle shift, but it's an essential one—it views teaching through the lens of learning, rather than focusing on teaching and letting the students learn as they can.

The course plan, and the syllabus, need to focus on the students. If you have designed a course which could theoretically be taught to an empty room of iPod recorders, without any real change in your course plan, you probably need to head back to the drawing board.

Just about every chapter you'll read in this book will address the importance of focusing on students and their learning, so I'll stop lecturing you at this point and begin letting the practical advice about syllabus construction enact this learning-centered pedagogical model. The rest of the chapter is organized around the elements that a syllabus should contain, with a discussion of the parts that require some decision-making or that might not occur to you on your first trip through the syllabus grinder. The following chapter, on the first days of the semester, will include some suggestions for ways to introduce the syllabus to your students.

Course Title, Time, and Location

If you need too much advice in this area, you might want to reconsider your career as a college professor. I will note that the room location and times of the course are worth including; in the first week or two of the semester I frequently have to glance at my syllabus, as I'm rushing across campus and spilling hot tea on myself, to remind myself what room I'm teaching in. Your students may be doing the same thing, so it's helpful for everyone to have that information at the front of the syllabus.

Contact Information

Provide your office number and your office hours (check with your department chair, if you don't know already, on how many office hours you are expected to hold per week; most colleges have a stated policy on this), as well as the best methods for reaching you outside of class. If you have a strong preference for either e-mail or the phone, give them that information.

The only sticky question here is whether to give students your home (or cell) telephone number. It is not at all necessary, since it's doubtful that any student will have such an emergency with the subjunctive mood in Spanish that they will need to interrupt you on a Friday evening. So if you're uncomfortable with the idea of students contacting you outside of the official channels of teacher-student communication (the classroom, office hours, office phone, and your school e-mail account), leave it off.

I know of only one good reason to include it, and it's the reason I have been putting it on my syllabus for the past six years. Offering on your syllabus your home or cell phone number can be a symbolic gesture that demonstrates to the students your eagerness to help them learn (as in: call me anytime you want to talk about *Beowulf,* kids; I'm always up for it). The gesture is small, but in the long and complicated relationship that you are trying to forge with your students, even the small things can help. And while students vary from campus to campus in their willingness to seek help from their professors outside of normal channels, I would estimate that during the six years of full-time teaching in which I have been putting my home phone number on the syllabus, I haven't received more than ten calls.

Course Description

Real thinking about the course begins here, at the front of your syllabus, the first place that should capture students' interest in the course. The course description should fit within the space of a paragraph or two, no more than half a page, and should function like an abstract for a scholarly article. It should provide a brief overview of the main elements of the course: the subject matter, the course promises, and the major assignments the students will complete.

I would argue, though, that the best course descriptions contain something more—an explanation of why the knowledge and skills you are offering to your students *matter:* how will their fifteen weeks with you and this material make them into a better student, a better citizen, or a better human being? Will they be better equipped with skills they will need for their other courses (writing, speaking, calculating, theorizing, and so forth)? Or better equipped to read and understand the daily news? Or more capable of making informed ethical decisions?

One means of helping students to see the importance of the course topic can be to frame the course as a whole with what a colleague of mine (Lucia Knoles, whom you will meet more formally in the second chapter) calls a "meta-question": a broad and important question which the content of the course will help them understand more deeply, and which ultimately will enable them to construct their own answer by the end of the term. My colleague teaches American literature and history, and her meta-question is a simple one: "What is an American?" Every book or essay they read during the semester, every work of art they consider or song they hear—all of them provide another bit of information or perspective to help students answer this question. By the end of the semester, the students are prepared to offer their own definitions of what it means to be an American. If you can identify a meta-question that will help you frame the course, the description is the place to ask that question and to help the students understand why it matters.

This section of the course description may sound a bit like a sales pitch, which is just fine. You want to convince them that they should take this course because it will be wonderful, not just because they have to fulfill a requirement. The course description offers you the first opportunity to make that case.

Course Promises

You won't see a section on the promises of the course on every syllabus you read, but the idea of the promises that you make to students has always struck me as an excellent way to entice them into the learning process. I am borrowing the idea of a "promising syllabus" from Ken Bain, who claims that the syllabi that he studied from outstanding teachers in higher education—though every one of them may not have used the exact same language—

all described in some way a series of promises that the course made to their students.

Promises can appear under different names—learning goals, learning objectives, course objectives, and so on—but the idea is that you are explaining to students what they will know and be able to do as a result of taking your course. Duffy and Jones make a distinction between "objectives" as measurable outcomes while "goals" are more impressionistic, hopeful outcomes (79–80)—but I'm not convinced that this distinction is important, so I am using the terms interchangeably here. Again, tune the language of this part of the syllabus to the frequency of student learning, rather than the language of material coverage. You should not promise, in other words, something like this:

- This course will review the history of western civilization from 1500 to the present, considering the historical forces that have shaped our contemporary American culture.

Promise this instead:

- Students will develop a rich understanding of western civilization from 1500 to the present, and will be able to analyze and discuss contemporary American culture in light of the historical forces that have helped to shape it.

Better still would be a set of more closely defined objectives that identify a handful of specific forces that you want them to understand.

Assuming that you can get this language down, and phrase your learning objectives as promises to your students, what kinds of promises should you be making to them? The literature on learning objectives in higher education, or the sorts of promises you can make to your students, is vast and ever-growing, so I'm going to jump backwards in time over most of it and return to a source that still carries weight in higher education today (although its widest influence has been in elementary and high school education): Benjamin Bloom's *Taxonomy of Educational Objectives,* written in 1956. In this book Bloom described a hierarchy of learning objectives that apply to all levels of schooling, including postsecondary education. Bloom's work has been revised and updated and argued about over the intervening half a century; one recent contributor to this discussion is Norman Gronlund, whose *Writing Instructional Objectives for Teaching and Assessment* is now in its seventh edition. But you can find Bloom's taxonomy easily enough by typing that phrase into any search engine; you'll come back with lots of hits, all of which will list and define the six broad cognitive skills that Bloom identified: knowledge, comprehension, application, analysis, synthesis, and evaluation. They ascend in difficulty, with the first levels serving as building blocks for future ones. So knowledge, for example, is required for comprehension, which encompasses both the ability to recall learned material and an awareness of its meaning and significance. Evaluation, or the ability to use criteria to make judgments of value, requires some development in all of the previous five categories.

How this translates practically into learning objectives for your syllabus requires thinking another step ahead. A useful article that makes use of both Bloom's and Gronlund's work in the context of higher education appeared in 2003 in the *Journal of Management Education;* it lists kinds of evidence that could be used to demonstrate a student's successful mastery of any of Bloom's categories. These examples of evidence coincide nicely with kinds of assignments you might give to your students, and with learning objectives you might list on your syllabus:

Knowledge: "definition, outlines, recall exercises and requests to reproduce knowledge acquisition";

Comprehension: "comparison and contrast, paraphrasing, extension, and summary";

Application: "classification, development, modification, organization, and prediction";

Analysis: "breaking down, categorizing, classifying, differentiating";

Synthesis: "creative behaviors such as development of a research proposal or a scheme for classifying information, and the creation of new patterns or structures";

Evaluation: "assessments, critiques, and evaluations" (536).

So, for example, you might promise students that they will leave your course with the ability to paraphrase a complex article in your field, which both describes a learning objective (under the category of comprehension) and sets in place one or more of your assignments for the semester.

Of course, you will want to push your learning objectives as far as you can toward the highest cognitive levels of the list; you certainly want to move beyond simply asking students to memorize definitions or engage in other activities that just test their ability to memorize the facts and formulas of your discipline. Much of the specific knowledge that we have to offer to students will be of limited value to them in their careers (or will be out of date by the time they get into their careers), especially in the kinds of introductory courses you are likely to teach in the first part of your career, when many of your students will not be majors in your discipline. So you should think hard about what kinds of intellectual skills you are offering to your students. Aside from whatever knowledge you want students to take away from your course, what skills—such as synthesis, analysis, or evaluation—can you promise that you will at least help them develop or hone in their fifteen weeks with you? Knowledge of a particular chemical formula, while necessary to pass your course, might not prove of much use to an eventual accountant; but that accountant's ability to evaluate the competing claims of two scientists on the reality of global warming will certainly affect decisions she makes as a citizen in a democracy and as a consumer.

Once you have identified both the knowledge and the intellectual skills that students will develop in your course, sketch them out in general terms on a piece of paper; then write them more specifically in relation to the knowledge base and terminology of your discipline; and finally, formulate them as the promises of your course. If you have framed the course with a meta-question, you will want to make sure to promise that you will help them answer the meta-question by the end of the semester.

Student Responsibilities/Course Policies

Of course, your promises to the students are premised on the assumption that they will make a good-faith effort to learn in the course. So the promises section of the course has to be balanced with a section outlining the responsibilities the students have in order to help you fulfill your promises to them. Many syllabi list what I am calling responsibilities here under a section called "policies," though I think the word "responsibilities" provides a nice complement to "promises."

In this section of the syllabus, outline all the expectations you have for students in terms of their behavior and work habits in the course (assignments and grading will be addressed in the next section). The three major issues that most syllabi address in this section are attendance, late work policies, and classroom behaviors. In all of these areas, keep in mind that there are no right answers. Talk to five different teachers, or read five different articles on these subjects, and you will hear five different opinions. Formulate these policies according to your personality and your developing teaching style.

On attendance, first, you have to decide whether you will take it and, if you do, how you will respond to students who do not attend. Eventually, after your first year or two of teaching, you will sort yourself into the kind of person who requires attendance or who doesn't; for now, here's a simple guideline. If you are teaching a class with twenty students or fewer, and will be teaching mostly through discussion, group work, and other interactive exercises, you should require attendance. Those kinds of activities depend upon students being in the classroom, and you will find attendance easy enough to take, after the first few weeks, by scanning seats or by checking names off when you collect or pass back work. Establish consequences for those who do not attend—some adjustment to the final grade for the course—though you should allow students an absence or two without penalty for emergencies that might arise.

If you are teaching a larger class, and are planning to rely more on lectures than discussion, you should still emphasize the importance of attending class, but you might also find that trying to keep track of attendance and calculate it into everyone's grades can be a tremendous time sink. I would hold off on requiring it for larger classes, at least in your first semester, and hang on until you've been through a few semesters before you decide what kind of attendance policies you want to set in your courses.

How you will handle late work—and you will get late work, I promise—is an equally open question. I know teachers who say that as long as the students do the work, they don't care when it comes in; I know others (including myself) who believe that students who turn in work late might be spending time on material we covered weeks ago, and not paying enough attention to the material we are covering now—and so we penalize or simply don't accept late work. I'll return to this topic in more detail in Chapter 6, so I'll stick with general advice for the moment. If you feel confident enough to set a firm policy on late work before you start teaching, set it and note it in your syllabus here; if not, use a generic phrase like "All assignments must be submitted in class on the due dates," and then handle late work on a case-by-case basis.

Finally, you should note on your syllabus any expectations you have about classroom behaviors, both positive and negative. If you expect students to participate in every class, say so—and say why it's important for them to do so (see the explanation on my sample syllabus in Appendix A). If you want them to take notes on your lectures, say so. If you think steam will come out of your ears if you hear a cell phone go off in class, then let them know that all cell phones must be turned off. Focus on the main behaviors that you want to encourage and discourage—don't legislate every possible behavior you can imagine in the classroom, or they may feel as if they are being treated like schoolchildren.

On the other hand, if you have pet peeves that you know may influence your attitude toward a student, or your grading of him, you owe it to the students to give them fair warning about those pet peeves on the syllabus. If nothing makes you more angry than people wearing red shirts before 10:00 in the morning, make sure you address that specifically.

Evaluation

There are no right answers or easily formulas here, either—and lots of decisions to make. Begin with the simplest and most important one—will the students' major graded assignments be timed examinations, take-home exams, papers, oral presentations, or some other product? You had four years of college yourself, and you'll undoubtedly speak with colleagues about their courses and assignments, so that will give you some ideas about the options available to you. You also probably have some idea about what constitutes a reasonable student workload in your discipline (if not, run the number and nature of your planned assignments by your department chair, and ask for her opinion).

Make your decisions here by looking back at your promises— don't just give three timed exams because that's what you think everyone else does, or assign a major research paper because that's what you had to do as an undergraduate. Look at each of the objectives you have established for the course, and then devise assignments that will let you know whether the students have achieved that objective.

Let's say you are teaching a media studies course, and you promise students that you will provide them with a vocabulary of terms to help them analyze the commercials they see on television outside of class. You have embedded two assignments in that promise: they need to have the knowledge of a set of media analysis tools, and they need to be able to use those terms to analyze a commercial they have never seen before. A two-part exam would fit the bill here: part one asks them to write definitions for the major terms of the course, and in part two you show them a commercial they have never seen before and ask them to provide a written analysis of it using the terms they have just defined.

An exam which asked these students to recite or remember analyses of videos you have already reviewed in class would not fulfill that objective; neither would a major research paper on the history of a particular film technique. You might of course have other objectives that such assignments would fulfill, but the key point here is that you should assign nothing that does not help them fulfill one of your course promises. If you have established a solid set of promises, and offered the students more than simply the drilling of content in your discipline, you will still have a wide enough variety of choices in the assignments you can give to them. Don't limit yourself to what you know from your undergraduate experiences and what you see your colleagues doing; be creative, and find different ways to help them demonstrate to you that they have learned what you have asked of them. Think about how your discipline's content and skills might be useful to them even after graduation, and design an assignment that will help show them that—have them design a website for a famous historical figure or event, or analyze newspaper stories about global warming, or collaborate on business memos about an ethics breach, or write letters to the editor addressing a political crisis, or give a report to shareholders about a new product, or provide annotations to a poem. You don't need to reinvent the nature of student work in higher education, but one creative assignment like this in your first semester can make a big difference in students' perceptions of your course (and, therefore, in your student evaluations).

Once you have settled on the major assignments, you will have to make decisions about the extent to which smaller assignments—quizzes, homeworks, lab reports—factor into the student grades. Until you have a firm grasp on the campus culture where you are teaching, I would recommend including some level of weekly assignment that will ensure that students are keeping up with the assigned reading, and that will help you to gauge their understanding of that reading. Such assignments will benefit the students by requiring them to stay on top of the assigned work for the course; they will benefit you by letting you know whether students are doing the work, and whether they are having problems in any specific areas. This does not necessarily mean daily quizzing, though that certainly is an option. A weekly quiz, as long as students don't know the day on which the quiz will be held, can serve the same purpose while requiring less grading from you.

A better option, one that should work in most disciplines, may be to give weekly writing exercises. A substantial amount of research has been done to demonstrate a link between writing and understanding—in other words, when you ask students to write out responses to a question or explanations of an issue or problem, it increases their understanding and retention of that issue (see Sorcinelli and Elbow in the "Resources" section at the end of the chapter). So one easy method to take advantage of this connection, and to ensure that students are keeping up with the work, is to take ten minutes at the beginning of one class per week and pose a thought question about that day's or week's reading; ask the students to write a paragraph or two in response to it, making sure they refer very specifically to the assigned work in their answers (see Chapter 4 for specific examples of these kinds of thought questions).

Grading such exercises does not have to represent a major time commitment. Instead of writing copious responses to each student, display a few sample responses on an overhead or a PowerPoint the first time you give the writing exercises back, and explain carefully what makes for a good response. Once you have done that, you can respond to the exercises with just a grade, and with a spoken explanation at the beginning of each class. Make the exercises count for something, but not much—in my classes, each writing exercise counts for 1 percent of the final grade.

This leads to the final issue to consider in grading, and in your syllabus—points, letter, or some combination of both? Chapter 6 offers a more detailed discussion of this issue and presents two different systems for you to consider, so I'll hold off on this question until then. But whatever system you decide upon, spell it out in this section of the syllabus.

Academic Honesty

Your institution or department may have a specific statement about academic honesty that you must include on your syllabus, so check with your department chair on that. The undergraduate handbook or catalog may also have a statement that all the students will have seen or heard at orientation, so another option would be to cite that statement to them on the syllabus. But even when such statements are mandated, the decision about how to handle various kinds of academic dishonesty—cheating on a test, plagiarizing, students turning in identical work—will likely be left to you.

That there will be consequences to academic dishonesty deserves a mention on your syllabus, since it allows you to explain to them what would constitute academic dishonesty in your course (and that can vary on such things as the acceptability of students doing homework together, for example).

As for identifying the consequences of academic dishonesty, experience has taught me to be firm and threatening, but not so specific that you are locked into the same policy for every case. An easy way to do this is to borrow the kind of "weasel" language that deals with crimes in our legal system: "Plagiarism may be punished by failure of the assignment or the course," or "Consequences for plagiarism can include zero points for the assignment, failure of the course, or expulsion from the college." These kinds of statements convey the seriousness of the issue but still give you some flexibility in determining the right response to a specific case. Much more on this topic can be found in Chapter 9, where I make specific recommendations on setting policies and handling breaches.

ADA Statement

Many schools also now require that the syllabus contain a statement that the institution and instructor will offer additional assistance to students with conditions that fall under the Americans with Disabilities Act. If your institution doesn't mandate such a statement, it is worth crafting a simple statement of your own indicating that students with special medical conditions or learning disabilities should come and speak with you about how you can ensure that their needs are accommodated in and out of the classroom in your course. Such a statement sends a positive message to the students about your ethos as a teacher, and of course it's also the right thing to do.

Schedule

My syllabi conclude with a detailed schedule that presents the readings, assignments, and topic of every class period throughout the semester; however, I have colleagues whose course schedules simply break the semester up into three or four big topic areas, give those areas a one-word title, and roughly correlate them with the weeks of the semester. The advantage of having a detailed schedule from the start is that it requires less thinking from me during the semester—I just have to check my syllabus to know what's coming on a particular day, as opposed to sitting down and doing course planning in the middle of the semester. The disadvantage is that the course never proceeds exactly as you hope it will, so in about half of my courses, I have to issue an updated course schedule at some point in the semester, with a new listing of assignments and due dates.

Keep in mind that the students—and you yourself—will be juggling multiple courses, as well as their extracurricular commitments and perhaps jobs and crises in their personal lives, so it seems only fair to inform them from the start about the due dates for the major course assignments or exams. It's also a good idea to minimize the amount of course planning you have to do while you're trying to keep your kayak afloat in the midst of the raging river of the semester. You'll have more time now, before the semester begins, to do the work of breaking the semester down into topics and texts on a weekly basis than you will in the midst of it.

But you do want to allow yourself some room to make adjustments on the fly, so a useful way to proceed with that first semester course schedule is just to provide fifteen weekly headings, listing the topics and texts to be covered in that week, and including the exam days and due dates for major assignments. Fill in the readings and other details as you go, and be prepared for the fact that you may have to send around a schedule update at some point. Don't stick to the syllabus schedule just because it's in print, if you think a modification midway through the semester will make for a better course.

The subject of teaching with technology, and of putting courses online, begins in the second-week chapter, but I should note here that having your course available online—either as its own website, or in a Blackboard-style environment—enables you to make the syllabus an interactive document that can lead the students wherever they need to be on a particular day. An online syllabus might have links to assignment sheets, to study questions, to events that you are encouraging students to attend, and to material on the Internet that you want them to see. If you keep a detailed schedule in your online syllabus, it will be much easier to make revisions to that schedule when your plans or due dates or assignments need adjustment in midstream. Even if you decide not to run a very technologically sophisticated course—which is a perfectly fine decision—it might be worthwhile to construct an interactive, online syllabus that contains the most up-to-date course schedule and serves as the official repository of the course's documents. Most institutions will have a virtual learning environment program (such as Blackboard) that enables you to do this very easily.

Finally, take a small step to help keep the chaos of your first semester at bay—something that I saw a colleague doing in her office and immediately adopted a few years ago. Wherever you do most of your school work—whether it's in your first office as a faculty member, or a shared office with other graduate students, or a corner of your basement—take the schedule sections of your syllabi (and you can annotate them as you go, filling in the details as you figure them out) and tape them to the wall, right next to each other. That way when you're trying to avoid grading papers or are finally finished watching that YouTube video someone e-mailed you and you are ready to start working, you'll be able to glance over and see exactly what you have coming from and for the students, and you can think more carefully and in advance about how to schedule your own time and work sessions throughout the semester.

Resources

Athanassiou, N., Jeanne McNett, and Carol Harvey. "Bloom's Taxonomy as a Learning Tool." *Journal of Management Education,* 47.5 (2003): 533–555.

This use of Bloom's taxonomy, unlike many sources you'll see on it, specifically applies to college and university teaching.

Bain, Ken. *What the Best College Teachers Do.* Cambridge, Mass.: Harvard University Press, 2004.
See pp. 74–75 for Bain's descriptions of the promising syllabus.

Bloom, Benjamin. *Taxonomy of Educational Objectives, Handbook I: Cognitive Domain.* New York: Addison-Wesley, 1956.
You'll find an edition of Bloom's book somewhere in your institution's library (perhaps even in your public library), sometimes in its original form, sometimes revised by later editors. The revised versions that I have seen have been aimed at K–12 teachers, so I think you're best off just heading back to the original work. But subsequent editions will probably be fine as well.

Duffy, Donna Killian, and Janet Wright Jones. "Stalking the Superior Syllabus." In *Teaching within the Rhythms of the Semester,* 55–119. San Francisco: Jossey-Bass, 1995.
Duffy and Jones offer a very full analysis of how differently students can react to a syllabus, and use that analysis to argue for what they call an "enriched" syllabus—a monster of a document, size-wise, but one that contains features I don't include here, and are worth thinking further about. For example, they advocate leaving numbered blank spaces on the syllabus for students to write *their* learning objectives for the course (84), which would make for a great opening-day activity that you might add to the list of possible opening-day techniques you'll find in the next chapter.

Gronlund, Norman E. *Writing Instructional Objectives for Teaching and Assessment,* 7th ed. Englewood Cliffs, N.J.: Prentice Hall, 2003.
Like some of the revisions you'll find of Bloom's work, this one

is aimed mostly at K–12 teachers. Still, the language of writing learning objectives will cross the boundaries into syllabus construction, so it might be worth a look.

Lang, James. "The Promising Syllabus." *The Chronicle of Higher Education,* 53.2 (September 1, 2006): C2.

This column on the syllabus includes additional thoughts from Ken Bain on the promising syllabus, which came from an interview I conducted with him on the topic.

Sorcinelli, Mary Deane, and Peter Elbow, eds. *Writing to Learn: Strategies for Assigning and Responding to Writing Across the Disciplines. New Directions for Teaching and Learning,* 69 (Spring 1997).

This issue of *New Directions for Teaching and Learning* contains a dozen essays on the use of writing in the college classroom, all of which are grounded firmly in research on writing and learning. It's an excellent starting point if you are interested in pursuing that research further, and it also describes some great practical strategies.

First Days of Class

I walked into my very first college course as a teacher three weeks before my twenty-second birthday, in late August of 1991, the first week of my first year of graduate school. It was English composition, 8:30 A.M., and I had seven students enrolled. Concerned about the fact that I was probably only three years older than the students I would find in the class, I decided to forget about trying to impress them with my authority, and to try instead to seem like one of them—so I was wearing sandals, a pair of navy-blue khakis that I had cut raggedly into shorts, and a white T-shirt. I was nervous, so I kept it short. I gave them the syllabus and the first assignment sheet for the course, read through both documents, and then let the students go.

I'm willing to shoulder only part of the blame for all of the bad decisions I've just described (if you think you can identify all of them, put your name and address on a postcard, send it to me, and you'll be eligible for a drawing for a free lunch). Like the other new graduate student instructors that year, I had spent a day or two at a teaching orientation sponsored by the university, and I was enrolled in a graduate course called "Teaching Writing" that would meet weekly throughout the semester (though it hadn't met yet). Despite these kindly (but flimsy) efforts by the university, I was massively underprepared for a very complex task—helping eighteen-year-old students learn to read, think, and write well enough to prepare them for success in college and life beyond.

My lack-of-training story is a familiar one in academic autobiographies, as Elaine Showalter points out in *Teaching Literature* (4–9), common to most of us who have been teaching for a half-dozen to a dozen years or more now. But times have changed, and few teachers will enter their first classroom with such a tiny amount of advance help and advice. Your commitment to reading this book, if you do nothing else, still puts you ahead of where I was on that first day. But more likely than not, you have already taken a graduate course on teaching, or you have spent time serving as a teaching assistant, or you have been through a more extensive orientation or training program than the one I experienced.

However much of this you have under your belt, I can promise you this: you will be nervous, and you will be glad when that first class is over. That's not necessarily a bad thing—nervousness produces an energy that you can channel into your opening day presentation, and no nerves whatsoever would probably mean that you aren't taking the job seriously enough. Showalter cites a colleague who offers an excellent description of this dynamic: "Of course you are scared of going into a classroom and performing in public. Who isn't? But that's where your energy will come from. Reinterpret your reluctance to perform as a desire to perform" (17). So accept the fact that you will be nervous, prepare for it if nerves produce physical symptoms for you—for instance, have a bottle of water for dehydration, or a handkerchief for sweaty palms—and rest assured that once you get into the room, that first class will fly by.

But while you're eagerly anticipating that opening day, you need to consider a handful of issues, and plan your course of action for that first day. I'll address below a few decisions you'll need to make before you step into the classroom, and then consider your pedagogical options for the first day of the semester.

What (Not) to Wear

Let's begin very specifically: don't wear navy-blue khaki cutoffs, sandals, and a white T-shirt. Moving to a more general level, don't wear the kinds of casual or unkempt outfits that you believe the students will think are cool, for two main reasons: you're not a student, and in any case you're probably wrong about what the students will think is cool.

The question of the kind of relationship you want to forge with your students, and what kind of teaching persona you want to construct, is a complex one. I will address it more fully in Chapter 15. But I will anticipate the ending here and say that the one relationship you should not imagine yourself having with your students is that of a friend or peer. However close you are to your student days yourself, you are now in a position of authority over the students in your class. You should certainly want them to feel comfortable with you, and to speak to you openly and honestly about their ideas and their lives, but keep in mind that you have control over their grades, and those grades, rightly or wrongly, can impact their lives in all kinds of significant ways—determining whether or not they maintain scholarships, are accepted into graduate or professional schools, and are offered the jobs they want. Trying to assume the role of a friend in their lives—either by your dress, or your interactions with them outside of the classroom, or your correspondence with them—is a disingenuous pose that obfuscates the nature of the real authority you have in their academic lives.

So, what should you wear? Styles change, and I don't follow fashion trends very closely, so I won't be too specific here. But wear attire that seems professional, and that helps to establish a boundary between you and the students (who will all mostly be wearing shorts, jeans, and various articles from Abercrombie and Fitch). Men will always be safe wearing long pants and a shirt with a collar; women can of course be safe wearing the same thing, though women will have more varied options for boundary-establishing dress. A great resource for the more complicated world of women's fashion in higher education is Emily Toth's *Ms. Mentor* guide, listed in the reference section of this chapter (you can also find some of her fashion advice online in the free archives of her column for *The Chronicle of Higher Education*).

But don't obsess about it. If you're really flummoxed about what to wear, then throw on the outfit you wore when you interviewed for the teaching position you now have, and for the first day or two of classes just see what everyone else is wearing.

Follow suit.

Free Day or Full Day?

Mistake number two, on my legendary opening day, was doing twenty minutes of syllabus reading and letting the students go early. Unfortunately, you will find that some of your colleagues treat the first day of class as a half-day, the only purpose of which is to pass out the syllabus and take questions (and there are almost never any questions). I see little harm in making a slight concession to this custom, and letting the class out five or ten or fifteen minutes early (depending upon the length of the session), but to offer no substantive pedagogy on the first day of the course is a mistake.

Much of what we do in the classroom has symbolic value on top of whatever face value it might have. So lecturing for an entire semester without allowing students any opportunity to speak sends the message that you have no interest in what they have to say; dressing in khaki cutoffs sends (or tries to send) the message that you're no different from the students; leaving your cell phone in view on your desk during class signals that cell phones are acceptable in class.

Opening the semester by introducing the students to the course topic or material in a substantive way sends the message that you are excited and eager to help the students learn in this course, and that the time they invest in coming to class matters. Not engaging with the course topic or material on the first day, by contrast, sends a message that the course meetings are a requirement that you both would rather not fulfill: you'll meet when you have to, but at every opportunity to cut things short (first and last days, or days before a break), you're as eager to avoid seeing them as they are to avoid seeing you.

Engaging with the course material on the first day does not mean delivering a full lecture—that seems to me as poor an idea as ending class early. Indeed, a research study by Perlman and McCann on teaching strategies that were most and least effective on the first day of class, published in the journal *Teaching of Psychology,* suggests that delivering a full session's worth of information on the first day proved counterproductive for many students, and turned them off to the course (278). Remember that students are usually beginning five new courses this first week, so offering too much information on that first day may prove a waste of time, since the students may be too overwhelmed to absorb it. Still, even within the limits of a (slightly) shortened class, you can easily make use of a few simple but substantive teaching techniques to introduce the course, pique the students' interest, and start the semester off right.

Adding and Dropping

Experienced faculty might reject the argument above for a reason that you will quickly become familiar with yourself—namely, that the first week of classes at most colleges and universities is add/drop week, meaning that students have the opportunity to make changes to their schedule through the first week of the semester, adding courses that might have opened up over break and dropping courses that no longer fit in their schedule. Some schools have developed a culture which views the first week almost as an opportunity for students to window-shop in various courses, visiting multiple classes which might be competing for the same slot in their schedule, and eventually picking the one with the best professor, or the right workload, or even just the most convenient times and days. Since a sizable percentage of students who attend the first day might not be here in a week, faculty members might wonder, why spend a lot of time planning for that first day?

Add/drop week is a necessary evil, since students will always have to deal with possible last-minute schedule changes in extracurricular activities, work commitments outside of school, internships, or other obligations. But reducing the first day of the semester to the equivalent of sticking your syllabus in the shop window, hoping to attract customers, helps to make this necessary evil into a regular feature of the campus culture. Although it may seem to stretch on endlessly to you now, the fifteen weeks of the semester will fly by, and you'll find yourself struggling to

accomplish all of the objectives you set for yourself in your syllabus. Don't sacrifice course time lightly; make the first day an important part of your course.

What should you do about adding and dropping students? You
don't have to do anything about students who drop, of course,
except be grateful about the fact that you now have one less set
of exams or papers to grade this semester.

Adding students presents a bit more of a challenge. In every
class that follows the first one in add/drop week, make a quick
announcement at the beginning of class that students who did
not attend on the first day should stop and see you after the class.
Hand them a syllabus, ask them to review it and e-mail questions
to you or bring them to the next class, and—most important—explain that they bear the full responsibility for material or assignments that were covered on days they have missed. If they can
get that information from a fellow student, fine; if not, point out
your office hours and ask them to come and see you so that you
can review for them what they have missed. Because you will be
sure to have a student or two in this situation, you might consider making your opening-day lecture or exercise available in
paper form, or posting it to the course website, so that you can
save yourself some time that first week by sending them away
from their visit to your office with a handout or worksheet or a
website address.

What to Do: Teaching the First Class

Whatever you decide to do on the first day, you should ensure
that you cover three bases: present the syllabus to the students;
introduce the course topic and/or some initial material; and require at least some students to participate.

This last point may be the most important one. Determining how students can participate in the course, and can make their voices heard in and outside of the classroom, should factor into every decision you make in your pedagogy, including decisions you make about the first day of the semester.

Symbolism plays a role here as well. Inviting—and perhaps requiring—students to participate in the first class of the semester sends the signal that students in this course will not be able to sit back and coast through the semester. They are expected to be in class, to be prepared, and to participate in every session. Here are a few specific techniques that can help you accomplish these objectives for your first day of the semester.

SYLLABUS REVIEW

For most classes I have taught, this part of the first day has consisted of my standing in front of the classroom and reading the syllabus aloud, which I have traditionally done for two reasons. The first one might be construed as vaguely legalistic: I want to be sure that everyone has heard the student responsibilities in the course and the policies on academic honesty, so that when I have to deal with problems in these areas, no student can claim ignorance of them. The second reason is that the reading-aloud exercise allows me to elaborate on various aspects of the syllabus that are worth noting, and might be skipped over if the students are just skimming through it to check for the workload and due dates.

Reading the syllabus aloud will certainly suffice to introduce them to the course, and I don't see anything wrong with it—as long as you are engaging the students more actively during some other segment of that first day. But, truth be told, both you and they will probably find it among the most boring moments of the semester; imagine if your department chair gave you the faculty policy document, and then sat across from you at a table and read it out loud to you. How boring and annoying would that be?

When I wrote a column for *The Chronicle of Higher Education* in the fall of 2006 about the boredom of the syllabus read-aloud, I received many e-mails from faculty members who had devised more interesting ways of introducing the students to the syllabus. The best idea came from Michael Gennert, a computer scientist who described his opening class in this way:

> I usually hand out a course description sheet that includes what the course covers, the required background, instructor and TA office hours, labs, homework and project expectations, exam dates, grading policy, and honesty policy. Then I tell students to find a partner—and wait for them to do so, because someone is going to want to be a loner—and ask them to work together to find 3 questions they want to know about the course that aren't on the sheet. Then I ask for, and try to answer, their questions. (Lang, C1)

The benefits, Gennert explains, are multiple: "They're awake, working collaboratively, taking responsibility for asking something, talking to each other and me, and engaged." All these qualities, of course, are ones you want to see in students throughout the semester, and Gennert's technique does an excellent job, it seems to me, of establishing the culture of participation that you should work for in your course, and begin with on your first day.

I would suggest only one small modification to this technique—namely, that the students can ask three questions either about what's not on the syllabus, or about what *is* on the syllabus. Although we might imagine our syllabus prose to be crystal-clear and in no need of elaboration or explanation, our students might not see it the same way.

ICE-BREAKERS

You've probably participated in ice-breakers at some point in your life—activities at the beginning of a group meeting or process which are designed to help the participants get to know one another, and feel comfortable with the group. This is an admirable goal, and certainly one you'll want to achieve somehow in your course, but I'll be honest here and advise that ice-breakers which are not tightly tied to the content of the course should be avoided, for two reasons: they can remind students of the kinds of activities that they hoped they left behind in their grade-school and high-school classrooms; and the students are being ice-breakered to death, I can assure you, in the orientations they are undergoing in the other parts of their campus lives—for the freshman class, for their dorms or floors, for their clubs and teams, and so on.

If you're really an ice-breaker kind of person, and you participated in an ice-breaker that changed your life and you have a missionary zeal to pass it on to others, go with it. I agree with Graham Bennett, who criticizes ice-breaking activities with the point that "our students are all very different, and for every student who revels in funky, creative edutainment, there is a student who is totally put off by anything resembling a game or gimmick" (Bennett, C2)—but his point also means that you'll have students who "revel" in ice-breakers (i.e., weirdos), and you won't please everyone no matter what you do. So if you're an ice-breaking type, ice-break away. On that note, in looking around for the least offensive ice-breaking activities I could find for this chapter, I came across two simple ways to get to know students informally that Donna Killian Duffy and Janet Wright Jones recommend, and that seemed quick and sufficiently removed from the summer-camp nature of many ice-breakers:

1. Arrive at the first class well before the starting time, and stand at the doorway and greet each student as they come in, shaking hands and introducing yourself to them by name; this can both help you learn names right away, and, as Duffy and Jones put it, "fosters a feeling of community" (141).
2. As students come into class, hand each one a piece of chalk and ask them to write their names on the board before they sit down; benefits here include again greeting each student individually, and the students "begin to share in the ownership of the classroom space" (141), which might help encourage greater participation down the line.

If neither of these activities appeal to you, and you don't like the idea of ice-breaking activities or such informal openings, try one of the more conventionally academic alternatives given below.

FIRST IMPRESSIONS

Research on learning theory suggests that students come into our classes with some prior "knowledge" of our subject matter, and they use what they already know to help them organize the information and ideas that you present to them (see Chapter 7 for more on this). I say "knowledge" because, as you may see it, what they have is not knowledge but misconceptions, stereotypes, and half-formed ideas or scattered bits of information. No matter—whatever they have, they will use it to help them process the information you give them, and they will attempt to fit new information into the categories their prior information has helped them to construct.

But my students, you might object, have no prior knowledge about the culture of Native American societies in the pre-Columbian era. Perhaps not, but they have ideas about Native Americans, and about pre-Columbian America—smatterings and bits of data picked up from other courses, from television and movies, or from their own reading. Those ideas—preconceptions about Native Americans, for example—will act as filters to help them process what they read and hear in your course. If their only perceptions of Native Americans come from the Disney movie *Pocahontas,* their first encounter with Native Americans in your course will fall into the categories of "Mmmm, they're just like Pocahontas!" or "Mmmm, they're nothing at all like Pocahontas!"

I'm simplifying here, of course, and you can check the resources I've listed at the end of the chapter for a fuller and more accurate picture of this issue. But what you can't do is change the way people learn, or process information. So the best way to confront this problem of the sometimes-faulty filters of students' prior knowledge is for you to figure out, during the first class or two of the semester, what the students know or think they know about the subject matter; once you have done this, you can spend time in the course addressing those preconceptions and affirming or attempting to correct them.

A simple method for gathering that information is to make use of student information sheets. At some point during the first class, pass out a paper to everyone which asks them to fill out their name, major or possible major, and e-mail address—you can use the latter if you need to send a message to the class for some reason (although many universities now enable you to do this more easily with Web-based e-mail systems, or through the virtual learning environments that I'll discuss in the next chapter). In addition to asking for this information, though, ask each student to write a short paragraph in response to two or three substantive questions about their past experiences with the course topic, or about their understanding of the ideas you will be presenting over the course of the semester. These questions can be very simple and general, even personal in scope:

1. In Art History: Describe for me one work of visual art that has really impressed or interested you; what made it stand out for you?
2. In Philosophy 101: What makes a person ethical?
3. In Human Biology: What fields or careers do you think depend heavily on an understanding of human biology?

Students' responses to these kinds of questions will help you gauge the extent to which they have thought about the course topic in advance, and can help you as well to make the case for why this course will prove useful to them in their academic and professional careers ("Every career depends heavily on the understanding of human biology, kids!"). You can—and probably should—think about the lectures or discussions you are conducting in the second and third classes of the semester in light of the information you will gather from these first impressions of the students.

Happily, you can also use these information sheets to achieve the goals of an ice-breaker, if you are so inclined. In classes of twenty-five or less, this activity takes no more than 15 or 20 minutes, and can go a long way toward easing the tensions that students may feel on the opening day, as well as humanizing you in their eyes, and vice versa. Once you have collected the sheets, use them to take attendance—not simply checking names against the names on your roster, but calling out names and putting those names with faces—and to engage in a brief conversation with each student as you take the opening-day roll (which can be saved for this point on the first day). As you glance through the information sheets, use their responses to allow you to ask each student a question or two about their academic plans or their ideas about the course topic: if they wrote "Undeclared" on the major question, for example, ask them what they are thinking about; if they claim the *Mona Lisa* as their favorite painting, ask them if they've been to Paris. These questions should not be overly familiar, obviously, but you also don't want to be perceived as grilling them on course content. Don't spend more than a minute with each student; in larger classes, you can be selective, and engage in conversation with a smaller number of them.

Finally, you can use the information sheets as the preparatory material for an opening class exercise in gathering the initial impressions of the group as a whole on the course topic. Formulate a question that you think will help you gain a picture of the group's overall perception of the course topic, and put it on the information sheet—for example, "Tell me the first five things that come to your mind when you think of Native Americans." After you have completed the roll call—with or without the personal banter—explain that you now would like to discuss with them their impressions. Pose the question from the sheet orally—"So let's hear what all of your first impressions are about Native Americans"—and ask for volunteer responses. If no one responds initially, ask a student or two simply to restate or explain their written response. This relieves the pressure for them of having to come up with an answer on the spot, and will usually encourage others to speak as well. As they explain their responses, write them on the board, putting people's ideas into categories or columns that relate to the major themes and ideas that you will cover throughout the semester (for instance, war and weaponry,

social organization, religious beliefs, etc.). In the closing minutes of the class, talk briefly about how the course will address—
or not address—the issues that they have identified in their responses.

Thomas Angelo and K. Patricia Cross, in *Classroom Assessment
Techniques*, describe a similar exercise called "Misconception/Pre-
conception Check." Acknowledging the existence of student preconceptions on common course topics, and pointing out that student preconceptions are usually misconceptions, they suggest
posing questions specifically designed to draw out common student misconceptions and allow the teacher to address them. They
give the example of a course in Native American history in which
the instructor poses three questions on the first day of class:

About how many people lived in North America in 1491?
About how long had they been on this continent by 1491?
What significant achievements had they made in that time?
(Angelo and Cross, 133)

When the instructor collects the responses, she shows students
the widely disparate answers that she receives, but does not provide them immediately with her answers to the questions. Instead, she spends the rest of the class discussing with them the
sources of their mistaken notions; then, for their first assignment, the students are asked to find more informed responses to
their questions through library research.

Whether you use such fact-based questions to prompt a discussion, or move instead directly to more conceptual questions,
you can use the information sheets or simply pose the questions
orally and get students' responses that way. However, because
students will be anxious and hence more likely to be quiet on the
first day of the semester, you should give them an opportunity to

think about your questions before you ask the class as a whole to respond. Try one of two simple techniques here:

1. Ask the students to spend five minutes writing a response to a question in their notebook, recording their impressions in paragraph form or even as simple notes or a list.
2. Ask the students to pair up with a partner to discuss their first impressions, and then have each pair identify three concrete impressions or pieces of information that they have agreed upon together.

Once they have had the chance to brainstorm in these low-pressure activities, they should feel more comfortable reporting their ideas to the class, since they can either read off their response or present their report as the work of a team (and thus help mitigate anxiety that they might give a wrong or stupid answer).

You may find, after gathering these initial impressions of your students over the first few semesters or years of teaching, that students give a pretty consistent picture of their preconceptions of the course topic—at which point you might decide to try alternatives to this opening-day strategy. But making some effort, through this method or another, to gather this information is a worthwhile activity that should help you plan your first semester of teaching more effectively.

A final advantage to the strategy of gathering information from students on the opening day of class (an advantage that I will describe in more detail in Chapter 14) is that you can return to that information during the final days of the semester and demonstrate to the students how far they have traveled from those initial impressions. This might prove a useful demonstration for you as well, one that you can use to gauge whether you have guided them as far away from those initial impressions as you would have liked.

BIG AND INTERESTING QUESTIONS

You may decide to save the information-gathering process for later in the first week, or use Blackboard or a writing assignment for that purpose. In that case you can consider a second possibility for your opening class, one captured nicely in a short article in the journal *College Teaching* by Kevin Bennett, who described a technique he used in teaching statistics—just the kind of course that probably needs a jump-start to pique the interest of students on the opening day.

Bennett describes opening his statistics course with a birthday celebration—or, more precisely, a celebration of the birthday paradox, which states that "once there are thirty people in a room, the probability that two people have the same birthday is more than 75 percent." Even before he passes out the syllabus, Bennett begins his statistics classes by explaining the paradox and polling the class for their birthday dates until they find a match (happily, he reports, he has found one every time). As we might expect of a statistician, Bennett has sought confirmation for the effectiveness of his technique through some statistical analysis—comparing student expectations for the course, after the first day, in a semester which began with this exercise and in one which did not. The rate of students who responded that they were looking forward to the course improved from 43 to 82 percent with the use of this birthday demonstration (Bennett, 106).

The struggle to capture and maintain student interest in a course lasts the entire semester, and the first day of the course may be your best opportunity to ensure a successful outcome for the dozens of days that will follow. Sharing intriguing questions, paradoxes, or mysteries that lie at the heart of your discipline, or even smaller ones that students might encounter along the way, resembles in some ways the narrative technique of beginning a novel or a film at a dramatic moment in the middle of the story— you are offering them a glimpse of the drama to come, and promising that your course will help them understand what now seems completely strange and mysterious.

Obviously, you will need to identify intriguing puzzles or questions in your particular discipline, or in the course topic, which might take a bit of thinking. One route that might lead to such discovery would be to reflect on the reasons you study what you study. You haven't always been interested, for example, in the mating habits of lobsters as your primary research question. Think back for a moment: what about your area of study do you find so fascinating that it keeps you up at night pondering the intricacies of lobster sex? What are the questions and intriguing mysteries that drew you to that area? What are the fields still left unexplored? Why does your subject matter to the world? You may have to take several steps along this route, getting to the more general questions that first interested you in your discipline, but by doing so you might rediscover some of the fascinating features of your discipline—even those you can touch upon in an introductory course—that you can use to connect with your students on the first day of the semester.

The questions or puzzles that you present do not need to be as dramatic or game-like as the birthday paradox. I use a simple exercise in my Introduction to Literature courses to try to interest students in the slippery nature of meaning in language and literature, and to interest them in the course. I put up on an overhead a poem that presents the reflections of an older narrator on a childhood experience with his father—one that I think many students will be able to identify with—and ask them to write down in their notebooks whether they believe the narrator's attitude toward this experience is a positive or a negative one. I ask them as well to note the specific words and phrases that would support their idea. After five minutes of this, I begin the discussion by getting volunteers to tell me which words and lines they highlighted. We analyze the poem like this for ten or fifteen minutes, at which point it becomes clear that the poet's feelings are mixed—he has both positive and negative associations with his experience. I help the students see that, and then explain that this process is one we will follow for the rest of the semester— reading works that can help to illuminate our own experiences, but also analyzing the written word, and using evidence to support our ideas.

In doing so, I hope to accomplish three objectives: to capture their interest by offering them a poem that can speak to their own lives; to demonstrate to them that they are capable of understanding and analyzing complex works of literature; and to convey to them that interpreting literature does not mean simply giving your opinion—it consists of using evidence to draw conclusions, an intellectual skill that they will need to use in every one of their college courses, as well as in just about every career you could imagine.

Gathering first impressions and introducing students to a central question or mystery of your discipline are just two of many possible openings for a course (see Davis and McKeachie below for other ideas), but they are simple and effective techniques for the first day of your first semester at the head of a college classroom.

As you gain more teaching experience, you may decide to use the first day for other purposes—to begin the slow, painful process of learning the students' names, for example (see Chapter 12 for more on this), or to provide a little bit of your own intellectual biography to the students in order to help them see your approach to the course. You'll grow into these decisions as a teacher. The techniques outlined above are all brief enough to allow for plenty of time for other course business on the first day, and yet are substantive enough to ensure that the first day of the semester is the moment when you begin to fulfill the promises you have made to the students on the syllabus.

Resources

Angelo, Thomas A., and K. Patricia Cross. *Classroom Assessment Techniques,* 2nd ed. San Francisco: Jossey-Bass, 1993.
See the section entitled "Assessing Prior Knowledge, Recall, and Understanding" (115–158) for suggestions on first-day-of-class activities.

Bennett, Graham. "(Dis)Orientation." *The Chronicle of Higher Education,* 53.9 (November 13, 2006): C2.
A witty description of ice-breaking activities gone bad, at an orientation for new faculty members.

Bennett, Kevin L. "How to Start Teaching a Tough Course: Dry Organization Versus Excitement on the First Day of Class." *College Teaching,* 52.3 (Summer 2004): 106.
Bennett's description of using the "birthday paradox" to open his statistics course.

Davis, Barbara Gross. "The First Day of Class." In *Tools for Teaching.* San Francisco: Jossey-Bass, 1993.
Davis's chapter on the first day of class offers a complete roster of just about everything that you need to address on the first

day, as well as a list of ice-breakers and other strategies, with very brief explanations of each.

Duffy, Donna Killian, and Janet Wright Jones. "The Opening Weeks: Establishing Community." In *Teaching Within the Rhythms of the Semester,* 121–157. San Francisco: Jossey-Bass, 1995.

Duffy and Jones list lots of strategies for opening the semester, and they are especially good on the more philosophical idea of the importance of fostering a community within the classroom during the first days of the semester.

Lang, James M. "Beyond Lecturing." *The Chronicle of Higher Education,* 53.6 (September 29, 2006): C1.

This includes my description of Michael Gennert's technique for introducing students to the syllabus on the opening day of the semester.

McKeachie, Wilbert, and Marilla Svinicki. *McKeachie's Teaching Tips: Strategies, Research, and Theory for College and University Teachers,* 12th ed. Boston: Houghton Mifflin, 2006.

McKeachie's book has long been a standard and comprehensive guidebook. See "Meeting a Class for the First Time" (21–28) for McKeachie's suggestions.

Perlman, Baron, and Lee I. McCann. "Student Perspectives on the First Day of Class." *Teaching of Psychology,* 26.4 (1999): 277–279.

The results of this article, a survey of 570 students taking psychology courses at a regional public university, provide an interesting perspective on student expectations for the first day of class, and how teachers can make a strong first impression.

Showalter, Elaine. *Teaching Literature.* Malden, Mass.: Blackwell, 2003.

See especially the opening chapter, "The Anxiety of Teaching," which describes all of the good reasons we have to be anxious about our first appearances in the classroom.

Toth, Emily. *Ms. Mentor's Impeccable Advice for Women in Academia.* Philadelphia: University of Pennsylvania Press, 2002.

An excellent and witty advice book for the audience described in the title.

Teaching with Technology

A few years ago a student in my English composition course wrote a narrative essay about the process of trying to draft a paper for her history class. The piece was well-written enough that it eventually appeared in the student newspaper, and it presented to the faculty on campus a somewhat disturbing picture of the thoroughness with which technology has penetrated the lives of our students. The student described sitting at her computer, trying to organize her thoughts about the essay topic, but never quite getting her head together amidst the constant interruptions of her ringing cell phone, instant messages from her friends, e-mails from her parents, the rotating selection of songs on her iPod, and the television in the other room blaring a DVD that her roommates were watching. I had a hard time imagining typing my name and address into the computer with all of those distractions, much less writing a history paper.

Walter Ong argued several decades ago, in *Orality and Literacy,* that writing was a technology that changed thought—that the shift from oral cultures to written ones had a profound impact on the way human beings reasoned and thought. Something similar seems to be happening to our students these days, as their brains learn to work under these conditions, and their creative energies

can be channeled through such a wide variety of technological
outlets. As Don Madigan points out, and as my student's essay clearly illustrated, this generation of students is "used to
multi-tasking" in ways that are less familiar to us older types
(2). A more forceful statement of the argument that a major shift
has taken place in the brains of our students appears in Marc
Prensky's controversial essay on "digital natives," which claims
that today's students "have changed radically," and that they "are
no longer the people our educational system was designed to
teach" (1). Prensky argues that we—the faculty, whom he refers
to as "digital immigrants"—need to radically change both the
content we teach and the methods we use to teach it in order to
accommodate these changes in our students. He refers to many
of the intellectual skills we now teach, things like "reading, writing, arithmetic, logical thinking," as "legacy" content that will
eventually give way to "future" content.

To which I can only respond: maybe. And I don't give that response with a raised eyebrow and a skeptical tone; I mean it sin-
cerely. It does seem possible to me that the onslaught of these
new technologies will transform our students, our curriculum,
and our teaching practices. But we are not there quite yet. We've
had a few thousand years to witness the transformations that literacy brought; the mental transformations that these new technologies will bring don't yet seem as visible to me as they do to
prophets like Prensky, although I do suspect they will eventually
manifest themselves in the way we structure learning environments in higher education. For the time being, though, today's
classrooms and curricula and educational frameworks are still
set up to integrate new technologies with traditional pedagogical
practices, and the larger structural elements of traditional pedagogies are not going away anytime soon. As a new instructor in
the early part of the twenty-first century, you will still find yourself in a classroom with chairs and desks and a board up front,

though that board may be green or white or designed to display digital images, and your students may have notebooks or desktops or laptops on their desks. There will be variations, but you will still stand in front of or next to the students and guide them into developing the skills you want them to have, and they will still need to read and write and speak in order to demonstrate those skills to you. So the basic work that we do, for the time being, will remain in place.

Moreover, the chances are decent that a new college instructor in the year 2008 or beyond will have grown up using e-mail, having a cell phone and an iPod or its equivalent, and maybe using IM to keep in touch with family or graduate school friends. So today's students, and their technology-soaked brains, won't be as far removed from you as they will be from the senior faculty on campus. You may be a digital native yourself. For that reason, you will not find me arguing in this book that you need to radically restructure how you think about education—nor will you see arguments here for throwing out textbooks and replacing them all with computer games. The importance of reading, writing, arithmetic, and logical thinking suggests to me that they will persevere, at least as long as you and I will be in the classroom. And I would argue further that the basic principles of teaching and learning, on which I am relying in this book, will still operate in whatever environment we and our students find ourselves—even in the environment of online and distance teaching and learning, in which you obviously will only stand in front of your students virtually, but will still need to understand the parameters of the basic teaching-learning transaction. So my intention throughout the book is to ensure that you have a fundamental awareness of how students learn, and to offer you concrete strategies to help them learn in a limited range of environments, both real and virtual; my assumption is that you are smart enough to figure out how to take that awareness, and those strategies, and shift and adapt them as new technologies become available to us.

None of this is to give short shrift to technology, although you might find this chapter less detailed than you would expect when it comes to explaining new pedagogical technologies. This is deliberate, for two reasons. First, you will find that while technology can work wonders in the classroom, it can wreak havoc on your schedule. Especially when you are making use of technology in the classroom for the first time, the start-up costs, in terms of time invested, can be tremendous. Tom Byers, a professor of management science and engineering, who also directs the Stanford Technology Ventures program and integrates technology heavily into his teaching, estimates that he spends eight hours of preparation for every two hours in the classroom. As a new faculty member, you *will not and should not* spend that much time on preparation (a general rule of thumb, which I will bring up again in the next chapter, is that you should shoot for two hours of preparation for every hour in the classroom). For your first year, stick with the basics—technology that you are familiar with, and that you can integrate into your classroom without a tremendous investment of time. I have kept my focus, in this chapter, on precisely those basic features of the technological landscape.

The second reason—an obvious one—is that technologies change. What will be available to you when you are holding this book in your hands, in 2008 or beyond, may not yet be invented at the time I am writing this, in early 2007. So I am hesitant to delve into too many specifics, in terms of software and pedagogical strategies, when those elements are constantly in danger of being superseded by the next wave of innovation. Again, my focus in both the book and this chapter is on ensuring that you have a solid foundation of teaching and learning theory to guide you through whatever our IT departments throw our way in the future.

With that said, I do want to spend time introducing you to a technological innovation that has become very common in college courses, and that seems destined to remain there in some form or another: Web-based learning management systems like Blackboard, currently the most popular educational software in the academy today (these programs are called by different names; I'm going with "virtual learning environment"). Programs like Blackboard—and its equivalents, such as Desire2Learn or open-source alternatives like Sakai or Moodle—are usually purchased for campus-wide licensing by your college or university, and then are available through the campus network to any faculty member who wishes to build a website for her course. Such programs provide space to post all course-related documents, to link to other sources and multi-media content, to accept and return assignments electronically, to send announcements, to facilitate dialogue among and with students through weblogs and chat, and even to allow students to build their own Web pages. If you have not been given information about such a program on your campus, check with your department chair or the information technology office on campus; just about every college in America has some kind of system in place along these lines. (This does not mean, however, that just about every faculty member in America is *using* these systems. Plenty of college and university faculty still teach with chalk and [small "b"] blackboard, or with more minimal forms of technological use, such as e-mail to communicate with students and PowerPoint for their lectures. I can't stress enough that there is absolutely nothing wrong with teaching a course that consists of nothing but you, your students, a chalkboard, and paper and pencils.)

Blackboard and its equivalents by no means exhaust what will be available to you on most college campuses right now. In an article that you can find online at the location listed in the Resources section of this chapter, Don Madigan provides an excellent and concise overview of the ten most common teaching and learning technologies on campus today: blogs, wiki, virtual learning environments, presentation software (for example, PowerPoint), Web tutorials, concept mapping software, webcasts, podcasts, electronic portfolios, and Personal Response Systems. The ones that might be less familiar to you, like concept mapping and Personal Response Systems (also sometimes called "clickers"), are the ones that require more work to incorporate into a course, and hence are not ones I recommend you try in your first semester. The more familiar ones—such as blogs and electronic portfolios—are all available to anyone who sets up a virtual learning environment like Blackboard for their courses, in addition to other features that these environments provide. Because of the widespread availability of virtual learning environments, their ability to incorporate other technological developments, and their relative ease of use, I will focus the rest of this chapter on working with them, reviewing the four main benefits that I think teaching with them can provide to faculty—as well as a few cautions and pitfalls to watch out for.

The necessary full disclosure here is that I am one of those faculty members who have been somewhat slow to embrace technology in the classroom, although that is changing. By the time you read this, I will be teaching with a virtual learning environment, as well as podcasting portions of my courses on the campus net. But because my experiences have been limited thus far, I asked a colleague of mine to play Virgil to my Dante as I set about to explore the role of virtual learning environments in the classroom for this chapter. Lucia Knoles teaches American literature, with a strong emphasis on its historical contexts, and has fully embraced the capacities of the Blackboard system that she uses for her courses. I have been guided by her wisdom throughout this chapter, so my thanks to Lucia for her help.

Building Community

The most important role that a Blackboard-style environment can play in your courses is to help build community among the students, and between the students and yourself. A course, after all, is a learning community, in which a group of citizens work together to accomplish the same goal: helping students understand something more deeply than they understood it before they entered that community. You are helping the students achieve this goal; they are helping themselves; and they certainly can and should be helping each other. But it can be difficult to build and sustain a learning community if your only interactions occur during three 50-minute sessions per week, some parts of which are inevitably taken up with administrative tasks, or students coming and going early, or breaks and holidays.

Virtual learning environments create a space that provides for interaction among the members of the learning community outside the classroom. Students and faculty can spend a few minutes with the community whenever they have the chance, and symbolically that space always exists only for the sake of your specific course—unlike your physical classroom space, which has a cheating heart and hosts all kinds of other learning communities when you leave it.

The main community-building feature in a virtual learning environment comes from the discussion boards or weblogs, which can either be left as an optional place for students to discuss course material or post problems or questions, or included as a regular assignment in the course. Lucia Knoles believes that leaving this interactive component as an option generally does not work—you will hear virtual crickets chirping in the silence, she assures me, if you simply tell students to post on a voluntary basis. Students have plenty of required work to do for their four or five courses; why on earth would they go out of their way to add to their workload by writing long posts to the course website?

Instead, Lucia advises making regular postings to a weblog or discussion board a requirement of the course. For her courses, students post a two- or three-paragraph response to the reading for every single class (they can miss three times without penalty). Before each class she skims the logs, which helps her discover the main ideas and problems that students had with the reading. Some programs, such as Blackboard, allow her to search for key words and phrases in the logs—so that, for example, she can conduct a search for the word "shoes" if she wants to find out whether any student noticed the symbolism of a pair of shoes in a poem she's teaching. This advance look at the students' ideas has also often helped her, she explains, prepare to deal with a problem or misconception that she did not expect—such as the students' annoyance and bafflement over spelling or punctuation conventions in eighteenth-century prose. In the classroom, the day starts with a discussion of common points that people have raised in the logs, or interesting questions or problems, and then moves into either more general discussions or whatever else Lucia has planned for the day.

Her assignment for the logs, incidentally, is the same for every class: find three quotes from the reading and analyze them in light of the overarching question or theme of the course. During the course of the semester, as the students repeat this exercise over and over and have the opportunity to view each other's logs, they get better and better at selecting key passages, analyzing them, and writing their logs. "Real learning," she says, "involves repeatedly using a certain set of questions and tools at an increasingly higher level." But of course you can assign anything you want for the weblogs—you might ask the students to post links to course-related sites, to post the results of their research on course projects, to post drafts of papers, to post in response to one another's work, and so on.

My first reaction to learning about Lucia's use of the weblogs was that it seemed like an enormous amount of work for the teacher. And it certainly can be—but it does not have to be quite this much work, and it may not even be as much work as it initially sounds. Lucia does not grade every single log that the students post. Checking to ensure that everyone has posted for each class takes only a minute, and this job can be saved until the end of the semester (since all posts are saved, and she can view the posts by student). The frequency of their posts helps determine their participation grade for the course. At the semester's midpoint, Lucia has them write a self-assessment of their own logs in relation to the best posts they have seen throughout the semester; she gives them a grade for that project, which she says really helps improve the quality of the logs during the second half of the course. Then, at the end of the semester, Lucia asks them to identify their three best logs—those are the only ones she grades individually. So grading logs or posts does not need to be as time-intensive as grading quizzes or papers.

Of course, you can also use the logs more sparingly, asking for one log per week, for example, or three logs over the course of the semester. A lot depends on how you plan to make use of them—but, again, Lucia advises that you should make some use of them, unless you want them to be nothing more than another requirement to fulfill. When the students post to the site, make sure that you use those posts in some way in the classroom, either to spark discussion or to help determine what you will lecture about.

In addition to the more philosophical objective of helping to create and sustain a learning community in the course, the logs help achieve a more practical pedagogical objective: they enable students who are quiet, and might feel anxiety about participating in the course, to make their voices heard to their peers and the instructor. You will have students in every class who either prefer to let others do the talking and coast through the class, or who simply feel anxiety about speaking in public and therefore don't participate in whole-class discussions (group work can sometimes enable these latter students to participate as well). Some teachers argue that shy students have to learn to participate in class, since we should be educating citizens and employees who are capable of making their voice heard when necessary. I am not entirely convinced of this, and we should remember that some students may have anxiety disorders which make speaking in public a difficult and potentially damaging ordeal; these students deserve an education as much as anyone else. The logs enable these students to participate in the larger course discussion without the pressures that accompany speaking in front of a big group of people—an anxiety that you might even share, and that most of us feel in smaller doses.

Weblogs and discussion boards, then, are the main features of virtual learning environments that help facilitate student participation in the course and build a learning community.

Intertextuality and Multimedia

In one of her courses, Lucia teaches a section from Maya Angelou's *I Know Why the Caged Bird Sings* which concludes with a powerful scene in which the main character stands up at a ceremony and sings the Negro National Anthem. In order to help students understand this scene more deeply, and to feel what that character might have felt, she puts a link to three different audio versions of the Negro National Anthem on the course website, which the students listen to when they have finished reading the story. They might also use those audio files in their papers—citing the lyrics to the song, or considering how those lyrics tie into the theme of the story.

Many faculty use multimedia resources in the classroom; I regularly show film clips, or play music, or show slides of artwork that relates to the works of literature we are reading. But that often involves lots of work—arranging for a slide projector to be in my classroom, or bringing in a CD player from home, or making a frantic call to the media technology people when the DVD player in my classroom doesn't work. Having these sorts of multimedia files available on the course website, where students can view them prior to class, as part of their homework, facilitates the use of such resources. You still may want to make use of them in the classroom, of course, and so will have to deal with the occasional hassle of importing the proper equipment—unless you are in a computer classroom, or know that all students have laptops, and your classroom is wired, in which case you can simply send everyone to the website—but at least you can be sure the students will have encountered the material when you are ready to discuss it with them.

Courses in every discipline can make use of the course website to link to supplemental material: for instance, you could link to audio files of animal calls, maps of countries or regions that play an important role in the global economy, online exhibitions of artifacts from lost civilizations, political advertisements, and so on. Again, build these elements into the required reading or study for the course; otherwise these optional sites for exploration might translate into lots of extra work for you in exchange for a small payoff. You might even consider an assignment in which students are asked to find two or three links to material that relates to the course topic, and to post them for the rest of the course; a follow-up assignment might ask the class to review all of those sites and select the best three, which then will become a permanent feature on the course website.

Multimedia capacity has been an especially welcome development in the sciences. Anatomy students at small colleges (where no cadavers are available) used to rely on cat dissection to study anatomical structures; now computer software enables them to get inside a virtual human body and explore. In chemistry courses, computer animation enables students to get a much clearer picture of chemical reactions and metabolic pathways. Even in social science courses, technology can help make students more active learners. An instructor might construct a spreadsheet that provides the equations to determine population growth, and then—up on the screen, before the eyes of the students—change the variables and allow the students to see how each tweaking of a variable affects the bigger picture. The students could do this same exercise themselves, at home, on the course website. These examples demonstrate how technology really can represent a substantial improvement in the teaching process, one of kind rather than degree. In an English literature course, it's more convenient for me to have all of my paintings and audio clips on the website, but I was always able to make those things available to my students; in an anatomy class, technology can give students access to something that was not available to them previously.

Organization

"I'm an intellectually organized person," Lucia said to me when we first sat down to review her website together, "but a physically disorganized one." Lucia's use of Blackboard has helped tidy up her messy office by ensuring that everything related to her courses remains filed and enclosed in a single space—on the servers of Assumption College (and, of course, backed up on her personal computers as well, just in case).

First and most obviously, the course website offers a convenient location for the syllabus, for all course handouts, for assignment sheets, and for any other pieces of paper that you normally need to give the students in class. But handouts do not have to exhaust the transition from paper to Web. In most virtual learning environments, students can turn in their written work online—and you can respond to that work online, inserting marginal comments in the text, highlighting passages that you think deserve praise or revision, and typing the final comment that you might normally scrawl across the back of their paper. Lucia asks students to write a note to her, when they turn in their papers, identifying the strengths and weaknesses of their own papers; her comments begin as a response to their self-assessment. The student logs, if you choose to use them, remain on the course website for the semester, and you have those handy for review at the end of the semester for grading purposes. The grades, finally, can be automatically computed by the software according to formulas that you establish, as long as you have been recording the students' grades in the system throughout the semester.

In other words, everything that you would normally hand to the students, and everything that they would normally hand to you—even, if you teach in a computer classroom, exams—can be shifted to the course website, leaving your desk free for things like the two or three pencil holders and paperweights I get from my children every year for Christmas and Father's Day.

This consolidation of work has some benefits that you might not appreciate until you've been through a semester of teaching:

1. No student can complain that he dropped a paper off in your mailbox, or under your door, and that it disappeared; you will have a record of the minute and second your students filed their papers or homework with the site.
2. You will not be cleaning out your office over the summer and find, behind the radiator, those three papers that you lost and, shamefacedly, had to ask the students to print out and turn in again.
3. You will not carry with you to class each day a folder which grows increasingly bulky and bulging with paper each week of the semester, expanding until it bursts open one day while you're hurrying across campus.
4. More seriously, since all student work will remain visible to you on the website until the end of the semester, you will easily be able to note improvement in the quality of any student's work over the course of the semester, something which you may choose to factor into final grade decisions.

Again, you can chart a middle course here. If you still would prefer to grade papers or exams at the local coffee shop, so you can hold out hope that one day you might actually work up the nerve to ask that good-looking barista on a date, then you can simply make the website available as a resource center containing all course documents; then when students miss class, or say that they have lost the syllabus, you can direct them to the website. Or you might have students turn in homework assignments online, but still hand in paper copies of their major assignments or exams. Whatever combination you choose, faculty at just about any level of technical competence can use a course website to help eliminate clutter in their teaching lives, and to reduce the amount of paper they are shuffling back and forth across their desk each day.

Reproducibility and Documentation

Even more practical than its ability to organize your course is the website's ability to reduce your workload in courses you will teach again, and to provide a convenient source of materials to document your teaching when you are under review for renewal, for tenure, or for promotion. Those issues might seem a long way off right now, but making this time investment at the start of your first semester can pay off handsomely at the start of the next semester, or when it comes time to compile documents for review.

First—especially if you are teaching an introductory course in your first semester, which the vast majority of graduate students and new faculty will be doing—you will teach the course again, perhaps even the next semester. You will discover, in your first semester, plenty that you wish you had done differently, and you will want to make changes to the course the next time around. Having everything—syllabus, assignment sheets, supplementary course material—saved to the website, and available for easy revision and transfer to a new website (a feature of most virtual learning environments), will speed that process along: you can pick and choose the elements of the old syllabus that you'd like to maintain, and add the new. You also might find it useful, as you are preparing the syllabus the second time around, to glance back at students' work and responses to homework assignments. Doing so might help you remember, for example, that students really did not understand a particular assignment, or that everyone made the same set of errors on the first paper, which you can easily forestall with some additional instructions on the assignment sheet.

Second, your course and your teaching will be subject to review by someone somewhere along the way. For adjuncts and graduate students, that might mean a classroom visit from your department chair, and a request to review your syllabus and major assignment descriptions. For first-year faculty on the tenure track, it might mean visits from the chair and the dean, and the obligation to compile a record of course materials. In either case, you will find the course website a convenient spot to locate and reproduce those materials, and a source of even more extensive information about the work your students have produced to which you can send curious administrative types. Tenure-track faculty, in particular, will benefit from having a website for each course, since you may undergo as many as three reviews by the time you receive tenure—such as a first-year, third-year, and tenure review, in my case—and for each of those reviews you may be expected to document your teaching practices and achievements in all of your courses. The websites provide an easy record for it all.

Most faculty will now be able to maintain a file of audio and video samples from their classrooms as well. Podcasting, which in its simplest form means that you audio- or video-tape portions of your class and then make those audio and video clips available on the course website, has become an increasingly common feature of campus life. After you have returned to your office and transferred the audio or video file to the campus network and to your website, students can review your lectures or course activities as they are preparing for exams, or catch portions of a lecture that they might have missed. The obvious danger of podcasting is that students will rely on the podcasts rather than actually coming to class. You can alleviate that problem if you keep the lecturing in your classes to a minimum, and rely on a wide range of teaching activities in your classroom. The experience of listening to the podcast of a class discussion will never match the experience of sitting in the midst of that discussion, and being capable of entering it.

Wading or Jumping In?

You will perhaps have realized by now that in this chapter the conceit of the book—that each chapter corresponds to a particular week in the semester—goes off track a bit. Your decision about how much technology to employ in the course will have to be made well before the second week, and in fact it should be made as you are planning the syllabus. But the second week is the time when you should start to see the benefits of using technology in the classroom, since you might begin to see the first written work by your students by the end of the second week, and you will realize then how quickly the paper can pile up for a course.

So, as a first-time faculty member, how much should you rely on technology for your course?

As I've already said, you do not need to make use of technology in any way to be an effective teacher. Most of the benefits I've described above as resulting from the use of virtual learning environments could be obtained from other pedagogical techniques, though they might require more work on your part, or different kinds of timing. You can be a brilliant teacher with nothing but paper, pens, chalk, and a blackboard. If you have little or no experience with technology, or you are not comfortable with computers, or you oppose the use of computers for any reason (for example, if you happen to be a famously Luddite writer and teacher like Wendell Berry), then forgo the technology this semester, and dip your toe in the water in your next semester or second year of teaching.

If you are a "digital immigrant" (Prensky's term), and have been living in this territory for a while now but don't have much experience building websites or working with new software programs, then put your course online via Blackboard or one of its equivalents, and use the program to organize and document the course, and perhaps experiment with links to course-related material or have an assignment or two turned in online. You should have a feel by the end of the semester whether you want to step it up in the future.

But I know that plenty of this book's readers will be "digital natives," will have constructed websites of their own, will have contributed to wikis, will visit discussion boards and chat rooms regularly, and will have their own blogs. For this group, I don't see any reason not to jump right in. The benefits that virtual learning environments can provide are important and pedagogically sound ones, not to mention ones that can make your life less chaotic in a semester that will, I promise, seem like four of the most chaotic months of your life thus far.

When you are ready to step beyond the virtual learning environment, and experiment with the latest technologies coming down the pipeline, two that seem to me to hold the most promise for the immediate future are Personal Response Systems and wikis. Personal Response Systems are hand-held devices or modules located at every student's seat that allow them to respond electronically to questions posed by the instructor—and that immediately relay those responses to you. You can use PRS technology to gather initial impressions of a topic, to take polls, to check students' understanding of a key lecture point, or to determine the opinions or experiences of the class on some controversial topic. PRS devices can give the instructor information that can be used to determine how to proceed in a lecture or discussion, and they involve students in the lesson in a way that just asking for questions or a show of hands might not.

Wikis are websites that allow for, in the words of Wikipedia, the ultimate wiki, "mass collaborative authoring." Such sites are constructed to allow users—who may or may not have to register—to add and remove and edit the content of the site. Wikistyled sites are becoming increasingly popular on the Web these days, in part because of the success of Wikipedia, and they present opportunities for collaboration among students that were certainly available before now, but would have been much more cumbersome to manage. An instructor might set up a wiki on the topic of a course, for example, and require a typical set of assignments—papers, exams, oral presentations—but ask as well that all students contribute to the course wiki. At the end of the semester, that wiki will document, and display to the students, the collective sum of the knowledge and skills they have developed over the semester.

PRS devices and wikis require either hardware or digital knowledge that not all new faculty will have, though, so I leave it up to interested readers to explore these pedagogies further on their own. To determine whether these teaching tools are available at your college or university, and to see what else might be available to you, start with the IT department on campus; they will either have the answers or can direct you to the office that has them. Many campuses now have a Center for Teaching/Learning and Technology, and those offices can provide you with assistance in integrating the latest technologies into your teaching.

Resources

Madden, Kendall. "'The Brave New World' of Classroom Technology." *The Stanford Report,* March 7, 2007.

This article references Tom Byers and his use of technology in the classroom.

Madigan, Don. "The Technology Literature Professoriate: Are We There Yet?" *IDEA Paper* 43 (March 2006): 1–6.

A concise but comprehensive overview of the technologies

----

you can incorporate into your classroom. The full text of this paper is available online through the ERIC database, or by visiting the IDEA center at Kansas State University, *http://www.idea .ksu.edu/*.

McClymer, John. "The AHA Guide to Teaching and Learning with the New Media." American Historical Association, 2007. *http://www.historians.org/pubs/free/mcclymer/acknowledgements .cfm*. January 29, 2007.

A great guide to teaching with technology, available online from the American Historical Association. The examples are from history courses, but the principles are easily transferred to other disciplines.

Ong, Walter J. *Orality and Literacy.* New York: Routledge, 2002.

This is the most recent edition of Ong's classic text. It has a few references to the digital age, but remains mostly important for the basic idea—the way changes in linguistic media affect how we think.

Poradzisz, Sarah. "Technology—from IM to TV—Brings a Culture of Distraction." *Le Provocateur,* March 29, 2005: Viewpoint.

The student essay that I cite at the opening of the chapter.

Prensky, Marc. "Digital Natives, Digital Immigrants." *On the Horizon,* 9.5 (October 2001): 1–2.

Prensky's original essay, also available online: *http://www .marcprensky.com/writing/default.asp*.

In the Classroom: Lectures

For a couple of years, the church my family and I attended was primarily staffed by two priests: a Monsignor in his fifties, a very formal and traditional priest who loved high ceremony; and a younger, more dynamic man in his mid-thirties, who had a much more informal approach to life. The differences between the two men were never more evident than in their sermons. Monsignor went up to the lectern on the altar in a measured, stately way, and read his sermons word for word from a text. They were well-crafted pieces of oratory: he always began with a personal story or a joke, followed by some reflection on the meaning of the story, and then tied that into the day's Gospel reading. Father Jim, on the other hand, came down from the altar and stood before the congregation, strolling up the aisle and into the first few rows as he spoke. His sermons were not so carefully sculpted; they tended to be more conversational. You often felt that he was making his point directly to you, rather than to the back of the church. One day after mass I asked him how extensive was the text he relied upon, and he pulled a sweat-stained index card out of his pocket and showed me his text—it had thirty words written on it at most, an outline of the main points he wanted to identify. His sermons were repetitive, but not in a boring or careless way; they continually circled back to two or three main ideas. He would highlight those ideas as he introduced them—"So the important thing in today's Gospel is this notion of *charity*"—and then at the end of the sermon he would quickly restate each of his main points, reminding us of the ideas his sermon had covered.

As I listened to these contrasting sermon styles for two years, it eventually occurred to me that my experiences in the pews were probably as close as I would come in my post–graduate school life to reliving the student experience of traveling from class to class, adjusting myself in each period to a different lecture or teaching style. And I came to appreciate the homiletic styles of both lecturers. Neither of them seemed necessarily better to me; they were different, and appealed to different parts of my brain and aesthetic sensibilities.

The contrasting styles of these two religious orators, and the fact that I was able to appreciate and take ideas away from each of them, helped remind me that effective lecturing can take many different forms: dazzling multimedia shows, rabble-rousing injunctions to action, intimate and conversational arguments, or quiet feats of exquisite oratory. It's a very small leap from that realization to the next: there is no one right way to lecture, no matter how many different prescriptions you might read. This principle is easily broadened in education: there is no one right way to teach, either. Effective teaching depends upon teachers knowing both the situation—the students, the classroom, the material—and themselves, with their own strengths and weaknesses.

So the final logical leap takes us to the principle that underpins every page of this book: Vary your teaching methods. No single teaching technique should constitute the sole pedagogical method in any classroom; the most effective teachers are those who use multiple approaches—some lecturing, some group discussion, some small-group work, some problem-solving sessions, and more. Each of us probably preferred one method of teaching when we were students, and for many of us who went on to advanced degrees, we preferred reading on our own and listening to lectures—but we also know that we can't generalize universally from our own experience. My wife tends to fidget through just about any kind of lecture; an elementary school teacher, she prefers learning by getting her hands on things, and getting the opportunity to vocalize her own ideas through discussion. So what worked for you might not work for all of your students, and the best solution to that problem is to vary your teaching methods, to ensure that as many students as possible can connect with the material in some way.

Don't interpret this principle too rigidly, and assume that you need to parcel out class time to these different teaching methods in equal increments. You may certainly find that you feel most comfortable as a teacher with giving lectures, or with students doing group work, and you may be most effective as a teacher with one of these strategies. I suspect that most of us rely on one strategy more than others, and that's just fine. You will develop your own style both within a strategy—giving formal lectures from a text, for example, versus speaking from notes—and in terms of how you move between strategies. Just don't let yourself become so comfortable with any one strategy that it excludes other possibilities.

So, again (circling back like Father Jim): vary your teaching methods. The lecture you give on Monday will appeal to some of your students; the small-group activity that involves filling out a worksheet on Wednesday will catch some different ones; the debate you moderate on Friday will interest yet another set of students (and the students who loved Monday's lecture may feel disconnected and uncertain about the purpose of the debate).

Cast as wide a net as possible with your teaching strategies in order to gather up the most possible students.

Lecturing: Theory and Background

Dip your pinky toe into the research that has been done on the effectiveness of lecturing as a teaching style, and you will soon come across statistics like the ones below, which offer a dour view of lecturing as a teaching method:

- Student retention of material covered in the first 10 minutes of a lecture is about 70%; in the final 10 minutes of the lecture, retention has dropped to around 20%.
- In a 50-minute lecture, students are attentive to the lecturer around 40% of the time.
- If an instructor speaks at a rate of 150 words per minute, the students will hear around 50 of those words. (Jones-Wilson, 42–43)

Michelle Jones-Wilson cites these statistics in the article listed in the Resources section of this chapter, but you will find statistics like these just about anywhere you look for information or ideas about lecturing in higher education (including McKeachie, Barbara Gross Davis, and all of the major guidebooks). You will also find dozens and perhaps hundreds of articles like the one I cite below by Hwang and Kim, which describes an experiment in which 70 students in a nursing program in Korea were divided into two separate classes: in one class the students primarily worked in small groups to solve problems designed by the instructor; in the other class, students were taught entirely by traditional lectures. At the end of the semester, the students—who had been sorted into groups of roughly equal background and preparation beforehand—were given a test on the material de-

signed by the instructors. The students in the lecture sections
scored significantly lower than those who worked on problems
in groups throughout the semester. Experiments like this one
have been conducted in many disciplines, and almost always
yield similar results.

To approach the matter more philosophically, you will find
plenty of writers and researchers on higher education who ask a
more basic question about the role of lectures in the classroom
today: why are we still relying on this teaching strategy that Joseph Lowman describes (96) as a "holdover from a pretechnolog-
ical age when books were scarce or nonexistent and the lecture
was the primary way students could gain information"? Since the
invention of the printing press, we have had at our disposal a
much more efficient means of getting information into the hands
of our students—the book. So what are we still doing lecturing in
the college classroom?

The response to this question is that we are, or should be, doing things other than just providing information when we lecture. Wilbert McKeachie points out five functions that lectures
may fulfill in the age of the printing press and the Internet, outlined here in my words:

1. Lectures can provide our students with the most up-to-
   date information and perspectives in our field, which—
   even with the Internet at our disposal—often take years to
   filter through academic journals or more conventional
   publications.
2. Lectures can summarize and compare multiple articles or
   books, allowing us to cover large areas of peripherally related content or background material quickly; then the
   students will have only the most important works as assigned reading.
3. Lectures, unlike print texts, can be adapted to the audi-

ence sitting directly in front of us. An article from a highly specialized or technical journal might contain information that I want my freshmen to understand, but I know they will spend countless unnecessary hours trying to translate that information into more basic concepts. A lecture can do that work for them.

4. Lectures can motivate students and inspire them to learn in ways that the written word cannot. We present ourselves as living models to our students, human beings who have found our course content fascinating and want to share our enthusiasm for it. A well-delivered lecture can arouse students' interest in our subject by humanizing it through the lecturer. You might think here about a teacher or scholar—or even a parent or friend—whom you respected and admired, and remember how their enthusiasm and interest in some area of study helped to spark your own.

5. Writing lectures, finally, may help the lecturer become more knowledgeable in his or her discipline, as the teacher is forced to review and identify and present the major concepts in a particular area—a selfish reason, perhaps, but not entirely so, since an instructor with more knowledge of the course content should benefit the students as well.

For all of these reasons, and perhaps others, we should not chuck the lecture out of higher education just yet. You will know from your own personal experience, I am guessing, that lectures can be intellectually charged learning experiences, when they are done well and the audience is prepared to listen to them. Like me, you may still enjoy going to lectures, and also listening to them in the shorter forms you may encounter in places like religious services or academic conferences.

So lecturing should remain in the repertoire of techniques we use in the college classroom, though it may play only a small part in some courses—in 10- or 15-minute sections at the beginning of class, or primarily during the first weeks of the semester. The role of the lecturer, though, should never become the exclusive one you play in the classroom, or perhaps not even the dominant one. Make lectures what Ken Bain calls "part of a larger quest, one element of a learning environment rather than the entire experience" (107). Religious services actually operate in a similar manner—the homilies or sermons that are delivered during the service usually account for only one part of the experience, which may also include singing, recitations of prayers, observances of rituals, and more.

But this doesn't mean that you have to devote part of each class session to singing dirges about the first law of thermodynamics. Instead, you need to plan your lectures so they fall into one of two kinds: brief, 15- to 20-minute presentations that will end while students are still retaining most of the ideas; or presentations that build in opportunities for interaction with, and feedback from, your audience. Below I'll offer a few tips on effective lecturing in general, and then some strategies for including interaction in longer lecture sessions.

Voice, Gesture, Movement

Although you may be reluctant to think about teaching as a performance—or at least as only a performance—it can't be denied that teaching has a performative side to it. For at least a few minutes of every class, even if only when we are introducing the day's activities, we are performing upon the classroom stage. It may help to remember that the role of a performer is to communicate something to an audience. So you might instead think about the teacher's role as having a communicative side to it, if you prefer not to imagine yourself as Brad Pitt or Angelina Jolie on the stage.

Effective communication depends on much more than the words that come out of our mouths—it depends upon how they come out of our mouths, what gestures we make, how and where our bodies move, and so on. And while these might not be the most important issues for a new teacher to consider, they do matter. I'm sure we have all seen speakers, for example, who we knew had interesting things to say, but whose monotone delivery and frozen persona made it difficult for us to stay awake. In this area of teaching, more than anywhere else, your personal style will play a huge role in determining your lecture style, so I am not going to rattle off a massive list of tips for effective oratory. You can probably get many of those tips by becoming more attentive to the speaking styles of the lecturers you encounter regularly—deans, other faculty at academic conferences, politicians, clergy—and noting to yourself what works and what doesn't.

But I do want to draw your attention to two simple areas in which even a first-time faculty member can become more deliberate and practiced in lecture-style communication. Trying to make use of these recommendations will feel very forced at first—and if you're not completely comfortable with your material, it might prove distracting as well. But even if you only think about these tips for the first few minutes of your lecture each day, eventually you will grow more comfortable with them, and find yourself using them unconsciously. I want to give credit where credit is due for these tips, though I have no print source to cite. For a few years, while I was at the teaching center at Northwestern University, we regularly sponsored workshops on effective classroom communication conducted by Ann Woodworth, an award-winning acting professor in Northwestern's theater program, who has been acting and teaching acting for some thirty years now. I attended her workshops a half-dozen times or more, and benefited enormously in my own teaching from following the strategies she recommended. In the Resources section at the end of the chapter, you will find a video by Nancy Houfek in which you can see a similar workshop on effective classroom communication and encounter other strategies in this area.

First, as any poet or poetry scholar will tell you, we tend to emphasize the nouns and verbs when we speak. Say that last phrase aloud—and say it loudly, which forces out the meter of the words more clearly—and it should sound like this: When we *speak,* we *tend* to *emphasize* the *nouns* and *verbs.* We do this for good reason—the nouns and verbs carry the meaning in most sentences. Poems work like this too. When poems have a regular meter, that meter usually puts the stress marks on the nouns and verbs in a line of poetry.

Public speaking, at its best, sounds like poetry. You will be writing too many lectures and lecture notes to have them shaped as carefully as poems, but you can improve your speaking skills by making a more conscious effort to highlight the nouns and verbs when you are speaking in class. Doing so helps ensure that your listeners, who will only be taking in a fraction of the words you speak, are getting the most important ones.

A second tip concerns the way that many of us let our sentences fade away as we approach the end of them. When we speak it sounds like this: I WENT TO THE store today. This is perfectly natural: we expel breath as we speak, and as we get closer to the end of the sentence, we have less breath available to provide vigor and emphasis to our words. The structure of many English sentences, though, places the meaning of the sentence in its final words. Take "its final words" out of the previous sentence, and you will see how that sentence loses its meaning completely. So that sentence needs to be spoken like this: "The STRUC-

TURE of MANY ENGLISH SENTENCES, though, PLACES the
MEANING of the SENTENCE [pause; dramatic finish] in its
FINAL WORDS." Most sentences will benefit from building to
their end, as that one does, rather than trailing away into silence.

Becoming aware of just these two simple vocal strategies will
go a long way toward improving your speaking style. You'll be
too busy worrying about what you have to say the first few times
you have to lecture to the class, but by the second or third week
of the semester, try to spend the first five minutes of your lecture
emphasizing the nouns and verbs and key concepts, and building
your sentences to a strong close. At least a few times, practice delivering the opening five or ten minutes of a planned lecture
while concentrating exclusively on the use of your voice. Once
you have practiced it in this way, you'll be more likely to use
these vocal strategies in the actual lecture.

The second issue to consider is movement, and here I want to
recommend a simple middle ground—don't stand stock-still, and
don't pace constantly. The first habit produces boredom; the second distraction. Keep your movements around the classroom
simple and occasional, stepping from the center of the stage or
from behind the lectern when you are preparing to emphasize a
key point—but make sure that you are standing still when you
deliver that point. Movement is generally best when you are
transitioning between ideas, or building up to a point. When you
are ready to utter the sentence that will change the lives of your
students, though, stay in one place. You want their attention on
the words at that point, not on a moving body.

You can also use movement in simple ways to help increase
communication in the classroom, and to give the lecture the feeling of a conversation, rather than a spoken-word performance.
Move out into the seats to speak to the back of the room; move to
different sides of the room to speak to the corners; move in front

of individual desks and speak for a minute to one person, as if you and she were standing on the quad exchanging ideas. When students speak or ask questions, move to the opposite side of the room, so that they have to speak to the entire class rather than just to you.

Advice on gesturing pretty much mirrors that on movement. Use gesture to emphasize main points—don't keep your arms at your sides like an automaton, but don't flail constantly like you're pulling 737s into the gate. With gesture, as with movement and voice, just putting these elements on your conscious radar is half the battle. Once you have done so, you should be able to rely on your experiences listening to and watching other speakers, and your natural instincts, to guide you into more effective practices.

Content

Here come the Zen koans again: when it comes to content, less is more.

You are not a book. Books can provide an endless number of concepts and ideas, and all the details to support those ideas, in a way that allows the reader to study them and return to them as often as possible until they are mastered. Let the books you have assigned in the course provide the comprehensive overviews, with all of the attendant details. Keeping in mind the statistics we saw earlier about lecturing and student retention, and McKeachie's list of the lecture's functions, limit yourself to activities like summarizing, highlighting, and clarifying. Set a goal of no more than three to five concepts or ideas that you want to emphasize in a lecture, and make those points as fully and clearly—and as often—as possible.

My eleven-year-old daughter writes essays for school which always begin with a short paragraph explaining what she's about to say, and then conclude with a short paragraph saying what she has just said. This drives me bonkers, until I remember that she's eleven and they teach them to write essays like this for a while. But this highlights again the differences between written and oral communication. Written arguments for college students do not need that kind of repetition, because students can use their highlighters to note the main points, and can return to them whenever they wish. Students can't highlight your lectures, however, so they need you to emphasize and repeat the main ideas of your lecture—and doing so at the beginning and end of the lecture, in addition to presenting the main ideas in the middle, probably is not such a bad idea.

It's difficult to be much more specific about handling content in a lecture without descending into details that will exclude some discipline or another, so I won't go much further here. Use humor if you have a sense of humor; a few studies have shown that humor can help retain students' attention during lectures. And, of course, make sure you fill in every concept or idea with plenty of concrete examples. This not only helps illustrate the ideas, but gives students the chance to get the concept down in their notes while you are expounding upon the examples.

Blackboards, Overheads, PowerPoints, Multimedia

You can be certain of one thing when you are lecturing: whatever you write on the blackboard, on an overhead, or on a PowerPoint slide, students will copy into their notebooks. Studies have actually been done of how students take notes during lectures, and one unsurprising finding has been that students copy down faithfully whatever they can see—as opposed to what they hear, which they tend to write down in a much more haphazard fashion. One of the first studies of this kind, by Edwin Locke, found that students wrote down approximately 90 percent of the material that was written on the board, as opposed to only 60 percent of the material that was delivered only orally, but that was considered important to the course content. This habit of student note-taking has two practical consequences for you as a lecturer, when you are thinking about what to write on the board or copy onto an overhead or put onto PowerPoint slides:

1. You certainly should use these visual displays to highlight the main concepts from the lecture, since what you put on the displays will remain in their notebooks and can be returned to for later study.
2. You should use these visual displays *only* to highlight the main concepts from the lecture; doing more than this will result in students copying down furiously every detail from your slide, and not listening to a word you are saying.

The first point seems obvious enough; the second one is probably the more important one for a new teacher to remember. In the first few years when I was using overheads in lectures, I received the same complaint on the evaluations at the end of every semester: the teacher goes through the overheads too quickly. I got this comment repeatedly, despite the fact that I tried each semester to go a little more slowly. Eventually, I slowed down to the point where I would put up the overhead, and then allow students a minute or two of silence to write down the definitions or ideas before I started talking. Only then did the complaints stop.

What's the point of having students write down ideas from the board or slides at all, you might be wondering, given the challenges of copying down lots of information that could just as easily be presented to them on handouts or in their virtual learning environments? The reason is that when students take notes, they are processing the information you are giving them, establishing connections and building meaning in ways that do not happen so easily when they are just listening, or when you simply hand them an outline. Having students take notes during a lecture, rather than just following a printed handout, *does* help improve their learning and understanding. So you should have some visual aid to highlight and organize the most important elements of your lecture—and you should encourage your students to take notes during lectures, if you don't see them doing so already—but the visual aid should be limited to topic sentences or phrases, brief definitions, key facts and statistics, and so on.

One faculty member I know tries to take advantage of student note-taking as a learning activity by organizing his lecture around questions, rather than topics. So the structure of his lecture derives from five or six broad, conceptual questions that he places on his PowerPoint slides; the different parts of his lecture come as a response to each of these questions. When students are taking notes in his lectures, they are not simply copying down headings and subheadings but instead are writing answers to questions—an activity that they will engage in later on papers and exams. Hence his lectures become opportunities both for learning and for practicing the intellectual skills required in the course. This structuring principle for lectures would work in any discipline; consider trying it for an opening lecture or two, and seeing whether it fits with your lecture style (see my article "Beyond Lecturing" in the Resources section for a fuller description of this strategy).

The spread of technology on college campuses, and the growth of computer-enhanced classrooms, means that we no longer have to limit ourselves to putting words on boards or computer screens. And I should note that the caveat I issued in the chapter on technology applies here as well—simply putting your lecture outlines and important information on a PowerPoint slide represents no great improvement from writing those same words on the blackboard or putting them into an overhead. You might find it more convenient, and it has the same advantage of reproducibility that putting your course in a virtual learning environment can offer—you can continually revise and reuse PowerPoint slides, and save yourself time in future courses. (On the negative side, you won't make it through a career in teaching without having some problem with the media in your classroom, so always be prepared with a backup plan if you are relying on computers or other media!)

Technology is useful in enabling us to add other elements to lectures, such as audio or video clips—or websites or even cartoons or advertisements or search engine results—that help to illustrate our subject matter. When you see opportunities to introduce these sorts of elements into a lecture, by all means do so. Keeping in mind that students' attention fades after the first 15 or 20 minutes, try to space the media and technology clips so that they help provide a natural break in the lecture every 10 to 20 minutes. If you know you want to show three clips from a film that addresses your topic, for example, don't show all three right away, and then lecture for 40 minutes; rearrange the lecture so that you can show a clip every 15 minutes. These elements will refresh the attention of students, and will give you a new window of opportunity to present content in a more traditional way.

Obviously, you want such elements to contribute substantively to the lecture whenever possible. You won't do much harm, though, if you throw in a funny or only mildly relevant clip every once in a while to help recapture the attention of your students—and such lighter moments can provide a break for you in the lecture as well, giving you the chance to catch your breath and prepare for the next section.

Breaking It Up

The use of media provides an opportunity to break up solid blocks of lecture time, but you can—and should—find other ways to accomplish the same thing if you know you have to speak for most of a class period (at least 30–45 minutes). You can do this by building in opportunities for students to write, to talk to each other, or to let you know how well they are taking in the material you are presenting.

Students will already be writing during the lecture, taking notes on what they see and what you say (and one of the strangest experiences you will have as a new faculty member will be to see people writing down the things you have to say, as if you actually knew what you were talking about). So you don't want to stop in the middle of the lecture and give them a 15-minute writing assignment—that tactic will likely produce not much more than complaints and hand cramps. But you can find ways to build quick writing opportunities into lectures, spacing them out every 15 or 20 minutes. For example, you might consider pausing once in the middle of a 50-minute lecture and giving the students 3 to 5 minutes to organize and fill out their notes. Encourage them to look at what they have written, to add information or ideas that are still fresh in their mind but that they didn't have time to copy down yet, and to draw connections between the ideas that already appear in their notebooks. Such activities will enhance student learning during lectures, and the students will be grateful for the opportunity to stop and process your presentation for a few minutes.

You can also use writing to break up a lecture by pausing once or twice during the hour to pose a question or problem, and asking the students to answer or solve it in their notebooks. Again, these questions should be brief enough that students can respond in five minutes or so; you might ask them to think about or work through an issue that has been raised by the material you have presented thus far. In practical terms, it's worth taking a stroll around the room during such an exercise, which will encourage students to stay on task rather than spending the five minutes doodling or text-messaging their friends or (if they are working with laptops in a wireless classroom) shopping for shoes. Just the possibility that you might walk by their seat is usually enough to keep them honest. Depending upon the size of the room, you might finish a brief exercise like this by having a handful of students tell you their response; if time or room size works against this, begin the next part of the lecture with an answer or solution.

You can also break up longer lectures by building in moments for students to interact with each other, in pairs or small groups. The dynamics and mechanics of small-group work in the classroom are covered in Chapter 5, but for the purpose of breaking up lectures for just a few moments, you can usually get away with having students pair up quickly with their closest neighbor. This strategy works best when used either in conjunction with, or as an alternative to, having students write in response to a problem or question. In other words, you can ask students to respond quickly to such a prompt in writing, and then have them discuss their answers with each other for a few moments, giving them the chance to change their minds or clarify their responses.

The faculty member I mentioned who structures his lectures around big questions uses those questions for just this purpose. Once or twice during the lecture, he will pose the next question and then stop for a few minutes to allow the students to have what he calls a "discussion moment," in which they speak with a neighbor and speculate about the answer to that question before he gives his response. For courses in which such a break might focus on solving problems or working with formulas, the discussion moment can allow students to compare their solutions and how they got them. In either case, giving them a minute or two to work on their own before they respond can often produce better and more thoughtful results, but time and course size should probably dictate exactly what your strategy will be.

One now-famous example of this strategy, which has become the subject of a short film and numerous articles, is Eric Mazur's technique of "peer instruction," which he developed in his physics courses at Harvard University. Mazur describes it like this:

> Lectures are interspersed with conceptual questions, called *ConcepTests,* designed to expose common difficulties in understanding the material. The students are given one to two minutes to think about the question and formulate their own answers; they then spend two to three minutes discussing their answers in groups of three to four, attempting to reach consensus on the correct answer. This process forces the students to think through the arguments being developed, and enables them (as well as the instructor) to assess their understanding of the concepts even before they leave the classroom.

Mazur's classes are held in rooms which allow the students to respond electronically (he uses the Personal Response System devices that I discussed in the previous chapter), so he can see immediately how well they understand the concept. Once he sees those responses, he either knows he can move on to new material or recognizes that he has to clarify what the students have not understood. You don't need a wired classroom to accomplish this, however—you can always have students raise their hands as you present the different possible answers. But more and more classrooms are equipped with the PRS technology, and you should consider using it to provide opportunities for interaction in lectures.

If you happen to teach physics, and this technique intrigues you, you're in luck—visit Mazur's website referenced at the end of the chapter, and you'll find a large data bank of questions you can pose to physics students. Faculty in other disciplines should focus on developing questions that will test the students' understanding of basic concepts or ideas, perhaps most simply by asking them to apply a just-reviewed concept in a new context, and seeing whether they are capable of doing so. Mazur's method has been adopted in classes in a variety of disciplines at many institutions, and with good reason: "Nothing clarifies ideas," Mazur says, "better than explaining them to others." Any strategy that you use to promote quick discussions during a lecture will benefit from this simple truth.

One more technique along these lines, which I discovered as I was sifting through different perspectives on lecturing (but have not yet tried myself), comes from Christopher Lucas and John Murry: "Have your students exchange notebooks with their neighbors and allow them time to review one another's notes for completeness and accuracy" (64). No student's notebook will look exactly like anyone else's, and being able to see what a neighbor thought was important will prompt students to look more critically at their own lecture notes. My one caveat here is that you should warn students at the beginning of the class that you'll be doing this, simply to ensure that everyone is indeed taking notes (and to make sure the students aren't whiling away the lecture hour drawing caricatures of their classmates).

Finally, you can always rely on the basic technique of pausing regularly to ask for students' questions. You will probably find, though, that simply stopping and asking for questions—especially in large lecture courses—will not yield much feedback from students. Students are often reluctant to ask questions in such a situation, in part because they are intimidated by speaking before crowds, and in part because they will suspect that everyone else understands the material, and their question will reveal them to be an ignoramus who doesn't belong in college. Moreover, they have been sitting quietly and taking notes, and for them to shift in an instant from that passive position to the more active behavior of formulating questions can prove difficult.

You can encourage better questions by combining this strategy with one of those described above—giving students a minute to write down a question in their notebook, for example, or having them stop and speak to a partner about the one thing that they find confusing in the material you have presented thus far. Soliciting questions after taking one of these steps will yield much better results.

One final note on communication in the lecture: Make sure that, when you attempt to solicit questions, you communicate a real desire to hear those questions. If you call for questions, glance at the room quickly, and then immediately begin talking again, students will understand that questions are not really part of the process. If you ask a question, stop talking for 10 or 20 or 30 seconds, and wait. Take a drink of water, walk to a different part of the room, or just scan the faces for half a minute. Only by stopping long enough to give students the time to formulate questions will you convey to them that you really want their questions—and only then will you actually get questions from them.

Resources

Bain, Ken. *What the Best College Teachers Do.* Cambridge, Mass.: Harvard University Press, 2004.

See pp. 117–126 for recommendations on the use of lectures in college courses today, as well as some practical suggestions for structuring them.

Gorham, Joan, and Diane Christophel. "The Relationship of Teachers' Use of Humor in the Classroom to Immediacy and Student Learning." *Communication Education*, 39.1 (1990): 46–62.
You would be surprised at the number of studies that have been done on the use of humor in the classroom, many of which have appeared in communication journals like this one.

Houfek, Nancy. *The Act of Teaching, Part I: Theatre Techniques for Classroom Presentation.* The Derek Bok Center for Teaching and Learning. San Francisco: Jossey-Bass, 2007.
A video workshop on improving communication skills in the classroom.

Hwang, Seon Young, and Mi Ja Kim. "A Comparison of Problem-based Learning and Lecture-based Learning in an Adult Health Nursing Course." *Nurse Education Today*, 26.4 (May 2006): 315–322.
This is one of many such experiments you can find demonstrating the problems that arise from relying exclusively on lecturing as a teaching method.

Jones-Wilson, T. Michelle. "Teaching Problem-Solving Skills without Sacrificing Course Content: Marrying Traditional Lecture and Active Learning in an Organic Chemistry Class." *Journal of College Science Teaching*, 35.1 (September 2005): 42–46.
A good article not only on the limitations of lecturing, but on how to combine it effectively with other teaching methods in a basic science course.

Lang, James. "Beyond Lecturing." *The Chronicle of Higher Education*, 53.6 (September 29, 2006): C1.
This includes my description of a lecture organized as a re-

sponse to questions, something that was suggested to me by a reader.

Locke, Edwin A. "An Empirical Study of Lecture Note-Taking Among College Students." *Journal of Educational Research,* 77 (1977): 93–99.
Locke conducted a very thorough study of what students did and didn't write down during a lecture, which produced the statistic I cite in this chapter, among other findings.

Lowman, Joseph. *Mastering the Techniques of Teaching.* San Francisco: Jossey-Bass, 1988.
An older, but still highly regarded, general guidebook for college teaching. See pp. 96–118 for material on lecturing.

Lucas, Christopher J., and John W. Murry, Jr. "Teaching: Lecture and Discussion." In *New Faculty: A Practical Guide for Academic Beginners,* 39–70. New York: Palgrave, 2002.
Lucas and Murry provide their own list of reasons for the continued use of the lecture in the college classroom (pp. 58–59), and offer a good list of general suggestions for writing and delivering lectures (pp. 62–63).

Mazur, Eric. "Chaos in the Classroom?" 2007. *http://mazurwww .harvard.edu/research/detailspage.php?ed=1&rowid=8.* January 5, 2007.
Visit Mazur's Web pages for more information on his techniques to get students involved in lectures, and—for physics instructors—for lots of questions that you can use to break up lectures.

McKeachie, Wilbert, and Marilla Svinicki. *McKeachie's Teaching Tips,* 12th ed. Boston: Houghton Mifflin, 2006.
Two chapters cover lecturing (pp. 57–73) and making large lecture courses more interactive (pp. 254–265).

In the Classroom: Discussions

It's midnight on Sunday, the night before the first day of the fourth week of your semester. You're sitting in front of your computer with a glass of wine, reviewing the material one last time before you get to bed, knowing that in nine hours you'll be standing in front of twenty students in their late teens, charged with teaching them to think about—let's say—the sociology of race in a new way. You've spent the first few weeks mostly lecturing, using some of the writing and discussion strategies outlined in the last chapter, but now you want to begin alternating your lectures with days of more lengthy discussions, since the students have been developing a solid background knowledge in the subject area.

For tomorrow you have planned 15 minutes of introductory lecturing, and then a really killer starter question for the discussion, followed by close to two dozen questions you can fall back on to continue provoking discussion. You won't need them, though; the class will be so engaged with your first question, which is just going to blow their minds, that they'll be jumping out of their seats to enter the discussion. You're jumping out of your seat now; you can't wait to get started.

You're not quite as certain about the killer nature of your starter question when you walk into class the next morning, and find fourteen groggy kids waiting for you to tell them what they need to know—just as you mostly have been doing for the first three weeks. But you move along as planned with the introductory stuff. You finally throw out the killer starter question, which yields just five minutes of superficial conversation; they seem baffled by it. Each follow-up question yields less and less conversation. Class ends ten minutes early, and you walk out dispirited, wondering what the hell happened. You're exhausted, too—the minutes you spent waiting for people to talk, facing what Peter Frederick calls "the terror of silences," were some of the longest and most emotionally draining moments of your life.

So what happened? Was it the cheap Shiraz? The fact that last night was the first game of the World Series, and no one seems to have done the reading? Is it their fault—the kids these days with their iPods and tattoos and short attention spans, that kind of thing?

No, what probably happened was that you imagined twenty students who had a morning just like yours. You were up at 7:00 A.M.; you showered and got ready; you bought yourself a latte on the way into school; you watched a funny video someone e-mailed you from YouTube; and then you spent 30 minutes before class reviewing the material for the course.

Your students, on the other hand, rolled out of bed at 8:48, threw on yesterday's clothes and slippers and a baseball hat, hurried to the classroom while talking to their roommate on their cell phone about where to meet for lunch, and are now sitting in their chairs wishing they could have a sip of your latte. They're tired, and the easiest thing for them to do right now would be to sit and write down what you have to say. Your deep question kind of confused them, because you asked it in four different ways, and you didn't really give them a chance to think about it in any event. Once they saw that no one was talking, they banked on the fact that shutting up themselves would ensure one of two favorable outcomes: you go back to talking and they go back to writing, or you end class early.

This scenario plays itself out far more often in college classrooms than most instructors would like to admit, and it leads many teachers—especially new ones—to fall back into the comfort of lecturing whenever planned discussions don't spring to life as the teacher hoped they would. Lecturing can be a comforting teaching method because it depends only upon you for its success; discussions and group work depend partly on the input of the students, which you can't fully control. But you need to ensure that you do not stay in this comfort zone; you should introduce discussions into your classrooms, in some form, for three reasons.

First, one theory of human learning tells us that the more ways you can engage your mind and body with new ideas or material, the more deeply you will learn that material (see the book by Paivio cited at the end of the chapter). So reading about an idea engages you at one level; listening to someone speak about it engages you at a second; reading it aloud yourself might engage you at a third; writing it in your notebook a fourth, and so on. If scientists could invent a way for us to smell ideas, we could perfume our classrooms with the major tenets of Romantic poetic theory, and our students could sniff their way to academic success. One of my children's elementary school teachers told me once that she never learned anything until she read it aloud, in addition to reading and thinking about it on her own.

You're probably discovering this principle in your own life right now, as you have been preparing the course and delivering your opening lectures and talking about the material with your students. The old axiom that you don't *really* learn something until you teach it stems from this principle—teaching the material requires that you engage it in a variety of ways, from reading and writing to speaking and listening to the responses of your students (Eric Mazur's description of peer instruction from the previous chapter refers to this same idea).

Second, discussion gives students the opportunity to try out ideas and theories which they can then develop further and more formally in their papers and exams. Your supervisory role in a discussion means that, in a course on Renaissance literature, you can intervene and point out the problem when a student explains his theory that Shakespeare's sonnet cycle contains a hidden layer of references to NASCAR. The student won't make that mistake in his paper, which would be far more costly in terms of his grade. Discussions should serve as a testing ground for students to engage with the material and develop their own ideas for their course work in a supportive and informed environment.

Finally, when you convey clearly and regularly to students that discussions are an essential part of the course, and that their contributions to the discussions are important and necessary, you are helping them understand something important about learning: that you are not the teapot of the sociology of race, and they are not the teacup.

Discussions can help students see how they can contribute to the shape of the course and to the understanding of their fellow students, as well as how their fellow students can contribute to their own understanding. Discussions (and your clear explanations of the role of discussions in the course, which are essential) reinforce the model of learning as a collaborative, constructive enterprise, a model that underpins this entire book. You set the parameters and conditions; you provide the information they need; you serve as a guide along the way—but they work by themselves and with their peers to construct their new understanding of the subject.

In this chapter I'll outline a handful of techniques that should help to jump-start and sustain a discussion in just about any kind of class. As you will see, some of these are fuller uses of the techniques I've already mentioned that you can use to break up lectures—the use of writing or pairs prior to a group discussion, for example—so perhaps you will have already tried them out in a brief format.

In the end, though, discussions depend upon lots of human beings, and human beings are unpredictable. No matter how carefully you may plan for a discussion, sometimes they fail. It may happen because the students haven't done the reading, or the topic doesn't hold their interest, or for any number of other reasons. For every discussion class you plan to teach, then, you should have two arrows in your sling: a deep knowledge of the material under consideration, and a backup plan.

Discussions require a deeper knowledge of the text than lectures, since you need to be prepared enough to respond to just about any comment a student could make about the course material. Prepare for a discussion as you would for a lecture, doing your own highlighting and note-taking on the essential points that you hope will arise in the class, and thinking about what kinds of connections your students might make between the day's material and the course as a whole, as well as their own lives.

As for backup plans, my alternative for a discussion class on a work of literature frequently consists of nothing more than a series of highlighted passages in the text that I could lecture about if necessary, as well as a handful of additional questions that I could throw out if my primary discussion topic induces a comatose classroom.

With a deep knowledge of the material and a backup plan in your pocket, you'll feel a lot less anxious about the discussion, and you'll be much less likely to abandon it the first time you encounter a minute of silence.

Discussion Starter Techniques

START DISCUSSIONS WITH LOW-STAKES WRITING

The writing theorist Peter Elbow makes a useful distinction between two kinds of writing that we can ask from our students: high-stakes and low-stakes assignments. Students do high-stakes writing on formal essays and exams, and their grades largely depend upon this kind of writing. But Elbow argues that we can and should use low-stakes writing as frequently as possible in our courses, in order to help students grapple with the material and develop their ideas about it throughout the course. As the name implies, low-stakes writing is either ungraded or counts for only a tiny percentage of the course grade—a piece of low-stakes writing to start a discussion, for example, might count for 1 or 2 points out of 100 available points for a course.

Low-stakes writing exercises, which I described briefly in the chapter on syllabus construction as one possible assignment, are the easiest and perhaps most reliable techniques you can use to start discussions in your courses. They can take many forms at the opening of a discussion class, but the simplest method is to take that killer question you have planned to open the discussion and ask students to spend 10 minutes writing a response to it before the discussion starts.

Another possibility, if the subject of the discussion lends itself to a debate, is to ask them to take the first 10 minutes to stake out their position in the debate on paper, as well as the reasons for that position. If the discussion depends upon a clear understanding by the students of some factual material, ask them to spend 10 minutes identifying all the facts that will be important for the discussion. If you have assigned them reading, ask them to spend 10 minutes responding to the ideas in the reading.

The options are almost endless, but this method of beginning a discussion with pre-writing solves several of the (very common) problems that our hapless hypothetical instructor encountered in the opening scenario of the chapter:

- The pre-writing will help students turn their minds away from last night's episode of *American Idol* and onto the course material; those 10 minutes of pre-writing can function as a transitional period from the world outside of your classroom to the world within it.
- The pre-writing ensures that they have time to think. Put yourself in their situation: imagine someone standing in front of you and demanding an on-spot answer to the most complex question you can think of in your discipline—"I'll serve you your latte, madam, but can you please first tell me why humanitarian interventions by powerful nation-states almost never achieve their goals—and there's a line forming behind you, so be quick about it." Ask a complex question and expect immediate answers, and you're going to get superficial stuff.
- The time spent on the pre-writing, and the fact that they know only a small portion of their grade will depend upon their response, ensures that they will seek clarification of your question if you have not posed it clearly enough.

- Once a student has written down a response or position for a discussion, you can feel more comfortable inviting everyone into the discussion, or calling on nonresponsive students, since even the shyest student can simply look down and read off all or part of his answer.

I use low-stakes pre-writing in all of my courses at least once a week; each writing exercise, as I call them, counts for 10 points out of the 1,000 points available for the entire semester. These exercises are easy to grade, and they contribute immeasurably, in my experience, to the quality and fullness of any classroom discussion.

USE OPENING OR CLOSING STATEMENTS

I first learned of a variation of this technique from a history professor named Arthur McEvoy, who called it the McEvoy Minute Around. He would take off his watch, hand it to the student next to him, and give that student one minute to speak about the day's topic; after a minute, the student passed the watch to the person next to him, who had a minute to speak, and so on around the classroom.

This strategy works only in classes of twenty or less; in larger classes it would eat up too much class time. You don't need the formality of the watch, or the restraint of a minute. Simply establish that at the beginning of the class, each student has a brief time period either to respond to a question you pose, or to explain what she thought was important, or relevant, or interesting about the reading or material for that day's class. As the students offer their statements, you take notes, and use their comments and ideas to fill out or alter whatever discussion questions you have planned.

Closing statements represent a simple variation on this technique. Reserve the final 20 minutes of class for them, and ask each student to spend one minute describing what they learned from the discussion, or what they still don't understand or haven't decided about, or what they still want to talk more about.

Both of these techniques address something that you will learn from your experience in discussion classes: the longer a student sits in a course without speaking, the less likely he is to speak at all in that course. This technique ensures that everyone will speak at least once in the class, and almost always leads to participation in the discussion by a greater number of students than usual. Used several times over the course of the semester, it should raise participation rates in the discussion by a noticeable level.

USE SMALL GROUPS OR PAIRS PRIOR TO DISCUSSION

If you haven't seen it yet, you will one day encounter in a workshop or conference environment the technique called "Think-Pair-Share"—it's a favorite of workshop leaders at conferences on education. Despite its vaguely *Sesame Street*-ish title, it relies on the simple idea that giving students the opportunity to share their ideas with one or two peers prior to the group discussion gives them more confidence in the worth and relevance of their ideas. Often a discussion will be slow to start because you have a class full of students wondering whether their ideas have any merit, or wondering whether they have misunderstood your question. Speaking with another student or two before having to contribute to the larger class will alleviate those concerns.

The think-pair-share works exactly as its name implies: students spend a moment or two thinking about the opening question or problem; they pair with a partner to discuss their initial ideas; then the larger class discussion begins. Each of these elements can be tweaked in different ways—the "thinking" might be done on paper, for example, or the sharing might occur among larger groups. Kenneth Bruffee's work on collaborative learning in the classroom offers some excellent models for managing the transitions from small groups to the larger discussion.

Teaching with small groups, and Bruffee's model for such teaching, will be considered more fully in the next chapter. Make sure that you follow the most important prescription that I'll give there, which is to ensure that the pair or groups have a task with a very clearly defined outcome.

MOVE FROM FACT-GATHERING INTO INTERPRETATION

At least until you have established a comfortable environment in which students feel free to express opinions that might be unpopular, or to stake out positions in complex arenas of ideas, you might find that students are more likely to respond to fact-based questions in class. It puts much less pressure on students to come up with a brilliant and coherent answer when you pose simple fact-gathering questions—"What does your text suggest were the three main contributing factors to the outbreak of the First World War?"—rather than ones that require deeper thought or interpretation—"What possible contributing factors to the outbreak of World War I does your text *not* consider?"

An effective way to ease into a discussion, then, can be to open the class with a period of gathering facts and collecting the evidence you will need for the discussion on the board. Once that material is available and visible to everyone, a more informed and participatory discussion should follow.

Coming up with questions for the fact-gathering portion of a class is not a mindless exercise, though. Students may clam up in bafflement at overly complex questions, but they are equally likely to clam up in resentment at questions that are too simplistic or obvious—"What's the title of the book you read last night?

What's the name of the main character?" If you are teaching a novel in a literature course, for example, begin by constructing on the board a map of the characters and their relationships to one another instead of simply asking students to name the main characters. In an economics course, ask them not just for the name of a theory covered in the reading for that day, but also for an example of the theory taken from their experiences as consumers on a college campus.

FORCED DEBATE

I first read about this technique in a classic essay on teaching through discussion by the historian Peter Frederick. I use it at least once a semester in every class I teach.

Identify an issue about which there are two clearly defined and opposed positions, and let students know one class in advance that they will be required to select a side and defend it. On the discussion day, divide the room physically into two sides and ask the students to sit on one side or the other. I usually follow Frederick's suggestion to leave a space in the middle for undecided students—who, however, have to move to one side or the other before the class has ended. In fact, any student who changes her mind can move during the class: from one side to the other, from one side to the center, and back again.

You can, of course, begin forced debates with a writing exercise, asking students to write a one-paragraph explanation of why they are sitting where they are sitting. Opening a forced debate is the easiest question you'll ask all year: "Why are you sitting on that side?" I will usually ask a handful of students on one side to respond to that question; by the time they are finished, the students on the other side are frantic to refute the points they are hearing.

The physical division of the classroom facilitates the discussion as well, since whenever someone moves, you can pause and ask them why; it also helps the students see that others are changing their minds as a result of the discussion, as they learn from their peers.

START EARLY IN THE SEMESTER!

Inertia is not just for physics anymore. Just as an individual student who doesn't speak in class will become less and less likely ever to contribute to class, a class full of students who spend the first three weeks listening to lectures will be far less likely to jump enthusiastically into discussions when you're finally ready to let them speak. Several weeks of listening to lectures will condition students into a passivity that will be harder and harder to break as the semester continues.

Therefore, you should build opportunities for discussion, if possible, into the first or second class period of the course. On those days, more than any others, invite as many students as possible into the discussion, and make it clear that discussions are discussions: if you encounter some long silences, don't break them by falling back into a lecture. Students are quick learners— if you rescue them from poor discussions, they will make sure you play that role as frequently as possible.

These techniques should help you open a discussion about any topic you can imagine, but they don't take into account some thorny issues that come up in classes that rely on student participation. So I'll finish this chapter with a set of FAQs on teaching through discussion.

Can I call on people, or should I rely only on volunteers?
The hesitation that many teachers feel to call on people probably stems from a fear that we will come across as drill sergeants,

putting our students on the spot and demanding answers like every law school professor you've ever seen in the movies. And certainly we know that some students do have real anxieties, especially in their first year, about speaking publicly in class.

But in order for students to construct their own understanding of your subject, they need as many opportunities as possible to put their ideas into words, and course discussions are one of the most frequent and best opportunities they will have to do this. We all expect a college graduate to be able to speak on her feet when called to do so, however much she may not like it—to paraphrase a joke from Jerry Seinfeld, we don't want to produce students who would be more afraid of giving the eulogy at a funeral than they would be of being in the coffin!

For these reasons, you should get into the habit of inviting students into the discussion even when they don't volunteer. To combat silence inertia, you should ensure that everyone speaks at some point within the first two weeks, whether they volunteer or not.

But you don't have to become John Houseman in *The Paper Chase* to accomplish this. Ken Bain makes an excellent distinction between two methods we can use to encourage students to participate in discussions. In the first, we challenge students to a duel—"I've said something interesting, now you say something interesting." In the second method, we are inviting students to bring a dish to a feast—"Listen to all of these terrific ideas and comments; can we hear your thoughts as well?" Which method you use depends entirely on your phrasing and demeanor as you issue the invitation, which may not seem like much—but it can make a world of difference to a shy student.

You can also mitigate any anxieties that quieter students may have by calling on non-participating students on the days when you begin with writing. Let them offer their initial contributions to the discussion by simply reporting what they wrote for the low-stakes exercise.

Should I grade students' contributions to discussion? How should I do it?

Many instructors do assign points in the category of class participation, and frequently will include attendance in that category—for example, 10 percent of the course grade will be determined by the students' attendance and participation. A common method of doing this is to give students a grade for participation at the end of the semester, and then deduct points from that grade for any absences over a certain number.

This seems sensible enough to me, as long as you have a fair and consistent method for determining their participation grade. I used to use this exact system myself, and felt confident that I could eyeball my course roster at the end of the term and give a ballpark participation grade for every student. Some semesters I have more than a hundred students, though, and at the end of the semester my brain is already halfway out the door by the time I'm ready to calculate final grades. Trying to remember whether Red Sox hat made more contributions than Yankees hat came to seem a much too random and imprecise grading method for me.

If you do choose to have a participation grade, consider a weekly self-reporting sheet like the one I have included in Appendix B, prepared by Maryanne Leone, a colleague of mine in foreign languages. Students fill out this sheet at the end of every week; Maryanne collects them, scans them and either approves the grade or modifies it according to her judgment, records them, and returns the sheets. At the end of the semester, she uses those grades to calculate students' participation grade for the course. In addition to creating a more reliable method of grading their participation, this worksheet has the added benefit of reminding students on a weekly basis of the importance of course participation, and giving them a sense of control over their grades.

If you are using a virtual learning environment in the course, you can use contributions that students make to that environment as a basis for participation grades, as Lucia Knoles does with her classes.

Sometimes the discussion veers off track, and the students end up discussing issues that are only tangentially related to the course. What should I do?

First of all, relax. Let them go on for a few minutes. Remember that establishing an environment in which everyone feels comfortable participating is half the battle, so allowing them a little freedom to veer off track will help contribute to that objective. The surest way to stifle future discussions is to clamp down on any conversation that doesn't fit your agenda for the day's class. If you've managed to engage twenty American teenagers in intellectual conversation, you're doing at least half of your job as a college instructor.

Still, discussions that go too far off track can become a problem, especially for inexperienced discussion leaders. You can try to pull them back in one of two ways. The first is simply to point out that the class has moved away from material that will be helpful to them for their exams or papers, and to throw out a new question or issue to restart the discussion in a more focused way. This can sometimes be a momentum-killer, though, and students might even resent losing the opportunity to talk about something that matters to them. A better strategy is to listen closely to off-track discussions and try to find threads that you can pull out and tug back into a more academic context. In other words, identify some pieces of the off-topic and see if you can get the students to help you reexamine those pieces through the lens of what they should be discussing. If a political discussion has veered away from the work of a particular theorist and into some hot contemporary issue, for example, pay attention to seemingly irrelevant comments that could be reconsidered in light of that theorist's work: "Do we have any way of knowing what Locke might have thought of what we are doing in Iraq? Are there clues in last night's reading that might reflect what his opinion might have been?"

I have two students who speak all the time, and the rest only occasionally or not at all. How can I balance out the contributions?

In my experience, this is the most difficult problem you will encounter in discussion classes, one that I have wrestled with continuously and never adequately resolved. Most advice on this topic suggests creating a system that prevents the problem—a gateway structure, for example, in which students can only make two contributions per class unless everyone else has spoken. Charles Hanson, a sociologist, makes use of a system in which students get Post-It notes at the beginning of class; each time they speak, they place a Post-It note on the front of their desk for everyone to see. They get one point each for their first two postings; beyond that, they can still contribute and place their Post-Its, but they earn no additional points. Hanson claims that this system discourages students from dominating the discussion, since the number of their contributions is visible to everyone in class.

Such systems seem like plausible ones to me when you have an extremely polarized classroom situation—one or two students doing all of the talking, and the rest completely silent. That level of polarization won't happen too often if you're making use of the techniques described above.

For less extreme situations, I have usually been able to muddle through the problem by handling it casually and with a sense of humor. When a repeat responder raises his hand for the third or fourth time and everyone else sits silently waiting for me to call on him, I will say something like: "C'mon, I'm not going to let Kevin do all the work today. Let me hear from some others first and then we'll come back to you, Kevin."

Again, the key here is to take this tack early, and not to let the rest of the class fall into the hope that they can rely on a few people to carry the burden in the discussion classes for the rest of the semester.

How much time do I give a lagging discussion before I jump ship?

Barbara Gross Davis says it best and most succinctly: "Do not be afraid of silence. Be patient."

One statistic you'll see cited frequently in the higher education literature (including McKeachie, in the reference given below) claims that the average teacher endures approximately two seconds of silence, after posing a question, before she either rewords it or answers it herself. Most experts recommend that you force yourself to wait ten seconds before stepping in to reword or respond. Those ten seconds can seem like a lifetime, but do your best to hold off until then. You can make them go by more quickly by moving to a new spot in the classroom during the silence, taking a drink of coffee or soda, or turning your back and writing something on the blackboard. Usually you'll see, after completing one of these gestures and turning back to the class, a hand rising tentatively into the silence.

But, as Davis also suggests, don't always jump in relief at that lone hand. If you can stand it, keep waiting until other hands begin to rise, which will convey as clearly as possible that you have no plans to step in and do their job for them.

Resources

Bain, Ken. "How Do They Conduct Class?" In *What the Best College Teachers Do*, 98–134. Cambridge, Mass.: Harvard University Press, 2004.

See especially the section entitled "Getting Students to Talk" (pp. 126–134), which addresses the issues of student inertia in the discussion classroom and inviting students into the conversation rather than challenging them. Bain also talks about the McEvoy Minute Around (first described in an unpublished talk by Arthur McEvoy, who was then professor of history at Northwestern).

Bruffee, Kenneth. "Consensus Groups: A Basic Model of Classroom Collaboration." In *Collaborative Learning: Higher Education, Interdependence, and the Authority of Knowledge*. Baltimore: Johns Hopkins University Press, 1993.

Bruffee's work on consensus groups informs both this chapter and the chapter on teaching with small groups.

Davis, Barbara Gross. *Tools for Teaching*. San Francisco: Jossey-Bass, 1995.

See pp. 85–88 for Davis's suggestions on the kinds of questions that work most effectively in discussions, and for her take on silence in the discussion classroom.

Elbow, Peter. "High Stakes and Low Stakes in Assigning and Responding to Writing." In *Assigning and Responding to Writing in the Disciplines*, ed. Mary Deane Sorcinelli and Peter Elbow. San Francisco: Jossey-Bass, 1997.

Elbow's explanation of low-stakes writing and its use in the classroom.

Frederick, Peter. "The Dreaded Discussion: Ten Ways to Start." *Improving College and University Teaching*, 29.3 (1980): 109–114.

You'll see this old standby cited in many essays about teaching with discussion, and widely reprinted on the Internet.

Hanson, Charles M. "Silence and Structure in the Classroom: From Seminar to Town Meeting via 'Post-Its.'" *The National Teaching and Learning Forum,* 9.6 (October 2000).

Hanson's "Post-It" technique addresses the dual problems of no participation and the dominant talker in a discussion.

McKeachie, Wilbert J. "Facilitating Discussions: Posing Problems, Listening, Questioning." In *McKeachie's Teaching Tips: Strategies, Research, and Theory for University and College Teachers,* 12th ed. Lexington, Mass.: D. C. Heath, 2001.

A good overview of discussion, as well as a thoughtful consideration of the problems that arise in discussions.

Paivio, Allan. *Imagery and Verbal Processes.* New York: Holt, Rinehart, and Winston, 1971.

Paivio's main idea, known as dual-coding theory, suggests that learning retention improves when learners receive both visual and auditory representations. The more general idea that multiple-sensory stimulation improves learning derives in part from this theory.

▬ ▬ ▬ ▬ ● ▬ ▬ ▬ ▬ ▬ ▬ ▬ ▬ ▬ ▬

In the Classroom:
Teaching with Small Groups

My inclination is to go into this chapter with my argumentative guns blazing, ready to counter the opinions I know you have about group work in the classroom as a complete waste of time and energy, as well as a source of irritation and discomfort for many students. I know you have these opinions for the obvious reason that, before I started teaching, I had those same opinions myself.

While I was doing the research for this chapter, in fact, I came across a survey that was designed to give a quick overview of an individual's preferred methods of learning. The VARK Inventory has been around since 1992, when it appeared in an educational journal called *To Improve the Academy*. It's a simple test, just sixteen questions, and your responses to these questions are designed to reflect your preferences and strengths as a learner in each of four categories: visual, aural, reading and writing, and kinesthetic. I took the test, and was absolutely unsurprised to learn that I had a very strong preference for learning through reading and writing, with a secondary preference for aural learning. This means that I prefer to read, write, and listen to lectures.

I was only half-joking when I said that I knew you were just like me, because in fact the VARK Inventory statistics—approximately eight to ten thousand people take the online version of the Inventory each month, and a post-test questionnaire gathers information about test-takers for statistical comparisons—show that teachers have a significantly higher preference for learning through reading and writing than their students do. So the chances are good that you are, in fact, like me, and prefer learning through reading and writing—and hence, like me, you may have been colossally annoyed as a student when you were told to get into groups and discuss things or do things or share things or be things.

But that same VARK statistic has an obvious flip side, which reminds us that many of our students prefer to learn in other ways—and one of those ways may be engaging in conversations or problem-solving tasks or other kinds of activities in small groups with their peers. I learned this from experience during my first few semesters of teaching, when I occasionally did use small groups, simply because I got tired of doing nothing but talking and holding whole-class discussions. I felt hesitant about using the groups, and imagined the students seething with resentment as they formed into groups, wishing they were down the hall in an anonymous chemistry lecture. At the end of the semester, though, I would always receive course evaluations which identified the small group work as one of the best features of the class. Much as I wanted to dismiss those comments as the ravings of a few crackpots, I began to understand that teaching in small groups really does benefit a certain portion of students.

Of course, since the learning preference for reading and writing is not a universal one among teachers, you may be one of those people who enjoy working with small groups, in which case you don't need to hear this argument. If you aren't one of those people, just remember that, as I argued in the chapter about lecturing, judgments about teaching strategies and their effectiveness should not be based exclusively on what we liked or disliked as students. Moreover, the arguments to be made for using small groups in the classroom, which come in many forms these days, are too numerous and well-supported to ignore.

I'll offer just three, but encourage you to dig into the references at the end of the chapter if you still need to be convinced of the value of small group work—or, as the literature usually refers to it, collaborative learning—in your classroom.

The first reason for using small groups stems more from simple thinking about the futures of our students than from concrete research, but you'll find this argument advanced in almost every book or article that argues for collaborative learning strategies. Mara Sapon-Shevin puts it this way: "It is hard to think of a single job today that doesn't involve working with others at some level. We can ill afford to graduate students who are competent but uncommunicative, skilled but unable to share those skills, capable of doing but not of teaching what they know" (xiii). In other words, much as students might prefer to learn by reading or listening, and then simply reporting back what they know on tests or papers, they won't be doing that a lot after they graduate. Assuming that at least part of the purpose of a college education is to prepare students to succeed in their career choices, we should take seriously the obligation not only to help them understand our disciplines and their related skills, but also to help them learn the communication and interaction skills they will need in their careers.

And Sapon-Shevin is certainly correct in saying that very few careers will allow an individual to avoid working in collaboration with others—whether they are presenting reports, pitching ideas, making sales, communicating with employers or customers, or even working in study groups or teams (in the case of students who are making their way through medical or law school).

Even if we don't explicitly *teach* students how to work in groups (although many writers on collaborative learning argue that we should do just that), we are still giving them a taste of an experience that will play a regular role in their futures, a glimpse of the challenges that face learning or working groups, and a sense of how well they respond to those challenges.

More convincing than this reason, to my mind, is the vast body of research that suggests that students who work collaboratively to solve problems and perform other learning tasks, as Barbara Gross Davis explains, "tend to learn more of what is taught and retain it longer than when the same content is presented in other instructional formats." She adds (as a bonus for first-year teachers desperate for good course evaluations) that "students who work in collaborative groups also appear more satisfied with their classes" (147). Many studies (like the one cited in Chapter 3 on Korean nursing students) have been conducted that offer comparisons between two or more sections of a course taught in different formats, one of which had the students working primarily in small groups; those studies have overwhelmingly established the benefits of small group learning for college and university students. Jack Tessier's article from a 2007 issue of the *Journal of College Science Teaching* offers one recent example of this exact paradigm—comparing the end-of-semester knowledge and skills of students taught in a collaborative learning-based course in general biology with those of students taught in a more traditional classroom environment. His results showed especially notable improvement for the students in the lower segments of the grade range. You can also see the opening chapters of *Collaborative Learning Techniques,* cited below in the references, for descriptions of some of the studies that have been done to test the effectiveness of this teaching method. As that book points out, too, the positive effects of collaborative learning extend beyond long retention—both students' satisfaction with their college experience and their persistence in obtaining the degree also increase among those who work in collaborative environments with their peers.

The third reason I would advance for collaborative learning is a more theoretical one, discussed in Kenneth Bruffee's excellent book, *Collaborative Learning: Higher Education, Interdependence, and the Authority of Knowledge*. Bruffee argues that collaborative learning helps establish and promote a better understanding of knowledge and learning in general:

> Most of us, including most college and university teachers, assume a foundational (or cognitive) understanding of knowledge. Knowledge is an entity that we transfer from one head to another—for example, from a teacher's head to a student's or from a staff member's head to the head of the boss. Collaborative learning assumes instead that knowledge is a consensus among the members of a community of knowledgeable peers—something people construct by talking together and reaching agreement. (3)

You won't find many learning theorists arguing these days for a foundational understanding of knowledge; I'm guessing if you look closely at your own experiences delving into the research in your discipline for your dissertation, in search of some elusive "fact," you've probably long ago abandoned the idea that the facts of a discipline exist on stone tablets to be memorized and passed on. The phenomenon of Wikipedia, perhaps more than anything else in our larger culture, has helped spread the idea that knowledge is a shared construction, one that comes into existence from the collaboration of knowledgeable experts. Bruffee's point is that while few of us would accept anymore the idea that knowledge came down with Moses on Mt. Sinai, we still teach as if it did. Collaborative learning, by contrast, models for students the idea that we construct knowledge together, and thus that they can construct knowledge together in their small groups. Their ability to see this point may be limited or partial, but that doesn't make it any less important for us to model it for them.

Before getting into strategies and problems with small group work, we need to define terms, and distinguish between two main forms of collaborative learning. First, you will hear this kind of teaching referred to variously as teaching or learning in small groups or teams, collaborative learning, cooperative learning, and many other names. There may be subtle differences in what these terms refer to, but you don't need to worry about that for now. They all describe a teaching strategy which puts students into small groups, from as few as two to as many as five or six, and requires those groups to complete some task. However, we do need to distinguish between two different ways in which college faculty typically work with small groups in their courses.

Informal learning groups are those which you might establish for all or part of a single class session, and which generally have a task or assignment that can be completed within that same class session. Having students pair up to compare their answers to a question for a few minutes (as in Eric Mazur's physics classes) would constitute the minimal use of informal learning groups; assigning students to groups of three or four to work through a complex mathematical problem in class, and to turn in their results for a quiz grade at the end, might constitute the most extensive use of informal learning groups. Occasionally I will set up informal learning groups to complete a task in a class session, and it will take longer than I expect; in those cases, the same groups might reconvene to finish the task during the next session, but without any expectation that they have worked on the assignment outside of class.

Formal learning groups, by contrast, are generally assigned a task that requires them to meet outside of class, such as writing a lab report or giving a presentation or building a website. These learning groups continue over longer periods of the semester; some teachers establish them at the beginning of the semester and maintain them for various tasks throughout the course. A journalism professor I know puts his students into writing groups that read and critique each other's writing throughout the semester. Formal learning groups come with a special set of challenges that don't present themselves quite as intensely in informal learning groups—in particular, formal learning groups can have problems if students don't cohere well in the group, or if one or more students dominate or slack off, or if they have trouble finding opportunities to meet (because, for example, the members of a group are all commuters with conflicting work schedules).

Because informal and formal learning groups create different opportunities and challenges, I've structured the rest of this chapter to address the strategies you can use, and problems you may encounter, in each format.

Informal Learning Groups

SETTING TASKS FOR SMALL GROUPS

The earlier chapters on discussions and lectures offered suggestions for tasks you might assign to pairs or small groups—such as having students attempt to answer a discussion question that you posed during a lecture, before you provide the answer yourself. The possibilities here are almost endless, and you might think about it like this: any question or problem or task that you might assign to students for homework, or ask them to complete on an exam, can usually be modified into an activity for small learning groups. In fact, you should design at least some small group tasks that will have students completing precisely the kind of work they will need to do on assignments and exams. Doing so gives them the opportunity to practice the skills they will need on those evaluated assignments, and lets them do this under your guidance, with the help and feedback of both you and their peers.

Here are some specific examples of tasks that you might assign to informal learning groups:

- Complete a complex mathematical equation, or solve a problem.
- Create a list of the five most essential concepts from last night's reading, in order of importance.
- Identify three real-world scenarios in which some abstract theorem or idea operates.
- Draw a chart that maps out the characters in a novel or film and their relationship to one another.
- Select a key passage from a reading and have the students "hyperlink" it by highlighting and explaining terms for which they can provide context.

You should notice one common feature in all of these tasks: each of them requires students to complete a task that has concrete, written results.

This is the most important rule for designing tasks for small groups, probably the only one that really matters. The surest recipe for both pointlessness and student dissatisfaction with small groups is to ask them simply to get into groups and discuss the reading, or tell each other what they think about it, or to, like, share their feelings, dude. Small groups need focus and direction to succeed, and they will get those things when they are working together on a task with results that can be recorded and explained if they are called upon to do so. Have students answer specific questions, or create lists, or map or chart things, or solve problems, or work on any other creative task that will lend itself to concrete results. Doing so will avoid some of the problems that otherwise can arise in group work—such as groups that go off task, or talk about their weekend plans instead of the course content. You are even more likely to avoid such problems if you give them some credit for their group work—have them turn in their work at the end of the class for a quiz grade, or for some other small fraction of their final grade for the course.

FORMING GROUPS

Putting the students into informal learning groups can be done in lots of ways, and many writers on group work argue that groups should be formed deliberately by the instructor so that they are heterogeneous. Ken Bain's study of effective teachers in higher education reports that his subjects frequently "found heterogeneous groupings more satisfactory than homogeneous ones, and created the diversity around issues of experience and proficiency with the material and the reasoning skills it required" (129). Put more bluntly, heterogeneity does not mean constructing a *Survivor*-esque mixture of blacks and whites, men and women, and so on; it means ensuring that each group has a smart kid, a . . . not-so-smart kid, and then various shades in between. The rationale usually advanced for this strategy is that the smart kids learn by helping the others in the group, while the others benefit from the smart kids' tutoring.

This makes sense to me, but not much research has been done in support of this argument, so I've always taken it with a grain of salt—especially because Bain goes on to point out that "some teachers let students form their own groups because it gave students control over their education" (129). In large classes it will prove too time-consuming for you to make deliberate pairings to produce heterogeneity, so I wouldn't worry about it. Either let the groups form by working with their neighbors, or assign them randomly. You can do this very simply by figuring out how many students you would like to have in each group and dividing that number into the total number of students in the class. The resulting figure is your total number of groups—have students count off around the room to that number, and then start again at one; when they are done instruct them to get together with everyone who counted the same number as they did. So in a class of twenty in which you want groups of four, you'll end up with five groups; in a class of twenty-five you'll end up with five groups of four and one group of five (it almost never works out evenly).

In smaller classes, where you might have the chance to group students more deliberately into heterogeneous groups according to their abilities, you could think about doing this as the semester progresses and you become familiar with their abilities. Until that point, let them form groups randomly or by counting off. If you delve deeply into the literature on collaborative learning and group formation, you will discover more complex schemes for grouping people according to their abilities, sometimes by having them line up according to some self-reported trait (*Collaborative Learning Techniques* describes a boatload of possible group-forming methods). To my mind, however, these kinds of exercises take up too much time to be worth the effort for informal learning groups.

MANAGING GROUPS IN THE CLASSROOM

"Everything in moderation," my father used to say to me, as he was dropping me off at college after every break. I think this was his way of telling me not to drink too much beer, but in fact this advice works well in many areas of life, including strategies for managing groups in the classroom: don't hover over the groups constantly, questioning their every decision, but don't sit at the front of the room and ignore them either.

No matter how well you design the task, you will still have students who don't understand it, and groups that wander off course, and students who will do their best to sit back and let others have the conversation without them. So you do need to provide some supervision of the groups, however minimal. At the same time, students will feel inhibited, and may clam up, if you plunk yourself down in a chair with a group right after you have set the task. Give the groups a few minutes to begin the process on their own, after you ensure that all the groups have understood the task and are making progress. Then move around the room, occasionally eavesdropping to check for problems, but primarily making yourself available for assistance. Envision your role here as an expert resource who can help students complete a task that someone else has assigned to them.

As you move around the room, you may encounter some of the following situations:

1. A group that began well, but has now fallen silent and seems unsure how to proceed. You can jump-start such a group by pointing out the next step they should take, or by asking a question or two.

2. A group in which you see three students working and one sitting back in his chair with a scowl and his arms folded. Listen to the group's discussion for a moment, and then ask that student what he thinks, forcing him to enter the conversation. Further along in the semester, when you might know that a particular student is likely to withdraw from a group exercise, you can help that person stay engaged by making sure each group has a designated re-

corder—that is, the person who writes down the group's responses—and simply designating that student as the recorder. Having to record the group's ideas will ensure at least some participation from the loner.

3. Groups talking about something other than the assignment. This problem will almost always correct itself simply by standing within earshot of them, which conveys to them that the teacher is watching and they had better get back on task.

4. Groups that complete the task as quickly as possible and then begin other work, or sit silently. If other groups are nearing completion, don't worry about this. But you can avoid this problem by designing tasks that allow for on-the-spot extensions or variations of the task. Ask a group that has finished to come up with two additional items for a list, or to consider how a slight change in the problem they are discussing would affect their answer, and so on. You can prepare them for this possibility by explaining at the outset that the next 20 minutes will be set aside for working in groups on a task, and that they need to watch the clock and time themselves accordingly; if they finish early, you will give them interesting variations of the assignment. This cuts off the expectation that they can rush through the task and then spend 10 minutes text-messaging their friends in the classroom next door.

In general, it can help to lay down some ground rules for the groups before you use them for the first time, even if those rules are relatively spare. In my composition courses, I have students get into informal learning groups a few times each semester to read and comment on each other's rough drafts, and before each session I remind them of my two rules for these working groups:

follow the golden rule by writing full commentaries on their peers' papers, with the kind of detailed feedback that they're hoping to get on their own papers; and make full use of the time allotted, so that if they complete the questions I use to direct their feedback, they should read back through the paper and use the time to offer additional thoughts or editing. I developed these rules after a few years in which a small number of students would provide the absolute minimum amount of feedback to their peers, and then would just sit back for the final 10 minutes of the session and stare at the wall. The rules have not completely eliminated this problem, but they have decreased its frequency.

PROCESSING INFORMAL GROUP WORK

Whenever a student, or a group of students, puts their ideas down on paper, they will want some kind of feedback or processing of their work. You should either allow time for this in class, or give them feedback on any written work that they turn in. The simplest means of processing small group work in the classroom is to ask each group, at the end of the exercise, to report to the class on their findings. This will do in a pinch, if you haven't had much opportunity to plan the processing stage, but I will warn you that this can be a stultifying exercise, as each group reports for two or three minutes and then sits silently listening (or, often, not listening) to six other groups respond to the exact same question they just answered. If you have more than six or seven groups, a full report from each group can really suck the life out of a room that had been buzzing with activity just a few minutes before.

Consider two alternatives to the orderly reporting of group work. First, treat the group work as pump-priming for a discussion: pose again to the class the question or problem that they have been working on, and let individuals and groups respond as they would normally in a whole-group discussion. This strategy puts some spontaneity back into the session and allows students to respond to each other's comments as they are made, rather than having to wait for other groups to report before they finally get their say. You can certainly still ensure that all groups speak by inviting a quiet group to give its response, but hold off on this until all of the volunteers have spoken—and you almost certainly will have volunteers when they have had the chance to tackle the issue in groups first.

Second, you might consider posing a different question or problem to help students process their group work—one that their task has helped prepare them for, but that also pushes them in a new direction. For example, if I have asked groups to draw a visual representation of the different characters in a novel and their relationships with one another on a posterboard (as I sometimes do), I might follow up by asking everyone to tell me what they learned about a specific character from this process. Or suppose you had asked the groups to use the information from the previous night's reading to identify the three best pieces of evidence in support of an argument for affirmative action policies; you might begin the processing by asking the groups to identify what they would see as the best piece of evidence *against* such policies. Questions like these draw on the thinking they have done in the groups, but push the class into new intellectual territory as well.

Formal Learning Groups

SETTING FORMAL GROUP TASKS

A common formal learning group task is to have students work together in pairs or groups on an assignment that requires an eventual classroom presentation. I suspect many teachers make presentations into group efforts for very practical reasons—it simply would take up too much class time to have students offer presentations individually, and it also relieves some of the immense pressure students feel at having to give presentations when they can split the burden of presentation time among them. Given that we do want students to be able to communicate effectively by the time they graduate, whether orally or in writing, presentations ensure that we are helping them develop that skill, and group presentations ensure that we do not sacrifice too much classroom time for this.

Save presentations for the second half of the semester, if you plan to use them, to allow students to feel more comfortable with each other than they would if they were standing in front of their peers in the second week of class. Use them to ask students to do research or develop perspectives that supplement what you are offering in the classroom; that way the students will have new content to teach their fellow students. In an introductory philosophy course, for example, the students might be asked to research and present biographical and historical contexts on the major philosophers who are being covered in the course, filling out the brief sketches that you offer for each new thinker. You can hold the students responsible for this material by letting them know that they will have to write one essay question on the final exam that links a philosopher's biography or historical era to his or her major work; if you don't hold them responsible for the content of the presentations in any way, they may treat the presentations of their fellow students as mental check-out time (just as they might do when other groups are reporting their results at the end of an informal learning groups session). Including some aspect of the material in the presentations on an exam will also help convince students that their research is more than busywork; it forms an integral part of the course.

But research presentations don't exhaust the possibilities for formal learning groups. Students working with lab partners would count as formal learning groups, as would problem-solving or study groups in mathematics or statistics. Students could work together to construct a website, present a written research report, develop a business plan for a fictitious company, write an entry for Wikipedia, film a documentary, stage a scene from a play, and so on.

The only real requirement for a formal learning group task is that it be easily divisible into parts. Students should be able to gather together as a group to come up with a direction or outline for the project, and then should be able to separate and conduct some of the work on their own. Given the large numbers of nontraditional students on campus today—students with work commitments and families and commutes—requiring students to work together on every detail of a group assignment may prove excessively burdensome. For this reason, formal papers written by groups may be a difficult assignment; such papers often end up looking like patchwork quilts, with four separate papers having been pieced together into a single document.

FORMING GROUPS

Because students working on formal learning group assignments will be spending more time with each other than those who are simply yoked together for 20 minutes to solve a problem in class, it would seem to make sense to spend a bit more time and energy considering how to form such groups. Unfortunately, no consensus exists in the research literature on collaborative learning regarding the proper strategy for constructing formal learning groups.

Barkley and her colleagues argue, for example, that "broadly speaking, research supports heterogenous grouping because working with diverse students exposes individuals to people with different ideas, backgrounds, and experiences . . . There is also some evidence that diverse groups are more productive and better suited for multidimensional tasks" (45). I had read some version of this statement often enough that I worked hard to create heterogeneous formal learning groups in my first few years of teaching, and found myself frequently frustrated. What I experienced, it turns out, was not unusual, according to a further consideration of this issue just a few paragraphs later by Barkley: "Homogenous grouping offers advantages for some kinds of learning activities . . . Homogenous groups may also master most efficiently highly-structured skill-building tasks, since students can communicate with each other starting from a similar level of knowledge" (45). When I had students in my advanced creative writing classes work on each other's essays in heterogeneous groups according to their writing abilities, for example, I found the exercise only moderately successful, and often frustrating to the students. The best students may have gained something from critiquing the work of their peers, but those excellent students tended to receive either little or poor advice from the weaker students, who floundered when they were asked to make suggestions on how to improve the papers of their more skillful peers.

These days, then, I tend to use either random or heterogeneous groupings for informal learning groups, and homogeneous ones—teaming up strong students with strong students, and weak students with weak ones—for formal learning groups. I know that many of my colleagues prefer to let students form their own groups when those groups will have to meet outside of the classroom, since the groups might self-select according to their schedules. Self-selection may also give students some of that sense of control over the task that Ken Bain refers to. However, self-selection can also lead to groups based purely on friendships, and friends who are assigned an intellectual task can easily fall into groupthink mode, unwilling to challenge each other or push against anyone's ideas for fear of disrupting the friendship.

I like a compromise proposed by Barbara Walvoord, who addresses the subject of group formation in her book about teaching writing and having students critique each other's writing in small groups. Walvoord suggests that you ask students to submit their preferences for group partners to you a class or two in advance of the official forming of the groups, if they have such preferences (many won't). Keeping those preferences in mind, you select the groups, with an eye toward whichever principle, heterogeneity or homogeneity, seems appropriate to you. If four students who sit in the back row and talk through every class request to be together, break them up; students who have expressed no preference can be grouped according to how well they have performed in the course, or the number of prior courses they have had in your discipline (this is something you can ask them on the student information sheets they fill out on the first day of the semester).

I've been happy using a version of this strategy for several years now—asking for the students' preferences, and then following those preferences as much as possible as I create homogeneous groups. And in fact I apply this strategy to other elements of the group's formation and task-setting. If I have constructed a list of possible research topics for students to choose from, I ask the groups to select their top three choices; if I have multiple possible presentation dates, again I ask them for their top two or three preferred presentation dates. In all of these cases, though, I make the final decision—which I hope gives them some sense of control over the groups and the assignment, but ultimately lets them know that I am responsible for what happens in the course.

MANAGING GROUPS IN AND OUT OF THE CLASSROOM

Because of the difficulties that students may have in finding meeting times outside of the class, you should set aside some time to allow students to work with their groups in class. This doesn't have to be extensive—20 or 30 minutes at the beginning of the process can be enough to allow them to coordinate their schedules and set up a plan of action; a half class or full class set aside for the groups to work on their projects at a later date provides an opportunity for them to begin combining their work, and also allows you the opportunity to circulate among the groups and check their progress. If you don't feel you have enough time for this in class, you do need to monitor the groups somehow and ensure that they are making adequate progress— perhaps by having them visit you once in your office, or send you two or three required e-mail updates, or turn in work in stages. Don't just form the groups, give the assignment, and expect everything to move smoothly along. This generally will not happen.

After the first year of using small groups for formal learning tasks, you will likely have encountered some of the following common problems:

1. One or two members of the group are not pulling their weight. You may find out about this from a hesitant e-mail or office visit from a conscientious group member, or you may notice it yourself during the classroom working time. You can often prevent this problem, or at least have means at your disposal to respond appropriately to it with your grading pen, by having both group and individual grades for the task. So the group might receive a single grade for their oral presentation, but individual members would receive grades based on the outlines and bibliographies they turn in for their portion of that presentation. You can also mitigate this problem by taking a few minutes to speak with each group, either in class or by requiring each group to make one office visit, and checking with each student to see what contributions they have made to the project thus far. These conversations will usually expose the slacking student to the

daylight in front of their peers, and often will spur him or her to avoid further embarrassment by getting to work.

2. Sometimes groups will claim that they simply disagree too sharply to work productively, and will request to be disbanded and dispersed into other groups, or one student will ask to switch groups. Unless the circumstances are really compelling (such as a student feeling threatened by other group members), you should resist any requests to reorganize groups. Help them sort their problems out, have them come talk to you in your office—but remember, they're big kids, and you are not asking more of them than they should be able to handle, or more than they will be expected to handle in their professional lives. Every class will contain a student who's about as enjoyable to work with as Steve Carell's character in *The Office* (or his British equivalent, Ricky Gervais), but those characters are funny because we all know people who are equally obnoxious, and sometimes you still have to work with them to sell paper goods.

3. Other problems that you might find in formal learning groups—such as students who wait until the last minute, or move in an unproductive direction—should be addressed by staying on top of their progress, and speaking with students about the status and direction of the group's work in their classroom sessions or in office visits.

PROCESSING FORMAL GROUP WORK

Processing this kind of group work primarily means grading it, and the major question here is whether you grade the students individually or as a group. Again, there are no clear answers here—group grades can reward or punish people whose contributions to the project don't match those of other group members, while individual grades can hurt the coherence of the group task, as each member focuses primarily on achieving a good grade for herself. The most practical and effective model for grading group work, then, is to combine the two, and assign a grade to the group as well as a grade based on the written contribution that each individual makes to the project. So, if the group gives a formal presentation which they have broken down into parts, ask each member of the group to provide a written outline of their part, as well as an annotated bibliography of the works they consulted for the presentation.

As for the specifics of grading projects, and grading individual work, and grading in general: all of that and more will be covered in the next chapter.

Resources

Bain, Ken. "How Do They Conduct Class?" In *What the Best College Teachers Do,* 98–134. Cambridge, Mass.: Harvard University Press, 2004.

This is the section of the book that covers in the most detail the nitty-gritty of classroom teaching.

Barkley, Elizabeth, et al. *Collaborative Learning Techniques: A Handbook for College Faculty.* San Francisco: Jossey-Bass, 2005.

After an opening section on the theoretical basis for collaborative learning, and tips on group work in general, this book describes thirty collaborative learning techniques, each filled out with examples from different disciplines.

Bruffee, Kenneth. *Collaborative Learning: Higher Education, Interdependence, and the Authority of Knowledge.* Baltimore: Johns Hopkins University Press, 1993.

This is a great book, one that deserves a full reading whether or not you commit yourself to collaborative learning. Bruffee presents the most philosophical perspective on the enterprise, as in: "Collaborative learning is a reacculturative process that helps students become members of knowledge communities whose common property is different from the common property of the knowledge communities they belong to" (3). If you find sentences like that one intriguing—and I'm a sucker for them—Bruffee's work will help refashion your perspective on higher education. His theories about knowledge and our acquisition of it have strong parallels to the ideas in Thomas Kuhn's *The Structure of Scientific Revolutions,* as Bruffee acknowledges.

Davis, Barbara Gross. "Collaborative and Experiential Strategies." In *Tools for Teaching,* 145–174. San Francisco: Jossey Bass, 1993.

This section covers not only collaborative learning but other alternatives to traditional teaching strategies, such as role playing and case studies—all worth a look.

Fleming, Neil. "VARK: A Guide to Learning Styles." 2006. *http://www.vark-learn.com/english/index.asp.* November 29, 2006.

The original questionnaire, first published in *To Improve the Academy,* has been updated several times, and you can now take it online at Fleming's VARK site. The statistics about teacher and student learning styles are from the FAQ section.

Fleming, Neil, and Colleen Mills. "Not Another Inventory, Rather a Catalyst for Reflection." *To Improve the Academy,* 11 (1992): 137–155.

The article that first presented the VARK inventory.

Sapon-Shevin, Mara. Foreword. In Ruth Federman Stein and Sandra Hurd, *Using Student Teams in the Classroom: A Faculty Guide,* xi–xiv. Bolton, Mass.: Anker, 2000.

Sapon-Shevin's Foreword contains a useful summary of why collaborative learning is important in today's academy. The book as a whole provides an overview of the theories behind collaborative learning, followed by two sections: techniques for forming and handling groups—these authors call them "teams"—in the classroom, both formal and informal; and several dozen examples of specific exercises in which faculty at Syracuse University have used teams in a wide variety of disciplines.

Tessier, Jack. "Small-Group Peer Teaching in an Introductory Biology Classroom." *Journal of College Science Teaching,* 36.4 (2007): 64–69.

Tessier's research is one of many comparative studies of this kind. Go to the ERIC or EXAC databases that your institution's library will subscribe to, type in the words "collaborative learning," and you will find study after study showing results similar to the ones I note above in this chapter.

Walvoord, Barbara. *Helping Students Write Well: A Guide for Teachers in All Disciplines.* New York: MLA, 1986.

Walvoord offers sensible suggestions on how to form groups by letting students express their preferences, but then reserving the actual selection process for the teacher.

Assignments and Grading

Most teachers will tell you that they would teach without grades if it were possible; that they dislike grading; and that grading turns out to be one of the most mentally taxing and anxiety-producing features of life as a teacher. As much as I would now like to announce proudly that I have invented an EZ Grader 2000 that will simplify your teaching life, I have to second Barbara Walvoord and Virginia Johnson Anderson's plain-spoken appeal to faculty who have grade anxiety: "We urge faculty to abandon false hopes that grading can be easy, uncomplicated, uncontested, or one-dimensional. Teachers must manage the power and complexity of the grading system rather than ignore or deny it" (xvii). So abandon those false hopes, all ye who enter here; grading is complicated, and it may be the least appealing activity you will undertake as a teacher—but it still has to be done.

Kenneth Eble offers one explanation for the bad feelings many of us have about grading: it "makes teaching uncomfortable because it threatens an amicable relationship" (143). Until grades enter the picture, in other words, you can envision the classroom as just a bunch of folks sitting around talking about physics. When the first grades come back, that fiction dies, and the uneven nature of the power relationship between teacher and student comes to the fore. Of course, dissatisfaction with grading has a more practical source as well—the time expenditures that grading requires, and the pressures that it produces as you have to turn around student work on short deadlines all through the semester.

I think the most disturbing aspect of grading, however, may be the lack of absolute standards or right and wrong answers in an area in which we are making judgments that take on absolute meanings. When you stamp a C on someone's work, it can feel like you've stamped it on her forehead; it now becomes visible to her, and her parents, and perhaps her peers, and to future employers or graduate schools. Knowing this, you wish desperately that you could point to some pre-existing or God-given scale against which students are measured and graded, in order to justify your evaluation of her. Yes, I gave her a C, but that's what she deserved because it says right here on these stone tablets that if students do X, Y, and Z, then they deserve a C.

Alas, those stone tablets don't exist, and learning to live with yourself as a grader means learning to accept that you establish the criteria according to which students are graded, that you evaluate them against that criteria, and that you and you alone are responsible for the grades you dispense. It's a painful realization, and you'll never stop wondering, at least occasionally, about the legitimacy of your grades—or about the legitimacy of a particular grade that you gave, and that a student is contesting, and that has you wondering whether he really has a point, and maybe you should change it? Having these anxieties and uncertainties about grading does not mean you have done anything wrong; it means you're a teacher, and you wish along with the rest of us that grading would just go away.

Given all that, I still want to provide some guidance in this area, at least by letting you know about the main challenges you will confront as a grader and outlining the different strategies you could take to approach these challenges. I've divided this chapter into the five stages of the grading process—giving assignments, collecting them from students, evaluating them, transforming those evaluated objects into numbers and letters, and returning them—with as much practical advice as I can give in each area.

Among the many works I consulted in my research for this chapter, I found the recommendations of Walvoord and Anderson to be the most sensible, and their overview of the grading process the most comprehensive. So I will cite their work frequently throughout the chapter, and if you have additional questions and concerns about grading, I encourage you to consult it yourself—their text in turn will point you to an extremely wide array of resources and perspectives on grading.

Assignments for Learning

Since I already discussed this topic in the chapter on the syllabus, I'll just give a quick reminder here that planning the sequence of assignments in your course, and actually drawing them up, should be tied to the learning objectives for the course. Your assignments should help to build the skills and knowledge that you want students to have, and should give you a way to know whether students are acquiring those skills and that knowledge. I think the best way to get a global perspective on this, and to design a coherent sequence of assignments, is to construct a course skeleton which identifies the nature and due dates of the major exams and assignments—mapping our their placement within the fifteen-week semester—and then to check those exams and assignments against the learning objectives on your syllabus (see

---

Walvoord and Anderson, 17–42, for several examples of course skeletons). Once you have created a good fit, you can fill in the remainder of the schedule.

As for the assignments themselves, here are three suggestions.

First, just as you offer a wide variety of teaching techniques in order to help as many students as possible learn in your course, you should offer a wide variety of assignment types in your classroom—everything from exams and papers to presentations to more creative kinds of assignments that I will mention below. As Christopher Lucas and John Murry argue, "Given the variety of ways that students learn and then respond to evaluations, and given the increasing diversity of educational sophistication in today's classrooms, it is clear that the more you can vary the nature of your evaluation instruments, the greater the number of students you will help to succeed" (97). For example, students who have strong test anxiety might fare poorly on high-pressure exams, and their poor performance might not reflect their understanding of the subject. Offer a paper assignment as well, and those students have their chance to shine. Students who have weaker writing skills, by contrast, will welcome a multiple-choice section on an exam. Any kind of assignment or exam that you give will appeal more to some students than others, and will lend itself to their particular talents, so vary those assignments and exams.

Second, if the culture of your discipline or department—or your own personal preference—dictates that you primarily give exams, then at least some of your exams should require students to write, even if that only entails very brief explanations of how or why a problem was solved. You can find research that tells you how to construct multiple-choice exams to promote thinking, but an easier route to producing thinking on such exams is to ensure that students have to do more than fill in the bubbles.

Your learning objectives will undoubtedly ask for more than the ability to select one correct answer out of four, so you need to find ways to test for those other objectives you have established, and requiring students to explain or analyze problems in writing can help accomplish this. Walvoord and Anderson cite the example of a math professor who gives exams and assignments divided into two columns: one column for solving the problem with numbers, the other for explaining the steps in writing (22). Explanations of the reasoning or problem-solving process, short-answer questions, one essay question at the end of an exam—all of these are options to push students into thinking harder during an exam. Adding writing to an exam will certainly add to the amount of time you have to devote to grading, but I'll give you a tip later about how to reduce this time.

Third, think creatively about the kinds of assignments you give. One way to come up with creative assignments is to think about what people who major in your field end up doing professionally, and try to design assignments that will give students a taste of what their professional lives might feel like. A historian I know has students research and write histories of local institutions; a business communications teacher has her students design websites and brochures for organizations on campus that want to increase their public profiles; a scientist might have his students prepare a brief on global warming for a local political leader; an anthropologist could ask students to write a literature review in preparation for an upcoming dig; a mathematician might ask students to prepare a lesson plan for teaching a specific problem-solving skill to high school students. A colleague in my own field has students write an article for *The Explicator*, a scholarly journal that publishes short essays offering new perspectives on world literature, based on very close readings or original research. The students have to do research on the journal and its submission policies, prepare an essay that meets those criteria, and write a cover letter to send with their article (whether they actually submit the essay is optional). All of these assignments remind students of a fact that sometimes becomes cloudy for them when they are nineteen years old and buried in school work: that we are teaching them things that should help them succeed in their lives or their careers.

Another way to move toward creative assignments is to use "starter" and interim assignments as part of the package of work you ask of students. In other words, consider the possibility of breaking down a larger assignment—such as a researched argumentative essay, or a major presentation—into component parts, and having each of those parts become a separate assignment. A major research paper could include such interim assignments as a prospectus, a literature review, an introduction and outline, a bibliography, and more. You can come up with the interim assignments by thinking about what skills students need or will have to develop to complete the major assignment. So, for a researched argument paper, students need to identify and review the relevant research to determine what position to take—hence the literature review as an interim assignment. You can even turn the interim assignments into the assignment itself, and skip the final product; I call these "starter" assignments. If you don't believe students will ever need the full battery of skills necessary to produce a major research paper in your discipline, for example, but you do believe that they should know how to conduct research and analyze and report their results, you might require them just to come up with a hypothesis and then supply the literature review that would help them support their hypothesis. Lucia Knoles's assignment to have students identify three quotes and write about them on Blackboard for each class constitutes a kind of starter assignment, since identifying quotes related to one another is one step you would take in writing a paper of literary analysis.

Finally, Walvoord and Anderson provide a list of close to a hundred different kinds of assignments in an appendix to *Effective Grading*. Some of the more creative of these are the following:

Advertisement
Briefing paper or "white paper"
Budget with rationale
Client report for an agency
Court brief
Diary of a fictional or real historical character
Executive summary
Instructional manual
Letter to the editor
Regulations, laws, rules
Research proposal addressed to a granting agency
Review of book, play, exhibit
Taxonomy of set of categories (193–195)

You'll notice that many of these creative assignments, both theirs and the ones I have suggested previously, involve asking students to present work to the public or to specific, hypothetical audiences that you would describe for them. Unless they are personal secretaries to a dictator, most professionals will not write research papers or reports for an audience of one (which is what students do for you), so asking them to produce assignments tailored to a specific audience or to the general public is a great way to introduce them to work that they might be doing after graduation.

A last issue to consider in giving assignments is the instructions you give to the students, which should be as full and precise as possible. If you are giving an exam, give explicit instructions orally or in the exam header; for other work, you should type up an instruction sheet for every major assignment and distribute it or post it to the course website, as well as reviewing it in class. Vague or unclear assignment instructions will not harm the best students in your class, who will succeed no matter what you ask of them. If you finish the semester by telling the students "Write me something interesting," the brilliant kids are going to write you something interesting. Everyone else will curse you, flounder around anxiously in search of something to write, or bother you with endless questions about it. So you should provide instructions that tell them not only the technical parameters of the assignment (e.g., ten pages long, or three paragraphs), but also the qualities that a successful assignment will have (e.g., a clear thesis statement, evidence supporting the argument in each paragraph). You might even tell them what your grading criteria will be for the assignment, to make it perfectly clear where they should focus their energies.

Ideally, you will give students the objectives for the assignment, or tell them specifically how the assignment helps develop or test one of the learning objectives of the course. You can do this in a brief header statement on an exam or instruction sheet, which might say something like this: "This assignment is designed to give you experience in conducting research for an audience of the general public. This means you will have to do research in the conventional manner which we have been practicing in this course, but then develop strategies to translate your technical findings into clear prose accessible to an educated American adult. Since many graduates in this field work in agencies that use research to influence public policy, that translation skill is an essential one to have." Assignment objectives give you a reason to point students back to the syllabus, to remind the students about the learning objectives of the course, and to help them see the priorities of the assignment. For tests, you might consider explaining the objectives of a particular exam to them a class or two in advance, so they can factor that into their decisions about what and how to study.

Collecting (Late) Assignments

How to collect work—whether to have the students pass their papers to the front of the row, or collect them from the students at their desks—is a complex issue which educational researchers have been debating for decades, and I want to make fourteen detailed recommendations about this.

No, just kidding. I'll let you handle that decision on your own.

The one issue here that deserves a moment of thought is how to handle late student work. Hopefully you have outlined a policy on late work on your syllabus, one that not only establishes the rule for how and whether students can turn in assignments late, but also provides a rationale for that rule. If that's the case, follow the rule as much as possible, though obviously you want to reserve the right to make exceptions for emergencies or for situations in which you think a student has a legitimate reason for late work.

Having said that, I want to complicate your view of late work. Most teachers who assign penalties for late work, if pressed, would argue that working professionals are responsible for completing work and meeting deadlines in a timely manner, so we should inculcate those skills in our students. Requiring students to meet deadlines and punishing them for not doing so mirrors a professional environment in which employees have to meet deadlines and may lose income or employment if they don't.

This has always seemed a reasonable argument to me, and I don't believe anyone should feel bad about asking people who are eighteen years old or older to turn in their work on time.

At least one researcher on effective teaching, Ken Bain, differs here. In *What the Best College Teachers Do,* Bain argues that penalizing late work puts an undue emphasis on the assignment as a performance, as opposed to seeing assignments as a learning experience. After all, he quotes one exemplary teacher as saying, assignments "might be late because [the students] decided to pursue some higher goal for the project or do more work on it" (154). In other words, does it make sense to penalize a student who has ambitious plans for a project, and who will learn more from it, when she is willing to do extra work but would have to turn it in a few days late? Bain also questions whether the rationale of teaching students to adhere to deadlines is a legitimate one: "Even those who cite such a policy as a learning objective can seldom if ever point to any evidence that it actually encourages students to be timely or that such habits are likely to stick beyond the confines of the classroom" (153–154). It's difficult to imagine how anyone could compile such evidence, so Bain's question seems on point here—does penalizing students for late work teach them not to be late in life? Even if it might, does it do so at the expense of potentially greater learning? One of my best friends is late for everything, all the time; he always has been, and I'm convinced he always will be. Anytime we are going somewhere, including out of state, and I ask him how long it will take, he estimates it at about twenty minutes. I don't think punishing him would help. He's missing the gene that helps the rest of us keep track of time.

This is one of the many reasons why grading and evaluation can prove so vexing. I don't see one right answer here, so my advice is that you should feel free to set your late policy as you please and stand by it. I do think that allowing students to turn work in late without penalty will prove difficult in your first year, since tracking and returning work away from the rest of the stack will prove to be one more hassle for you, and will be conducive to misplacing papers or assignments. I recommend that you revisit this issue in your second and third year, considering Bain's perspective, but that for now you do the following: state clearly on the syllabus and on assignment instruction sheets that requests for extensions require at least one day's advance notice; grant requests that seem legitimate; create some small disincentive for work that comes in late without the extension request (a grade reduction, for example, or a slower turnaround time from you). See how it goes, and think about this issue again next year.

Evaluating Assignments

This is the numbers portion of the book, which means that things are going to remain pretty basic, because I'm a word guy. But the more basic the better in your first experiences with grading, so my lack here is your gain.

The first numbers issue here is the number of hours you spend grading, which will be lots and lots. But you can take two steps to reduce the number of hours you have to spend examining and marking student work. For smaller items, such as quizzes or short essays or even brief presentations, you can do much of your substantive evaluation orally in class, and limit yourself to marking a letter or number on the student's work. You can do this by writing brief notes to yourself on the most common problems or wrong answers you see in an assignment as you grade them, and then offer a quick presentation in class on those issues right after you have handed back the assignment. If every student is misusing the semicolon in a writing assignment (and they always do), you can save yourself time by presenting a two-minute overview of the semicolon in class rather than writing that rule in the margins of student work fifteen times. Even for larger assignments, you can do this for less important errors that you see frequently, although on the major assignments for the course students do deserve more individualized feedback from you to help them improve their work for the next assignment.

You can also save time on your grading, and establish clear standards for evaluation that you can communicate to students, by using a grading rubric for assignments and exams. A rubric is simply a set of categories or criteria that you construct in order to help you evaluate student work consistently; it might take the form of a grid that you fill in as you grade the student's work, or it might exist only in your head, as you evaluate each paper for four specific qualities. Rubrics have three major advantages. First, as Kathleen Montgomery points out (36), they help you determine what matters in an assignment, and thus can remind you to focus your teaching on the things that matter. Second, they ensure that you are grading a set of student work consistently, focusing on the same elements for everyone and weighing those elements in the same manner in determining your grade. Finally, rubrics can save time: they restrict you to focusing on a limited number of issues, and you can explain those issues to the students when you return their work, and present orally to them what you otherwise might have been writing on a dozen different papers. Walvoord and Anderson argue for the use of a rubric called a "primary trait analysis" or PTA, which "identifies the factors or traits that will count for scoring . . . builds a scale for scoring the student's performance on that trait . . . and evaluates the student's performance against that criteria" (67). They recommend constructing such a PTA scale for every major assignment.

To give a quick concrete example, for students writing an argumentative paper, you might construct a rubric that looks like this, given a paper worth 100 points:

Category	Points	Comments
Clear Thesis	(20 pts)	
Organization	(20 pts)	
Focused Paragraphs	(20 pts)	
Use of Evidence	(20 pts)	
Clean Grammar	(10 pts)	
Effective Introduction/Conclusion	(10 pts)	

Final Comment:

Evaluating a paper with a rubric like this consists of watching out for these six elements as you read, assigning a point total in each category, writing very brief explanations for your scores in the "Comments" box, and then using the "Final Comment" to tell students how they should focus their energies in order to improve their work. Add up the points in each category, and you have your score out of one hundred. A rubric like this can be a real blessing when you have a massive stack of papers or other student work to grade. Reading each student paper afresh, without a rubric on paper or in your mind, can really tax your intellectual energy, as you rack your brain every ten minutes to figure out what each student did and didn't do well. In addition, as Montgomery points out (36), rubrics will be especially useful for complex assignments (multi-stage research papers or presentations) which require multiple skills and kinds of work, and which might otherwise overwhelm you with possible issues to evaluate.

Rubrics also can help improve students' performance, especially if you let them see or know about the rubric before they complete the assignment. The rubric will communicate to them what matters most to you about the assignment, and will reinforce the most important skills that you hope the assignment will teach them. The downside to this positive quality is that the rubric can restrict your ability to reward or penalize a student for anything that does not fit into one of your categories. If a student does an exemplary job of conducting outside research, for example, and goes well beyond what her classmates did, or if a student turns in a solid technical performance, but uses wildly inappropriate language or racist or sexist sentiments, you have no way of responding to those elements with the grade. Don't fret too much about this. When you use the rubric you have designed for your first batch of papers, you will discover one or two categories that you need to add, and maybe one that you want to drop, and so you'll revise it. The next time you'll revise it again, until you have seen enough student work to know what they are likely to do and not do, and thus what categories will cover all of the things that matter to you.

Assigning Numbers and Letters

Calculating how to reduce the number of hours you spend grading constitutes the easy section of this mathematical chapter; now we turn to the more complex topic of grading systems. Before we look at the numbers, you will have to make a decision about whether to grade on a curve—that is, designate in advance that only a certain number or percentage of students can receive an A, and define the standards for an A in such a way that the numbers work out. I'm going to be blunt and directive here: don't grade on a curve. Grades should not be a precious commodity that students compete for; students should measure their learning against the standards that you have set for them, not against the performance of their peers. Grading on a curve, in short, puts numbers and letters ahead of learning, and makes learning a game that students try to win—exactly the opposite of the attitude you should want to foster in them. What if everyone meets the learning objectives that you set for the course? Why would you want to make tiny distinctions between students in order to knock some of them down a grade? They'll be upset, you won't feel good about it, and you will have taught them that your evaluation of their work depends upon factors outside of their control. Don't do it.

The one reason faculty members continue to grade on a curve, in my experience, is that it allows them to boost up student grades when their tests are so hard that no one does well, or it helps them keep the grades down when everyone is doing well. Curving the grades in order to correct these problems just means that you are playing with the numbers, when what you really need to do is look harder at your teaching. If you are designing tests that only one or two students can do well on, either your tests are too hard or you are not teaching effectively enough to help students do well on them. Either way, you need to go back to the drawing board and think about readjusting the standards you have set so that you can realistically help students reach them. Designing a test that no student can finish, or an assignment that most students would fail without a curved grade, means that you are a tough grader, for sure, but—contrary to popular opinion—tough does not necessarily mean good. If everyone fails an assignment, the chances are far better that you have screwed up, rather than your students. Don't take the easy way out and fall back to the curve; go back to the drawing board and rethink what you expect of your students.

Now that we've settled that, I'll offer two simple systems for calculating your grades. Let's start with the letters. If you want to

grade using letters, you begin by finding out how many gradations your school offers in its letter grade assignments, and then
assign each letter a point total. At my college we have A, A−,
B+, B, B−, C+, C, C−, D, and F (no A+, D+, or D−), that is, ten
gradations. Since F equals 0, that means the rest of the letters receive a point designation from 1 to 9, with A receiving 9 points,
A− 8 points, and so on. Once you have that information, you're
ready to roll.

Let's say, to keep this simple, that your students will take three
tests, write two papers, and do a presentation. You first have to
determine how to weight these things in the determination of
your final grade. You think the tests and papers are roughly equivalent in terms of importance, and the presentation less so; you
also want the final test to be worth more than the others. So you
come up with this:

Tests: 50% (15%, 15%, 20%)
Papers: 40% (20%, 20%)
Presentation: 10%

Johnny Student gets the following grades:

Tests: B, B+, C
Papers: A, A−
Presentation: B

Convert each of those letter grades into their numerical equivalents, so now you have:

Tests: 6, 7, 3
Papers: 9, 8
Presentation: 6

Take each of those numbers, and multiply it by the percentage that it is worth—since the first test is worth 15%, you will multiply his numerical score on that exam (6) by .15 to receive a raw number (in this case, .9). Do this for all of Johnny's grades, and it looks like this:

Tests: .15 × 6 = .9; .15 × 7 = 1.05, .2 × 3 = .6
Papers: .2 × 9 = 1.8; .2 × 8 = 1.6
Presentation: .1 × 6 = .6

Add up the raw numbers—.9 + 1.05 + .6 + 1.8 + 1.6 + .6—and you get 6.55. Convert that number back into a letter, based on the system you are using—rounding down to 6 will give you a B; rounding up to 7 will give you a B+. Many teachers make decisions about whether to round up or down based upon a student's effort or improvement, so you can use those intangible factors to reward students who you feel deserve extra consideration. Depending upon how you round, Johnny ends up with a B or a B+.

This is the grading system—we'll call it letters and percentages—that I used for my first few years of teaching, and it worked perfectly fine. You can save yourself from doing all the math by plugging the raw scores (i.e., the numbers) and the percentages into a spreadsheet, and writing the formulas to have it do the calculations for you. (I was clueless about how to do this, but an economist friend explained it to me; go hang around in the economics department with your gradebook, looking forlorn, and someone will eventually take pity on you and help.) Blackboard and its equivalents will also do much of the mathematical work for you. A final option would be to use a software program like Gradekeeper, or one of its many equivalents, which you can download from the Web either for free or for a small fee. Many faculty swear by such programs, since they save time and help you avoid simple calculation errors.

A second system involves working with numbers from the start—converting your numbers into percentages, and then into letters at the end of the semester according to a pre-established scale; we'll call this the total points system. Generally scales look something like this:

A+	97–100
A	94–96
A−	90–93
B+	87–89
B	84–86

And so on down the line, with an F as anything under 60 points. The simplest system here involves making the entire semester worth 1,000 points. The tests in our previous example are then worth 150 points or 200 points, the papers worth 200 points each, and the presentation 100 points. Give grades in terms of points throughout the semester (you can give students the numbers-to-letter equivalency scale on the syllabus, so that both you and they can convert their numerical scores to letters if desired), and then simply add up the points at the end of the semester and convert their total to the matching percentage, and then to the letter using the scale above. It can be a little strange at first to think about giving a number to an assignment like an essay or a presentation, but you can always give students a letter grade in your head, and then just give them the equivalent in points of the letter (that is, if you would give the paper a B, then give them 85 points out of 100). Eventually, you'll find yourself thinking in terms of the numbers.

An obvious alternative to the 1,000-point system is the 100-

point system, which again keeps things nice and round and makes calculating the percentages a very simple task. The 100-point system leaves you fewer gradations to work with, which has advantages and disadvantages. Having fewer gradations means easier calculations, but it also blunts your ability to make finer distinctions with your grading pen.

The table below, provided to me by Paul Umbach, lays out the three alternatives I have just described in an easy-to-read visual format for all of you visual learners.

I would recommend the total points system for your first semester or two because it's simple and involves nothing more mathematically complex than addition, which even a mathematical moron like me can handle. It also makes it very easy for students to keep track of their own grades—they can tote up their points as the semester goes on. I ultimately switched to the total points system for a different reason, though. One semester, back

		Test 1	Test 2	Final exam	Paper 1	Paper 2	Presentation	Final grade
	Total value	15%	15%	20%	20%	20%	10%	
Letters/	Points earned	6	7	3	9	8	6	
Percentages	(Raw)	.9	1.05	.6	1.8	1.6	.6	6.55
	Grade earned	B	B+	C	A	A−	B	B to B+
	Total value	150	150	200	200	200	100	
Total Points: 1000	Amount earned	127	132	148	190	182	85 =	864
	Grade earned	B	B+	C	A	A−	B	B to B+
	Total value	15	15	20	20	20	10	
Total Points: 100	Amount earned	13	13	15	19	18	8.5 =	86.5
	Grade earned	B/B+	B/B+	C	A	A−	B	B to B+

when I was using letters and weighted percentages, I had a student who plagiarized blatantly on a major paper, one that was worth a fifth of the semester's grade. I gave him a zero on the paper, in part because I thought he should have to take the course again, and I was certain that losing 20% of the semester's total would make it difficult for him to pass. But when it came to the end of the semester, I found that he ended up with a C, which astonished me. That was when I discovered that a zero in a letters/weighted percentage system doesn't hurt nearly as much as a zero in a points system. Simplify the example to this: there are two assignments, each worth 50% of the grade, or 500 points in the points system. A student gets a B− on one, and doesn't turn in the other. Should such a student pass the course? In the points system, he wouldn't: even if he aced the one assignment he turned in, he only has 500 points, which is in the F range. In a weighted percentage system, he gets a 0 for his missing assignment, and for the second he receives 6 points, which you multiply by .5, which gives him a 3 for his final grade total. Add 0 and 3, and you get 3; convert that to a letter, and you get C−. Not great, but still passing.

This simple example reveals a major difference between the two systems. In the weighted percentage system, as long as the student does any kind of work whatsoever, he will end up with some points, which will put him above 0 on the grading scale. The only way for a student to fail in that system is to do no work at all, and have 0 points. In the points system, however, students will fail if they have anything below 600 points—so missing a major assignment, or not doing required coursework, will almost always lead to failure.

Now obviously you can still use the weighted percentage system and get around this problem with a short statement on the syllabus that students must complete all of the assignments for the course in order to pass. And I'm not advocating the points system because I like to fail as many students as possible. But I do prefer to have the grading system as transparent to the students as possible, so that even the slowest of them can follow their point totals and can see how a missed or plagiarized paper can sink them in the course. You also may find, as I have, that you feel a subtle—and sometimes not so subtle—pressure from your department chair, or dean, or colleagues, to battle the grade inflation that you hear about frequently in the news, or hear faculty complain about in the hallway. (See Kohn, in the Resources section below, for a healthy perspective on the "problem" of grade inflation today; his historical overview of grading in America leads to the following conclusion: "The bottom line: No one has ever demonstrated that students today get A's for the same work that used to receive B's or C's. We simply do not have the data to support such a claim" [B8].) The grades I gave were definitely higher with the weighted percentage system than they have been with points, and I believe the points-system grades have more accurately reflected my evaluation of my students. For these reasons, and for the sake of keeping your life simple, I recommend starting your teaching career with the points system.

Ultimately, whatever system you choose, strive for transparency. Students should have no trouble understanding the system, and should be able to calculate their own grades at any time in the course. Put yourself in their position, and you can see that this is basic human decency, in addition to being pedagogically sound. Grades make a difference in their lives, and they deserve to know where they stand in order to help them make decisions about how to concentrate their energies over their five courses, and to help them see whether their grades will qualify them for scholarships or other opportunities for which they might apply. You can facilitate their ability to keep track of their own grades either electronically or on paper: Blackboard and other software programs can show the students their "running" average as the semester progresses; or if you are still working with flattened tree pulp only, you can include a tear-sheet or space on the syllabus that lists each assignment, with a place for them to fill in their grades. It's also worth mentioning to the students, either on the syllabus or in class, that you are always willing to give them their current course grade during office visits.

Returning Assignments

Finally, I'll offer a principle and two practical suggestions on how you communicate with students about their work when you return their assignments.

The principle is one that you'll see repeated in just about every resource you consult on grading: your focus in giving assignments and grading student work should be on helping them learn, not on justifying your grade. (As Lucas and Murry say, "Ideally, testing should serve to reinforce the process of learning.")

Your first inclination, when you return student work with your written comments, will be to point out everything the student did wrong, in order to explain to him why he received the grade he did. This inclination will stem from that anxiety you'll feel, noted at the beginning of the chapter, about the lack of absolute standards for grading. And of course you do need to point out the major problems in students' papers or presentations or exams, and help them see what they did wrong. But the bulk of your comments to students should focus on how they could improve their writing, or their analysis, or their speaking, or whatever, for the next assignment. Give practical advice whenever you can— coach them into studying or thinking or writing techniques that will improve the quality of their future work, and that will help them develop good academic habits. If a student's paper is disorganized, advise her to construct an outline of the paper either before or after she has written it; if an essay or an exam has no clear point to it, suggest beginning with a one-sentence thesis next time. Getting to those suggestions will obviously entail pointing out the problems in students' work, and that's fine. But move quickly from there into constructive criticism.

And of course you should not neglect to tell them what they did right. Students will learn not only from your corrections of their mistakes, but from your praise of what they did well. A standard format for responding to student work, one that I think a vast majority of teachers follow, is to begin with praise of the positives, and follow that with the problems. Don't make that praise a throwaway comment, either, one that seems like a formulaic phrase to soften the blow of what follows, as in: "Your paper was clearly written, but had fourteen problems that I will now dissect in detail." My wife, an elementary school teacher, once explained to me that when one of my children showed me their artwork, I was supposed to be very specific in my praise: "I like the way you used yellow for the sun," or "The dragon who is eating that man has a very beautiful tail"—that sort of thing. The same principle applies here. Be specific about what the student did well, and make that section of your response substantial.

The principle of grading to learn, rather than to justify, leads to two very practical recommendations for grading, with which I'll end this chapter.

First, do your best to return student work as quickly as possible. If you expect students to learn from their previous work, you need to get it back to them soon after they have completed it. At the very least, they should have it back a class or two before the next assignment of a similar nature is due, so they have time to reflect on your comments and make changes to their work habits and strategies. At best, student work should be turned around within one week. Given all the things that students have going on in their lives, you can be sure they will hardly remember a paper you give back to them three weeks after they have turned in, much less look carefully at your comments and think about how those comments could help them improve. You probably know this from your own experience. Have you ever turned in a dissertation chapter or sent off a submission to a scholarly journal, not received a response for many months, and then finally got it back with detailed comments on how you should revise it—at which point you were two chapters ahead, or had moved on to a new project entirely? If so, you might remember feeling like just chucking that old work, and avoiding all the hard work of revising, in order to concentrate on the new stuff. By contrast, if you get feedback on your work immediately, when you still have the fire in your belly for it, you know how easy it is to jump right back in and make revisions. The same dynamic holds true for student work—so make every effort to turn it around quickly.

Second, you should be careful about overloading students with your written comments, whether they are positive or negative or constructive. You may feel as if you are doing lots of useful work if you scrawl comments in the margins of every page, and then write a detailed endnote offering the student seven suggestions for improving his work. But probably what you're really doing is inspiring the student to shake his head, conclude that the paper stunk, and try to put it out of his mind. If teachers write too many comments, students tend to be overwhelmed and to focus on the superficial problems with their papers rather than the substantive ones. One educational researcher interviewed students after they had gotten back papers with written commentary and found that when papers had comments about stylistic issues as well as substantive ones, the students tended to focus on the minor stylistic elements and ignore the larger picture (Walvoord and Anderson, 124; Sommers). This doesn't mean that you can't correct grammar or make stylistic suggestions. The most effective method for responding to student work is to identify the two or three most important areas in which the student needs to improve his work, and limit yourself to addressing those two or three elements (a rubric can help you limit yourself in this way, as we've already seen). You can make a specific stylistic issue or grammatical problem one of those issues, if you wish, but you should not add a dozen grammatical corrections to the two or three elements that you are trying to guide them into correcting. Focus both their energies and yours by identifying the most important areas of concern, and coaching them to improve in those areas for the next assignment. This is an essential part of grading to learn, and will also help save you time by limiting the quantity of your comments. Students will sometimes wonder why they received a low grade when you pointed out only two problems to them, so it would be useful to explain your grading practice to the class before you return the papers, and mention that anyone who would like a more detailed explanation of the reasons for their grade can receive it in office hours.

Whew! This concludes the mathematical portion of the book, with the best advice I can give in the most complex area of teaching you will face. In the next chapter we'll take a break from all of this practical advice, and step back to take a wider look at what we know about how students learn in our classrooms.

Resources

Bain, Ken. *What the Best College Teachers Do.* Cambridge, Mass.: Harvard University Press, 2004.
See pp. 150–163 for thoughts on grading.

Eble, Kenneth. *The Craft of Teaching,* 2nd ed. San Francisco: Jossey-Bass, 1988.
An older general guidebook, still worth reading. See pp. 153–163 for Eble's advice on grading.

Gradekeeper. *http://www.gradekeepr.com.* January 23, 2007.

Kohn, Alfie. "The Dangerous Myth of Grade Inflation." *The Chronicle of Higher Education,* 49.11 (November 8, 2002): B7.
An excellent and clear analysis of talk about grade inflation.

Lucas, Christopher J., and John W. Murry, Jr. "Active Learning and Other Instructional Management Issues." In *New Faculty: A Practical Guide for Academic Beginners,* 71–104. New York: Palgrave, 2002.
Sensible suggestions on grading for new faculty members.

Montgomery, Kathleen. "Authentic Tasks and Rubrics: Going Beyond Traditional Assessments in College Teaching." *College Teaching,* 50.1 (2002): 34–39.
This article provides concrete examples of grading rubrics from a number of different disciplines, and makes an argument as well for creative, real-world assignments in the college classroom.

Sommers, Nancy. "Responding to Student Writing." *College Composition and Communication,* 33.2 (1982): 148–156.
In this study, also cited by Walvoord and Anderson, the researcher interviewed students as they read through comments on their papers.

Walvoord, Barbara, and Virginia Johnson Anderson. *Effective Grading: A Tool for Learning and Assessment.* San Francisco: Jossey-Bass, 1998.
A good and comprehensive advice text on creating assignments and exams and grading them. The final section, which focuses on assessment, can be safely skipped by new faculty members, which leaves you only about 140 pages to read.

Students as Learners

Picture a well-meaning parent who decides to become a football coach for his son's team. This father played football himself, has watched football on television for many years, and has even carefully observed how other coaches have worked with his child for a year or two. So he feels he has learned enough from his own experience and observations to handle the job of conditioning and coaching these young bodies to play a physical sport that he knows well.

On the first day of practice, the kids arrive, and he asks them to spend a few minutes warming up. He instructs them to stretch as he is used to stretching, and as he is accustomed to seeing athletes or actors on television stretching: bending some part of your body in this or that direction, and bouncing back and forth until the muscle is loosened up. After five minutes of this stretching over various leg and arm muscles, he has them up and running—all of them now working twice as hard, however, against the muscles that his "stretching" exercise has helped to contract.

Many of us engage in what my physical therapist friend Patty calls this "bounce stretch," a common-sense version of stretching that actually has the complete opposite effect on the muscle. When physical therapists or physicians need to make a muscle contract, they will use tapping and bouncing motions to induce it to do so. Actually stretching a muscle involves bending the body into the correct position and holding it there for at least ten seconds, the minimum amount of time it takes for the muscle to begin to loosen. Even people who have a vague understanding of this rarely hold the position for the required ten full seconds, according to Patty.

Our football coach, though, is in a teaching position, and is attempting to help his charges learn to use their bodies more effectively. Unfortunately, he is doing so without knowing very much about how the human body works—relying only on his own experience, his observations of what other people do, and his common sense. All of that is leading him not only to ineffective conditioning, but to actions that actually may cause harm to his kids. If he had even the most basic knowledge of the human body, it would make a huge difference in his ability to help prepare them for practices and games.

Can you see yet where I'm going with this?

Most college and university faculty believe that they can help other human beings learn complex subject matter simply by relying upon their own experience as learners, casual observations of their fellow teachers, common sense, and their own big brains. But we all know perfectly well the dangers of generalizing too broadly from our own experiences, and we all know from our own disciplines how misleading common sense can be when it comes to complex subject matter. Observing our fellow teachers won't help us much either, if they're all in the same boat as we are.

You may think of yourself primarily as a scholar, but if you are reading this book you are also a teacher (or about to become one), which means that you are in the business of helping other human beings learn. Learning is a complex process that evolves as we age, and there is a huge body of research literature on the neurological and psychological processes that allow human beings to acquire new knowledge and skills. You may have just finished writing the document which chronicled your travels through mountains of research literature in your discipline, and which earned you your doctorate, so the thought of wading through another mountain of such literature probably does not sound too appealing.

My goal here is not to send you back for a second doctorate in learning theory (would there be anything more cool, though, than having two doctorates?), but to convince you that your responsibilities as a teacher obligate you to acquaint yourself with one or two of the major explanations for how adult human beings learn, and to think about how those explanations might affect what you do in the classroom. Doing this can be a much less painful process than you might imagine—the half-dozen books on teaching that I will recommend in the final chapter will give you a solid foundation in the basics of those theories, along with plenty of practical advice on what to do in the classroom. Even brief articles that you might find in specialized journals on teaching, such as the *Journal of College Science Teaching* or the *Journal of Teaching Sociology,* will usually begin with an overview of whatever learning theory or teaching philosophy animated their experiment or classroom technique.

I'm going to get you started on this process by providing an introduction to two basic theories of how students learn and develop intellectually during their college years. I have reserved this information for the seventh week of our semester together because, while of course this knowledge should be helpful to you from the start, I know from experience that the overwhelming nature of teaching for the first time can push all but the most practical considerations out of your head for the first month or two in the classroom. You'll be thinking about little beyond how to survive the next few days, or how to turn around the next set of papers or exams, or how to deal with some baffling and unexpected situation with a troublesome student. So my recommendation would be to read this chapter through now as you are reading the entire book, but then to go back to it at midsemester—you might have a few days' break in the fall around now, or a full week's break in the spring—and read it again, seeing whether the experiences you have had with students thus far match the ideas about how human beings learn that I am about to describe to you.

These two different theories don't cover the same territory— one offers a basic model for how human beings process new information and knowledge, beginning in childhood, while the other is a more specific theory about a series of intellectual stages that students go through during their four years in college, stages that affect profoundly how they hear and respond to what happens in our classrooms. You will find plenty of books and essays that elaborate on these two theories, as well as plenty of arguments against them, or in support of alternative theories, or in support of modifying or updating those theories. This is not the time to become overwhelmed by these debates. Dip a toe in by starting here, and then wade in a little deeper, with a new book or a few articles on teaching and learning, over every summer break.

Mental Models

I introduced the idea of mental models—or "schemas," as they are sometimes called—in Chapter 1, so I'll elaborate on that conception a bit more here. This particular learning theory is difficult to attribute to any one thinker or text, although the educational theorist Jean Piaget would have as strong a claim on its origins as anyone. Piaget analyzed how children acquire knowledge, and posited a process in which children use their interactions with the world to construct models of objects and patterns of action. Those models of reality are subject to frequent revision by the child as she comes in contact with new objects and experiences; over time, the child slowly builds her mental models into increasingly more complex patterns and ideas. The important part of this process for our purposes is the fact that this learning process means the child is constantly revising—and transferring to other areas, and abstracting into general patterns—her already existing ideas or mental models. So what the child already knows plays a crucial role in how she encounters new experiences and objects, as the child works to fit new elements into the patterns she already understands. Piaget identified two primary parts of the learning process: *assimilation,* in which the child takes new information and slots it into her pre-existing mental frameworks; and *accommodation,* in which the child encounters new information that requires her to make changes to her current mental models. (All of this is a gross oversimplification—but Piaget's prose can be tough sledding, so be grateful for what you're getting; see Singer and Revenson, 12–26, for a basic and very readable overview.)

I'll give you a concrete example from my own experience in raising five small children, two of whom just passed their second birthday. We have a piano in our house, which I play and which the twins like to bang on whenever possible. Their act of banging on the piano keys to produce noise has helped form for them a mental model of a piano, and the pattern according to which it can produce sound. When the twins go to my neighbor's house next door (blessed relief!), their understanding of the mental model of the piano enables them to walk right up to my neighbor's small spinet and produce similar noises on it, despite its very different appearance from our upright piano. Their mental model serves them well in that respect, helping them negotiate what otherwise might be an unfamiliar object; they are able to *assimilate* the new object into their model of a piano. However, recently I bought an electronic piano (if all goes according to plan, you will know me better as a rock star than an academic by the time you are reading this), which requires either headphones or an amplifier to make noise—neither of which I had for a while. When I brought the new instrument into the house and set it up, the twins immediately went over to it and began banging on the keys—much puzzled, for the next few minutes, by its silence in the face of their actions. The electronic piano will require an *accommodation* of their mental model of these black-and-white-keyed objects—some of them respond to banging with noise, and some don't. It may take several years for them to clarify the situation and put those objects into two separate categories: pianos, and electric pianos or keyboards. Shortly after they gave up trying to play the piano, I found the boy twin climbing on the instrument, perhaps searching for a new mental model—jungle gym?—for what must initially have seemed to him like such a familiar object.

The process of forming and maintaining mental models becomes more complex as we age, but the basic idea still applies to the students who come into our college classrooms with mental models of our subject matter. I mentioned earlier the mental models of Native American culture that students might bring into an anthropology course. A great deal of research has been done, in particular, on the mental models of motion that students bring into physics courses. Craig Nelson, a scientist who writes and speaks extensively about how we teach critical thinking in the sciences, describes one such study and its results in this way:

Suppose I toss a ball into the air, catch it, and then ask students what forces act on the ball on the way up. Only about 10 percent of the students in an introductory college physics course have entered the seventeenth century. These few Newtonians will answer that the only significant force is gravity, which acts to slow the ball's rise. The other students will give answers that reflect alternative, non-Newtonian views of reality. Much of the students' direct prior experience has been that, when one stops pushing something—for example, a desk across a carpet—it stops moving. Typical physics courses produce no significant change in the percentage of students who eschew such Aristotelian notions. (46)

In other words, students take their experiences in moving things and watching them move to form common-sense theories of motion, and the forces that create and impede motion. Such theories are not stupid—many of them match the theories that Aristotle developed, and Aristotle was hardly a moron. But they don't take into account basic developments in science over the past four hundred years, and—what is most disturbing, as Nelson points out at the end of the passage—introductory physics courses often produce no change in the common-sense theories of motion that students bring to those courses.

All of this means that students are capable of encountering new information about motion, and theories of motion, and cramming that new information into their common-sense, Aristotelian mental models—assimilating rather than accommodating. So they may be able to "learn" physics, and perform well on exams, without making the fundamental changes to their mental models of motion—that is, moving from post-Aristotle to post-

Newton—that any physics teacher would want to see her students make. Our mental models can have such a powerful hold on us that we will perform all kinds of intellectual gymnastics in order to avoid abandoning them for new ones. My twins, for example, understand what it means for something to be broken, so they could maintain their simple mental model of a piano by concluding that my electronic piano is simply a *broken* piano rather than a different kind of piano, or something altogether different from a piano (they are a bit young to articulate to me exactly what they think, so I'm hypothesizing here). For them to make this intellectual move, joining the idea of *piano* with the idea of *broken,* costs them a lot less mental energy than it does for them to build up an entirely new mental model of a completely different kind of piano, or something altogether different that happens to resemble a piano. Such idea-building has an emotional cost as well—every time a child or student encounters an object or pattern that does not fit into one of his existing models, he has entered a temporarily unfamiliar space, a world which does not work as expected, and coming to grips with that and determining how to proceed can be a frightening and exhausting experience, depending upon the nature of the question. It probably didn't cost much emotional energy for the twins to revise their model of a piano, but it might take tremendous energy for a student with strong religious beliefs to encounter scientific theories that call into question her basic assumptions about the creation of the world—and she might fight tooth and nail to assimilate as much of that scientific information into her religious mental models as she can, and ignore the rest.

Another perspective on all of this, one developed by Jack Mezirow, comes from a theory that uses slightly different language to make a similar distinction between *transformative* learning and *assimilative* learning. Assimilative learning, as with Piaget, means that students simply absorb knowledge and fit it into their current knowledge structures, or mental models; transformative learning entails students tearing down their current structures or models and rebuilding them with the new knowledge we are offering to them. Kelly McGonigal describes the limitations of assimilative learning with the familiar example of students learning (or not learning) in physics: "In the sciences and mathematics, it is common for students to have learned an oversimplified definition or approach in high school. Students making the shift from classical to modern physics, for example, cannot simply layer new information onto old understanding" (1). Layering new information onto old understanding is assimilative learning, of the kind that Craig Nelson described. By contrast, transformative learning, as Mezirow puts it, is a complex process that includes

> becoming critically aware of how and why our assumptions have come to constrain the way we perceive, understand, and feel about our world; changing these structures of habitual expectation to make possible a more inclusive, discriminating, and integrating perspective; and finally, making choices or otherwise acting upon these new understandings. (167)

The language is slightly different, but the ideas are the same. Transformative learning means becoming aware of our mental models or schemas ("assumptions" in the quote above), recognizing their limitations, and revising them to accommodate the new knowledge we are receiving.

Two points deserve special emphasis here. First, students bring mental models to every course, and those models influence what they see and hear from us. As I argued in Chapter 1, you should attempt to devise methods to discern the mental models that students will typically bring to your courses. You can do that with exercises or worksheets in the first week of the semester, but you can also get a good deal of information by looking at articles on teaching in your area; you can find these in journals devoted to teaching in specific disciplines, or in articles or sections in the flagship journals of your discipline. A major journal in political science, for example—*PS: Political Science and Politics*—has a section in each issue devoted to articles and debates on teaching political science. However you get the information on students' mental models of your subject matter, your awareness of those models will allow you to address them and work more effectively to revise them or help the students dismantle them and build new ones.

Second, remember that abandoning old models of reality, or building new ones, is difficult work that may challenge assumptions and beliefs that students have carried with them for long periods of time. It's perfectly sensible for human beings to want to integrate unfamiliar ideas or objects into their existing models, and perfectly understandable why they might resist doing otherwise. Sometimes you will encounter students, either in class or in your office, whose ignorance can seem downright willful, or who give back to you such a distorted picture of what you have presented that you might be tempted to conclude that they are complete ignoramuses. My colleague Lucia Knoles told me that some of her students in an American literature class who read accounts of slavery in the United States before the Civil War were amazed to learn that some slaves worked as servants in houses rather than being out in the fields picking cotton and getting horsewhipped, and therefore they concluded that slaves had it much easier than they ever realized. Lucia was aghast, but realized that these were students who had never had large-scale evil or injustice thrust in their faces, and had therefore been carrying around with them the basic belief that the world was a just place, and that people were mostly good. Instead of letting the history of slavery challenge or complicate that belief, they immediately pounced on a tiny piece of the history of slavery and used it to slot the entire phenomenon into their unchanged worldview.

So keep this in mind when you encounter students who either seem resistant to what you have to teach them, or who just don't seem to get it. Be compassionate in the first case—what might seem like willfulness or defiance might be fear and anxiety at the prospect of having to tear down a familiar or deeply rooted mental model. In the second case, instead of just hammering away at them with the same facts and ideas, stop and take stock—are there mental models that are preventing the student from properly processing what you have to offer? If so, can you find a way to address those models, and point out to the student why they need revision?

The theory of mental models can help you in the classroom, though it may take some time for you to determine exactly how to discover and address the models that students bring to your class. The same is true of the second theory I want to tell you about, one that focuses specifically on learning and the intellectual development of students in their college years, as opposed to the more general theory of how human beings learn.

William Perry's Theory of Intellectual Development in College

You'll have to read around in a few different sources to get a fuller picture of the mental models theory (start with the *Piaget Primer*, and then try Driscoll's overview), but the second theory I want to introduce to you comes handily packaged in a single book. And if you like to read about research conducted in the old-fashioned way—that is, by chain-smoking professors working for offices with vaguely KGB-like names—then you will enjoy your trip through William Perry's *Forms of Intellectual and Ethical Development in the College Years: A Scheme,* first published in 1968, and still influencing the way many of us understand our students today.

Perry worked for the Bureau of Study Counsel at Harvard University in the 1950s, an office which advised students who were having difficulties with their academic work. In 1953, Perry explains, the office staff set out to "document the experiences of undergraduates in Harvard and Radcliffe over their four years of college" (3). They worked with a number of different means of obtaining this documentation, over the course of the next half-dozen years, until they finally hit upon the method that Perry describes in his study: administering questionnaires to the students about their attitudes toward teaching, learning, and knowledge at the beginning and end of each of their four years of college, and then conducting long and extremely open-ended interviews with the students about their responses to the questionnaires. Items on the questionnaire asked students to express different levels of agreement or disagreement with statements like this one: "One thing is certain: even if there is an absolute truth, man will never know about it and therefore must learn to choose and venture in uncertainty" (69). The oral interviews began with this question: "So what would you say stands out for you most about the year, as you look back?" (69), and from there the interviewer simply followed the direction of the student's remarks. Perry and his colleagues ended up with 464 interviews, which covered 84 students over the four-year sequence, and from all of this data he developed his scheme.

You'll be able to find quick and easy summaries of Perry's research on the Internet, and updated versions of his scheme in many places (the same is true with Piaget's work), but the original book remains worth reading, not least for the glimpse you get into the protocols, and lack thereof, of interviewing and producing scholarly research on human subjects in the 1950s. In one amusing interview transcript, the interviewer interrupts his subject with the question "Join?" and the italicized narrative explains that he has offered him a cigarette. You can almost picture him there in some white room in a basement of the Harvard campus, with a tape recorder the size of a minibus, wearing a gray suit, black-framed glasses, and a crewcut, holding out his packet of cigarettes to a fidgeting undergraduate. The language of the study is hopelessly gender-specific, with lots of talk about "mankind" and "man" believing this or doing that. And despite multiple protestations to the contrary, it seems clear to me that the idea for the scheme developed early on in Perry's mind, and many of his questions and interviews pushed subsequent students to help him confirm it.

Despite all of this, Perry's work remains influential for many college faculty, no doubt because the three main stages of intellectual and ethical development that he claims college students experience during their four years on campus will strike anyone with teaching experience as immediately insightful. The stages or forms that Perry describes are distinct from any specific content or discipline; he defines them as "the formal properties of the assumptions and expectancies a person holds at a given time in regard to the nature and origins of knowledge and value" (42), examples of which include terms like "dualistic" and "relativistic." The overall scheme posits three major stages of intellectual development that students work through in college, with three subpositions in each stage. However, the students do not march through these stages with arms linked, chanting the college fight song. Some students never leave the first stage, or they may reach a later stage but then remain stuck there; and students may show evidence of being in different stages when they are in different kinds of courses (for example, in their major courses they may exhibit sophisticated, stage-three thinking, but in a general course in another discipline they may still be in stage one). Perry clearly believes that movement through the stages represents intellectual and ethical progress, although you do not need to share that view to recognize that his scheme pinpoints a set of attitudes and perceptions about knowledge that you will see displayed in your classrooms and office hours.

The first stage Perry identifies is that of dualism, which moves from simple to complex forms over the three subpositions of that stage. Students in the dualistic mode of thought believe in absolute truth, which exists somewhere out in the world, and which their professors have somehow gained access to. The job of the professor is to take that absolute knowledge and pass it along to the students; the job of the student is to obey authority and absorb the truth. Students at this stage will naturally prefer lectures, and will probably chafe against too much discussion or small group work in the classroom. "I'm paying to learn from the expert," you might hear a student like this say, "so why do I have to sit here and listen to what a bunch of my classmates have to say?" They also will expect teachers to present theories and facts in a straightforward, uncomplicated way, and will be unsettled when this does not happen. Perry quotes from an interviewed student who expresses unease at the difference between history as taught in high school and history as taught at Harvard:

Well, in high school we took a course like that, a history course. In that course the teacher would be telling you exact facts and here it's altogether different. I don't know. I like the work better when they . . . I suppose it's more immature, but I like it better when they give you something concrete, exactly what happened—not go off on a tangent on some phase that appears on the surface not to have anything to do with the subject. I don't particularly care for that. (76)

The student's desire for the "exact facts," and for something "concrete," demonstrates his commitment to dualistic thinking, which would involve a mode of teaching that relates the "true" historical narrative without bringing in alternative histories or alternative versions of the facts that are presented. He is searching, in other words, for a kind of history that you simply won't find on college campuses today, where the very notion of a historical fact has been called into question by our awareness of the multiple and competing narratives of the past, each highlighting different facts and different understandings of the common facts.

It would be difficult for a student to last long on a college campus today with this attitude toward the world, and in fact I suspect many students who leave college do so because they can't reconcile dualistic thinking with what they hear and experience in their classrooms—and the world of dualism is a comfortable one, since answers exist for every question, so abandoning it can cause some emotional distress. Perry in fact argues that it is rare to see complete dualism even in entering freshmen, and that most students who enter college have begun to see the limitations of this worldview. One clear path to seeing those limitations comes when students realize either that two experts in a subject may disagree—they might learn this from taking two different courses in the same discipline, with professors who

fundamentally disagree about the nature of the discipline—or
that in all disciplines there remain areas of doubt and uncertainty. A student confronted by these issues moves into the transitional positions of stage one, believing perhaps that while absolute knowledge must exist somewhere, we just haven't found all
of the answers yet.

Most students, however, according to Perry, move from these
transitional positions of dualism into the three possible positions
of stage two, or relativism. The first move into relativism is a lib-
erating one in which the students feel that, since no one has
the correct answers, then all answers are equal—including their
own. "That's the great thing about a book like *Moby Dick*," Perry
cites one student as saying. "*Nobody* understands it!" (98). That
nobody understands it, on the positive side, might free the student into venturing her own opinion about the book, in a way
that she might not have wished to under dualism (since the professor has the right answer anyway, why risk being wrong?). On
the negative side, students newly entered into this position will
question grades defiantly, wondering what gives their professors
the right to take points off their answers, since everyone has a
right to his opinion—and students in the early position of this
stage will see opinions and answers and arguments as all one and
the same. If not defiant, they may be bewildered, unclear why
one paper receives an A and another a C. "If I present [a paper] in
the right manner it is well received," one student says, trying to
reason it out in his mind, but then giving up. "Or it is received
. . . I don't know, I still haven't exactly caught onto what, what
they want" (90). So relativism will come with feelings of liberation for some, but fear and unease for others, as they find themselves floating in a sea without any landmarks to help chart their
course.

For all students, though, this stage will come with an accompanying sense of academics as gamesmanship, in which the student has to figure out what each professor wants, and conform to each faculty member's individual whims, in order to do well in school. The students understand now that answers no longer exist in the sky; they understand as well that grades are determined by human beings, and therefore they have to learn to provide the answers that these different human beings want. Students in the later positions of this stage will develop a procedural mentality in which they spend some initial time each semester figuring out what the professor wants, and then spend the rest of the semester doing their best to give that to her. I've heard some of my smartest students, speaking to me during my office hours, describing very explicitly the importance of learning to write to each professor's particular biases—these are students engaged in procedural knowing. There is, of course, some truth to this recognition on the part of the students, since all teachers will tend to emphasize certain writing skills or habits over others, and we will never achieve universal, objective grading standards. But students at this stage will operate under an exaggerated sense of completely variable standards from one faculty member to the next, and from one course to the next.

A student who has reached this stage, and is capable of discerning and working up the standards of each professor, could graduate with honors and succeed easily in the world—and so, in that sense, could be counted as a successful college student. But we don't want our graduates to be chameleons who are perfectly willing to camouflage themselves against whatever color appears in the background, without making any judgments about it at all. Therefore, most of us who teach want to push our students into one of the positions of Perry's final stage, which entails the students making commitments to the values and knowledge that matter to them in a pluralistic world.

As Perry points out, doing this is an emotionally trying experience, and a cyclical one as well—students might make their initial commitments to a certain set of ethical values, for example, and imagine themselves done with that trying decision, only to stumble immediately into all of the complications and extenuating circumstances that make ethical decisions so challenging. One of Perry's students offers this description of making a commitment but then realizing that nothing is final: "It's a real, definite commitment, with a possibility of [laughs] of withdrawing from the commitment, which I think is the only realistic kind of commitment I can make, because there *is* a possibility of change here" (161). I think this is exactly the kind of student we should strive to produce in a pluralistic, democratic society—a person who understands the importance of making a commitment to a specific set of values and knowledge, but who recognizes the contingent nature of that commitment and keeps an open mind about the possibility that his values might one day change. Such a student would also recognize the contingent nature of the values of his peers, and hopefully would respect those values even while he maintains his own commitments.

I should note here that producing such students does not in any way require them—or you—to give up religious faith. Perry addresses this issue frequently in the book, and compares stage-one dualism to blind belief, while stage-three commitment resembles a mature and informed religious faith. Whatever our students' religious convictions may be, we are preparing them to live in a pluralistic society which leaves most decisions about values up to individual citizens, and requires that we respect the decisions that our fellow citizens make.

So what does all of this mean for you as a teacher? First, an awareness of these three stages can help you understand how students are hearing and seeing what happens in your classroom. As you encounter students in these different stages, you'll begin to recognize characteristic comments and behaviors. You'll have dualistic students who come to your office and plead with you to give them the definitive reading of a poem or solution to a problem, or who come crying to you over their most recent paper, not because they want to complain about the grade but because they believe that everyone else knows the answers but they don't. You'll have relativistic students who will point out to you that Professor X taught them differently, and they would just like to know what *you* prefer, and they'll be happy to give it to you. You'll have students fumbling their way toward commitment in their junior or senior years, arguing with you in class about a basic assumption in your discipline, or confessing to you during an advising session that they think they are going to enter the Peace Corps.

Second, and more important, the ability to recognize students in these different stages can make you a more compassionate and effective teacher. On top of everything else we are trying to accomplish in the classroom, we ultimately want to push students as far along the path toward commitment as possible. Dualistic students can be frustrating ones, and we can sometimes mistake their tight grip on dualism for stupidity (just as we might see stupidity in a student who holds tightly to a failing mental model). Understanding the perspective of these students can help us understand how to interact with them more effectively in the office, or even in the classroom, gently nudging them toward the realization that knowledge does not exist out in the sky, but in the minds of other human beings like themselves. I make it a point to begin each course I teach in Introduction to Literature with the argument that no single, correct interpretation exists of a poem or a story, a speech which is aimed at the dualists. But I continue the speech for the relativists—although no single, correct interpretation exists, not all interpretations are equal. I want students to come up with their own interpretation, based on the reasoning tools I will give them in class, and to defend their interpretations in class and in their papers.

Do freshmen in my Introduction to Literature class immediately jump from dualism or relativism to commitment after hearing this stirring speech? Of course not. But one or two might come around to this way of thinking by the end of the semester, and the rest have heard it, and might remember it when they hear it again in another class, or begin to sort it out in late-night debates in their dorm. Pushing students toward commitment presents even more of a challenge, and at least one study of Perry's scheme, or a modified version of it, suggests that the majority of students don't begin to make serious commitments until their first year or two after college. That doesn't mean that teachers shouldn't still push students in that direction, but it does mean that we should be realistic about what we can expect to accomplish in our classrooms.

I owe it to you as a reader to conclude my summary of Perry by noting that his theories have been extensively debated over the years since their first appearance, and that educational theorists today would be far more likely to cite more contemporary works and authors than Perry. Throwing around Perry's name at a cocktail party of educational theorists wouldn't be nearly as bad as authoritatively quoting Freud at a psychology convention—more like citing Newton rather than Feynman at the annual physics department picnic. And of course my summary has been a simplified one; students will not move through the stages so neatly, and they can be in different stages in different areas of their thinking, and so on—imagine any possible complication that someone might pose to a simple scheme like Perry's, and someone has probably proposed it. Still, the idea of seeing students in these specific phases, and seeing them move gradually from dualism toward commitments, has always rung true to me in terms of my experiences with them, and this continues to be true for many faculty members today.

- - - - - - - - -

You will, of course, come into your first semester of college teaching with a mental model of how students learn, one derived primarily from your own experiences as a learner. That model may be hard for you to abandon, since you have spent much of your life learning, and you have obviously been largely successful in doing so. One goal of this chapter has been to encourage you to take a second look at that model—to consider whether theories about learning and intellectual development in the college years might help you develop it further, and reshape it so that you can more effectively help students learn in and out of your classroom.

Think about your model of student learning, and the teaching strategies that work best with that model, as one that should remain subject to frequent revision and improvement for the next thirty or forty years, as you draw upon both your personal experience and your occasional glimpse into the latest research on student learning and teaching to deepen your understanding of the ways in which human beings learn. I'm with Christopher Lucas and John Murry in setting a second, and very modest, goal for the way in which theories about student learning might influence your teaching:

> Possibly the best that can be hoped for, first, is that college teachers will develop enhanced sensitivity to the fact that students do appear to differ in how they learn, even if the variability cannot always be fixed with scientific precision. Second, so far as learning modalities and age-related char-

acteristics are concerned, faculty must learn to eschew reliance on any single teaching approach—for example, on 'chalk and talk' alone, to the virtual exclusion of a broad range of other possibilities. (86)

Resources

If you approach the literature on learning theory without a degree in psychology, or neurobiology, or education, as I have, you will probably find what I have found—that the theories of how we learn are numerous, usually overlapping, and sometimes conflicting. Each of them seems sensible on its own, at first blush, and each of them draws critics who enumerate its shortcomings. The best approach, in my opinion, is to do for yourself what I have done here—seek out summaries or overviews of the major theories, mostly available on the Internet, and then look more deeply at the ones that seem to make the most sense to you and begin to think about how those theories could influence your teaching. In addition to the theorists I have discussed in this chapter, I have listed below a few alternative learning models by Gardner and Kolb, as well as one text (Belenky et al.) that updates Perry's work by considering how students' gender may impact their learning. You could spend a lifetime of reading on this material.

Belenky, Mary, et al. *Women's Ways of Knowing.* New York: Basic Books, 1986.

These researchers offer an updated and/or alternative theory to Perry; they focus, as the title implies, on how women might have a distinct learning style. Their theory still matches Perry's in its basic progression, as they see students moving through four beliefs about the nature of knowledge: seeing it first as received, then as subjective, then moving into procedural and finally constructed perspectives. If Perry's work appeals to you, this book deserves a look as well.

Driscoll, Marcy. *Psychology of Learning for Instruction,* 3rd ed. Boston: Allyn and Bacon, 2004.
Designed as a student textbook, this book nonetheless presents a very comprehensive overview of learning theories and their implications for teaching. Have your library order it for you, since its price will be tough on a new faculty member's budget.

Gardner, Howard. *Multiple Intelligences: The Theory in Practice.* New York: Basic Books, 1993.
You've probably heard of this theory in some form or another, although most of Gardner's research has been done on K–12 students. Gardner argues for the existence of seven types of intelligence—linguistic, musical, logical-mathematical, spatial, bodily-kinesthetic, interpersonal, and intrapersonal—and says that conventional schooling tends to reward only one or two of those intelligence types. Proponents of his theory work to help students express their intelligences in other forms—through music, hands-on learning, and so on.

Kolb, David. *Experiential Learning: Experience as the Source of Learning and Development.* Englewood Cliffs, N.J.: Prentice-Hall, 1984.
Kolb's theory of learning posits a four-stage process: concrete experience, observation and reflection, formation of abstract concepts, and experimentation in new situations. This isn't all that far removed from the mental models theory. Advocates of Kolb's ideas suggest that students need to begin the learning process with a concrete experience, some kind of activity that will introduce them to an issue and provoke reflection. This is simple enough to envision in a science course but a little more difficult

----

to imagine in a literature course, though asking students to write a poem might do the trick before they begin the study of poetry.

Lucas, Christopher J., and John W. Murry, Jr. "Active Learning and Other Instructional Management Issues." In *New Faculty: A Practical Guide for Academic Beginners*, 71–104. New York: Palgrave, 2002.
You could start here, especially pp. 81–86, for a good overview of different learning theories and their implications for teaching.

McGonigal, Kelly. "Teaching for Transformation: From Learning Theory to Teaching Strategies." *Speaking of Teaching*, 14.2 (Spring 2005): 1–4; *http://ctl.stanford.edu/Newsletter/transformation.pdf* (January 21, 2007).
A good overview of Mezirow's work; it concludes with a section on practical classroom applications. Available online.

Mezirow, Jack. *Transformative Dimensions of Adult Learning.* San Francisco: Jossey-Bass, 1991.
The theory of assimilative versus transformative learning, which in some ways falls in line with the mental models theory developed by Piaget.

Nelson, Craig. "Cultural Thinking and Collaborative Learning." *New Directions for Teaching and Learning*, 59 (Fall 1994): 45–58.

Perry, William. *Forms of Intellectual and Ethical Development in the College Years: A Scheme.* New York: Holt, Rinehart and Winston, 1968.
Perry's original text.

Piaget, Jean, and Barbel Inhelder. *The Psychology of the Child.* New York: Basic Books, 2000.

As good as it gets by Piaget, which, as I said, can be tough reading. Clear style was not his strong suit.

Singer, Dorothy, and Tracey Revenson. *A Piaget Primer: How a Child Thinks,* rev. ed. Madison, Wis.: International Universities Press, 1997.

A very readable overview of Piaget, and introduction to his work. I found this book quite interesting as both a teacher and a parent.

Students as People

I was talking to a colleague of mine at a restaurant one evening while I was working on this book, and the subject of some mutual friends came up, a couple who had been married for a dozen years or more. My colleague knew this couple much better than I did, and mentioned casually that he was glad they had worked out their recent marital difficulties.

"What marital difficulties?" I said.

"They were right on the edge a couple of years back," he said. "Didn't you know? They were talking divorce. It could have gone either way, but they eventually worked it out."

"Geez, I had no idea," I said. I shook my head. "It's amazing how much stuff you don't know about other people's lives."

"Yeah," he said, "and for the most part, the less you know the better."

In most cases, with your students, you'll be just like me in this scenario, ignorant about all of the stuff that is happening in their lives outside of the classroom—and when you do catch the occasional glimpse of things that are happening in their personal lives, you'll probably agree with the sentiment of my colleague, and wish you could return to your state of blissful ignorance.

To illustrate, let me tell you two stories (with details changed) about how much stuff I didn't know about the lives of two students who passed through my classroom in the last couple of years.

I had a female student in my freshman composition class whose first paper indicated that she could write as well or better than most senior English majors in our department. I rejoiced that she had ended up in my section, happily anticipating both her contributions in class and the remainder of her papers for the semester, which would be easy to read and simple to grade. However, as the semester proceeded, she was more and more frequently absent from class. She turned in papers late or not at all, and though the papers she did turn in showed continued evidence of her immense writing talent, they were also filled with sloppy mistakes. I used my comments on her papers initially to give her pep talks about how she should not waste her writing talents like this, and then—when those comments seemed to have no effect—to try and scare her into taking the class more seriously by warning her about the consequences on her grade if she continued to turn in late and sloppy work. And then one day, near the end of the semester, she came to me in my office and told me, very matter-of-factly, that her mother was dying of cancer, and that she was living at home to take care of her and commuting to the college. I had just watched my own mother die of cancer a year or two before, so all the horror of the experience was fresh in my mind. After she left my office, I felt sick to my stomach to think that I had been using the threat of low grades to motivate this girl to pay more attention to my assignment sheets while she was caring for her dying mother.

That same year I had a student in the gateway course for English majors who was competent but not outstanding in any respect; she was quiet, kept completely to herself, worked hard, but occasionally seemed to have trouble grasping the major concepts of the course, or completing an assignment. When that happened, she would come to see me in my office and ask for help, which I would give her. The next year she took my upper-level course in creative nonfiction writing, and there she seemed a different person. She had a different hairstyle, wore different clothes, socialized with her classmates more, and spoke more in class. Her writing had clearly improved, and she definitely seemed more emotionally committed to the class than she had in the gateway course (where she had seemed to me just to be plodding toward a degree requirement). However, she also seemed less conscientious about the particulars of her course work—she missed a few classes, turned in a paper late, and hadn't always done the reading. In the final paper she wrote for the class, I learned the reason for the changes in her behavior. She had been engaged, since her sophomore year in college, to her longtime sweetheart, who was a soldier; during the time she was in my gateway class, he had been away at an army base, and she spent most of her time writing him letters and visiting with his mother. After he returned home, he began to drink heavily and became abusive to her. She broke off their engagement, was free to date and socialize with her peers for the first time in her life, and began to nurture her long-suppressed hopes of becoming a writer— hopes that her ex-fiancé had done his best to discourage. All of this had happened just before she took the creative writing class with me; what I had seen in that class were the sometimes conflicting feelings she was experiencing of liberation, on the one hand, and a new commitment to her intellectual life, on the other.

The important point about these two stories is not that they are especially compelling tales of hardship and struggle—they may be, but if you probed into the details of the lives of all your students, you would be astonished to discover how many compelling tales of hardship and struggle are walking in and out of your classroom every day. The point is that we see only the tiniest slices of our students' lives, and those tiny slices rarely reveal to us what matters to them most, or what major events or people are shaping their lives right now. Students in their late teens and early twenties are watching their grandparents die (and sometimes even their parents), are falling in and out of love for the first time, are learning (or not learning) how to handle drugs and alcohol, are living away from home for the first time and trying to get along with roommates, and are trying to decide how they will spend the rest of their lives. Any one of these events or transitions has the potential to drain much of the emotional and intellectual energy of a human being—and most of our students are dealing with several or all of them, and then trying to stay on top of four or five completely different intellectual journeys each semester.

This course you are teaching, then, while it occupies a substantial portion of your time and energy at the moment, occupies a much smaller space in the hearts and minds of most of your students. It *should* matter more to you than it does to them— it's your life's work, after all, while for them it represents a way station on a journey whose destination remains unknown to them.

I'm telling you all this not to encourage you to delve into your students' personal lives and to adjust your grading or attendance policies for every student with a hardship story—in fact, I think both those things would be terrible ideas. These stories and my reflections on them are meant to prepare you for a handful of guidelines that should help steer you through your first year of working with students as human beings, each with a complex life outside of your classroom, while allowing you to maintain professional standards of conduct.

Stick Compassionately to Your Standards

Students who have read your syllabus, and stayed in your course beyond add/drop week, have agreed to complete a certain amount of work for you. You should not decrease or substantially modify that workload for the sake of students who might be having personal problems. It is certainly true that every face in your classroom may be a mask behind which is a story like one of the two stories I just told. But you will also have students who turn in work late or miss classes for the not-so-good reasons that they were out at clubs the night before, or were too busy playing X-Box in their dorm rooms, or simply forgot the assignment. When you are first confronted with a student who seems to be heading off the rails in your course, be courteous but firm. Enforce whatever relevant policies you have in the course. Hold opposing possibilities in your head—the student might be trying to take advantage of you, or he might actually have a dying mother at home. Since you can't know which is true, you are obligated to treat the students consistently and in line with the standards you've established for the course. Resist the temptation to motivate students with threats, and don't get angry; those moves will only worsen an already difficult situation for a student who really is in trouble. Remind the student of the course policies and enforce them.

If a student does open up to you about a specific hardship that is causing her problems in the course, do your best to accommodate her when you can—you might remove penalties for late work, extend deadlines, or allow a commuting student to work on an individual research paper rather than a group presentation. But do not simply pass students through if they don't complete the work for the course. If a situation arises in which it seems likely that a student will not have completed the necessary work to pass your course by the end of the semester, contact your department chair or the administrator at your college who handles students who are having academic difficulties—this person will usually be a dean, frequently the Dean of Students. At many colleges this dean can intervene in situations like this, find out the extent of the student's problems, and work with you to ensure that they complete their coursework, or take an incomplete, or take a pause in their studies. Remember this—a student who is having difficulties like this in your course is probably having them in other courses as well, and will be best helped by talking with a single person who can see the situation as a whole, and who has experience dealing with such situations (i.e., not you).

Listen, but Don't Counsel

Over the course of your career, you will eventually have a student in your office who wants to do more than confess a hardship in order to seek accommodations for grading purposes. You will have students who want to make confessions simply because you are a person that they respect and perhaps admire, and they want your counsel in dealing with crises they are undergoing in their lives. I've had students in my office or in their written work reveal their homosexuality, their problems with alcohol, abusive situations at home, and more. Sometimes those students have explicitly asked me for advice; sometimes they have simply told their story. I don't have the kind of warm and welcoming personality that invites such confessions from students, and the handful of them that I have received have been scattered over a half-dozen years; faculty members I know who do have warmer personalities—and especially female faculty members, who can be mistaken by students for surrogate mother figures—may hear multiple such confessions every semester.

You will be tempted, when such a confession falls into your lap, to offer your counsel, drawing upon your life experience and your instincts and common sense. Resist that temptation. Degree programs in counseling exist for a reason—helping students negotiate these complex issues in their lives is a complex task. Unless you happen to be teaching counseling, do not usurp the role of the professionals on your campus whose job is to help students manage their lives outside of the classroom.

Somewhere on your campus an office will exist with a title like Counseling and Student Development, and that office has trained staff who meet with students individually and help them with their life problems. That office also will have brochures or pamphlets or business cards with information about how to contact them and schedule an appointment. Before the semester starts, find that office and grab a handful of those brochures. When students come to you seeking advice on their life crises, listen patiently and compassionately, and then give them a brochure and direct them to the counseling offices. The first time you do this, it will feel cruel—but counseling is not part of your job, and your unfamiliarity both with the student and with the complexities of counseling means that you might ultimately do more harm than good by relying on your experiences and instincts to offer advice.

Know Your Campus

The counseling office may not be the only one you need to refer students to, even in your first semester of teaching. There may be a separate office for drug and alcohol counseling (frequently housed with the general student counseling offices); there will be a Dean's office for students with academic problems; there will be offices for health services, public safety, student life, and many more. Your campus may have a brochure or reference guide that lists all of the major offices that students might need to consult for emergencies or unusual situations—see if you can get your hands on it, if there is one. If not, check the opening pages of the campus phone book, or look at the campus website, and familiarize yourself generally with the roster of these kinds of offices. You should be familiar enough with them and their scope to know when to refer students in trouble to each of them.

The most important person you need to know on campus, though—and the one to whom you should be especially friendly, including stopping to chat whenever possible and remembering that person at the holidays—is your departmental assistant or secretary. These are the individuals who know the location and availability of resources on campus and in your department, and they can often point you in the right direction when you are confronted with a baffling situation with a student—or any kind of baffling situation at the college, for that matter. Your departmental assistant, in fact, may be the first person you'll want to consult whenever you have a question about policies or campus culture; unless they are brand new, they have probably heard someone else ask the question you are asking, and they usually know who has the answers, if they don't have the answers themselves. One of your very first activities as a new graduate student or faculty member should be to put on a big smile, introduce yourself to the department secretary, and be friendly.

(Departmental assistants, by the way, can also be great sources of institutional or departmental history, which means they will know the juiciest gossip about everyone in the department. Nothing makes your department chair less intimidating than knowing he paints Civil War figurines in his spare time, or has produced a CD of himself playing Christmas music on the recorder.)

Protect Yourself

One of the reasons I am discouraging you from getting too involved in the lives of your students is, unfortunately, a legal one—the closer you get to an individual student, the more you open yourself up to the possibility of being accused of inappropriate behavior, ranging from sexual harassment to bending school policy to simply offering poor advice. If you are in your first year of teaching, you are either a graduate student, an adjunct, or in your first year on the tenure track, which means that *you are vulnerable*. Again: *YOU ARE VULNERABLE*. You are vulnerable to being removed from the classroom for the duration of your program, or to not having your contract renewed. You will never do harm to yourself by being professional and listening to students and their problems, and then referring them to the appropriate office on campus and maintaining your policies and standards. Stepping beyond those boundaries opens you up to the possibility of both doing harm and being harmed professionally.

To further ensure that you do not become vulnerable to students' charges of inappropriate behavior, take two precautionary measures. First, document every interaction you have with a student that seems out of the ordinary to you. Save e-mails, or open a file on your computer and note down the dates of meetings with a student and the substance of the conversations. Second, and most important, *never meet students in your office behind a closed door*. Always leave your door partway open, even just a sliver, when you are meeting with a student; this tactic will prevent students from seeing your office as a confessional, or a boudoir, or anything other than a place to discuss their courses and academic lives.

I am fully aware that this advice has the potential to make me sound cold-hearted and uncaring. You may have been drawn into teaching because you have a warm heart and want to help students, and over the course of your academic career you may come to feel confident in your abilities to offer sage advice to students about the issues that you see them confronting each semester. If so, good luck.

But this semester, or this year, two facts should take precedence in your mind: you will not have the time to get emotionally involved in the personal lives of your students, and you cannot afford the professional risk of doing so. Be compassionate, listen when students need to talk, and then step back and let the experts on campus step in.

I want to finish this chapter by giving you some statistics on the demographics of today's college students in four areas, with quick reflections on what some of these demographics might mean for your interactions with students in and out of the classroom. Of course, the national demographics won't precisely match the demographics at your school. The specific demographics at your campus will almost always be available to you, however, from an office of institutional research on campus (on a smaller campus, this might be a single person rather than an office, and that person might have other roles on campus as well). Statistics on your students should be available from that office, and are frequently posted on the institution's website as well (you can also sometimes get this information from other tenured or tenure-track faculty members). The national statistics presented below come from two reports by the National Center for Education Statistics,

----

an office of the U.S. Department of Education, and are available online (see the Resources section).

AGE

If you've followed the literature on higher education over the past decade or two, you will have noticed an increasing amount of attention paid to the rise of non-traditional-age students—that is, students who are either coming to college or returning to it well beyond the approximate age range of traditional students (usually defined as from 18 to 24). Certainly this non-traditional population deserves the special attention it has received, since a 40-year-old who is going to college while working full-time and raising a family will present different challenges to an institution than an 18-year-old will, both in and out of the classroom; likewise, a 40-year-old returning to the classroom after twenty years may learn differently than an 18-year-old student fresh out of high school does (think of Perry here). Faculty at community colleges, in particular, will see a substantial portion of their populations falling outside of the traditional age range of college students.

The majority of students in higher education still remain in the traditional range, and the NCES predicts that trend will increase slightly over the next half-dozen years. In 1992, approximately 57 percent of the postsecondary student population were in the age group 18 to 24; that number increased to 60 percent in 2000, and is expected to rise to 61 percent by 2012 (*Projections of Education Statistics*). But the chances are excellent that you will have at least some older students in your first year of teaching, no matter what kind of school you teach at.

You might find yourself intimidated at the prospect of teaching someone twenty years your senior, as I was when I had to do it in my third semester of college teaching, at the tender age of 22.

Just remember what you learned about wild animals when you were a kid—usually they are more scared of you than you are of them. You may have a rare adult student who challenges your authority, or speaks condescendingly to students who don't share their richer life experiences. Such issues are usually best handled with one-on-one conferences with the student.

But returning and adult students are often excellent additions to the classroom, because they understand the full value of the education they are receiving (unlike traditional students, who often have parents footing the bill), and they want to get their money's worth by contributing and learning as much as possible. The main point to remember here, though, is that adult students often do need the kind of unique accommodations that students need when they are struggling with special hardships. Adult students usually have jobs, and they might be married and have children—all features of their lives that can, and probably should, take precedence over their school work in a way that a night at the bars or a breakup with a girlfriend or a spontaneous road trip should not. Again, this does not mean excusing adult students from work, but doing your best to acknowledge the greater complexities of their lives, and helping them get the work done.

GENDER

It has been the case for quite some time now that women outnumber men in colleges and universities. Women constituted 55 percent of college enrollment in 1990, 56 percent in 2000, and are expected to make up 57 percent of the total enrolled population by 2012 *[Projections of Education Statistics]*. This will vary according to discipline—faculty in English or education departments may find themselves, as I have on more than one occasion, in classes that are entirely female; faculty in economics or hard sciences might find themselves in classes dominated by males. Gender differences in college students may not seem all that significant for the classroom, unless you believe that girls should study poetry and be teachers and boys should get to build bridges and blow things up (not necessarily in that order).

However, a substantial body of literature has sprung up, much of it drawing upon or refuting older learning theories, that argues that women and men have distinctive learning styles—and that, therefore, they will respond more or less successfully to different teaching strategies. I think there may be some truth to this, based on my own experiences in the classroom, but I haven't been convinced enough by this research to believe we need to somehow formulate two different kinds of lesson plans in our classrooms. Practically speaking, at any rate, this would be a very difficult maneuver. If your first year of teaching suggests to you that there is more to this theory than I am allowing, begin by checking out Belenky's *Women's Ways of Knowing*, referred to in the previous chapter and noted again in the Resources section below. And see the conclusion of this chapter, where I offer some general thoughts on how changing demographics and possible differences in learning styles should affect what we do in the classroom.

One point is worth noting here, though. Some researchers have argued that the classroom climate for women can be a "chilly" one, especially in traditionally male-dominated fields like engineering and the hard sciences (see Sandler, Silverberg, and Hall). For example, faculty members might be less likely to invite or accept contributions from female students in a "chilly" classroom. Subsequent studies have called this phenomenon into question (see Drew and Work), but since it *may* be the case that some classrooms are less welcoming to women, it's worth reminding ourselves that we should take care to treat male and female students equally, and work to make the classroom a welcoming place for all.

ATTENDANCE STATUS

In raw numbers, 9 million students were enrolled in college full-time in 2000; the NCES predicts that number will rise to 10.1 million in 2012. The number of part-time students was 6.3 million in 2000, with an expected increase to 6.9 million in 2012 *(Projections of Education Statistics)*. Thus the full-time enrollment in higher education institutions is slightly less than two out of three students, although the institutional type will make a huge difference here. The vast majority of students at Ivy League institutions will be enrolled full-time, while the number of part-time students at community colleges will be much higher.

Part-time students, of course, are mostly part-time because they are doing something else as well—working, or raising a family, or caring for a sick relative. You won't always know when students are in part-time status, but again, as with older students, keep in mind that they might request or need special accommodations more than full-time students.

RACE/ETHNICITY

From 1976 to 2004, the percentage of minorities enrolled in higher education institutions in America rose from 15 to 30 percent, largely driven by an increase in the enrollment of Asian and Hispanic students. Asian/Pacific Islander enrollment rose from 1 to 6 percent during that time period, and Hispanic enrollment from 4 to 10 percent of the total college population. Black student enrollment increased as well, from 9 to 13 percent *(Digest of Education Statistics)*.

As with gender, some researchers have suggested that students from non-Western cultures have different learning strategies or styles than students from the majority culture in America. (Again, see the conclusion to this chapter for my thoughts on this.) Outside of that issue, the primary pedagogical pitfall that accompanies a diverse classroom lies in courses in the humanities or social sciences that ask students to confront and discuss controversies about race. In such classes, both instructors and fellow students can sometimes single out minority students and expect them to provide "the" Hispanic or Asian or black perspective. Obviously, the burden of speaking for an entire race or ethnicity is not one that any student should be asked to bear. My suspicion is that this usually happens unintentionally—for instance, an instructor poses a question about the effects of racism in people's lives and then lets his eyes fall on the only black student in the room, or the rest of the class clams up, waiting expectantly for that student to tell his story.

Some minority students may want to speak in this situation, but most will rightly resent the expectation that their experiences could be representative of an entire race. In these situations, watch your own nonverbal communication, and work more actively to ensure that contributions to a discussion come from as many students as possible.

Conclusion: Race and Gender in the Classroom

These thoughts have remained at a pretty general level, a necessity given how widely demographics will vary from institution to institution. The points I have made here will take on more importance if the demographics of your institution are skewed toward students whose presence is newer to the academy—older students, part-time students, minority students—and should guide the direction and extent of your following up on the resources below. If you are teaching at a mostly female college, look into the literature that argues for separate ways of knowing and learning for women; if you are teaching at an ethnically diverse community college, look more deeply at resources on teaching about race. Even faculty members teaching at institutions that still consist primarily of traditional students, as I do, will find their perspectives on teaching and learning enlarged by considering these issues more fully.

A more relevant question for a teaching guidebook is how and whether theories about the learning styles and strategies of a diverse student population should affect the way we teach. M. Lee Upcraft, who has conducted research on diverse populations in higher education for many years, draws two conclusions about this in an article published a dozen years ago, when many of the demographic shifts I outlined above were first becoming noticeable. "The first implication of changing student demography and characteristics," he writes, "is a call for a more diverse and varied style of instruction" (34), which would ensure that as many students as possible are learning in the classroom. Second, "even though students may be different from their teachers, they do have much in common with their fellow students. They can and should be encouraged to learn with and from each other" (35–36). In other words, instructors should provide opportunities for collaborative learning more frequently.

Although my attitude concerning the impact of changing demographics on our classrooms may seem a bit laissez-faire to you, a guiding principle of this book is to push teachers toward "a more diverse and varied style of instruction," including teaching techniques that rely on collaborative learning. So following the recommendations I have been making all along goes as far toward addressing a diverse student population as I think most education specialists are willing to go these days, until much more concrete evidence exists about effective and very specific techniques for serving different populations in our classrooms.

Many of the teaching guidebooks in print today, published over the past two dozen years, make lots of noise about the shock you should expect to receive at seeing these diverse populations in your classroom. But my guess is that the readers of this book, teaching for the first time—even if you were an undergraduate a dozen years ago—swam in those same waters as an undergraduate, so you won't feel the culture shock that I could spend many pages warning you about. Students today are very different from the students of thirty years ago, no doubt. But the students of today are not so different from the students of five or ten years ago—and, reassuringly and in all likelihood, not so different from yourself.

Resources

Belenky, Mary, et al. *Women's Ways of Knowing.* New York: Basic Books: 1986.
A scheme similar to Perry's, but focused on women.

Digest of Education Statistics: 2005. National Center for Education Statistics, U.S. Department of Education, June 2006. *http://nces.ed.gov/programs/digest/d05/ack.asp,* November 11, 2006.

Projections of Education Statistics to 2012, 31st ed. National Center for Education Statistics, U.S. Department of Education, October 2002. *http://nces.ed.gov/pubs2002/2002030.pdf,* November 11, 2006.

The Department of Education has lots of these demographic reports and statistics, all available through its website.

Drew, Todd, and Gerald Work. "Gender-Based Differences in Perception of Experiences in Higher Education: Gaining a Broader Perspective." *Journal of Higher Education*, 69.5 (September-October 1995): 542–555.

Drew and Work's research does not find any evidence of the chilly climate.

Sandler, Bernice, Lisa Silverberg, and Roberta Hall. *The Chilly Classroom Climate: A Guide to Improve the Education of Women.* Washington, D.C.: National Association for Women in Education, 1996.

This book contains information about the original study of the "chilly classroom," published back in the early 1980s, as well as recommendations for warming it up.

Upcraft, M. Lee. "Teaching and Today's College Students." In *Teaching on Solid Ground: Using Scholarship to Improve Practice.* San Francisco: Jossey-Bass, 1996.

Although the demographics he writes about are a dozen years out of date, Upcraft's point about the necessity of varying instructional formats still seems like a solid one to me.

Academic Honesty

In December of 2005, a graduate student with the pseudonym of "Michael Thompson" published a confessional essay in the *Chronicle of Higher Education* about how he had plagiarized a draft chapter of his dissertation from a handful of different sources in a foreign language, translating them and then cutting and splicing them together and padding out the mixture with some of his own insights. Fortunately or unfortunately for him, he received a lukewarm response to the chapter by his dissertation committee, and a growing sense of unease at his actions compelled him to scrap the chapter and rewrite it without the plagiarism, so it never made it into his final product. The author of this essay tries to explain why he plagiarized, but the effort is a weak one, filled with half-excuses—he was turned off to academic work at the time, he felt hopeless about completing the project and obtaining an academic job, he was only following the example of politicians and business leaders and clergy who were making constant headlines for their dishonesty. This may be the most surprising part of the essay—not that he plagiarized, but that he really had very little explanation or understanding of why he did it.

But that inability to see cheating and plagiarism as anything unusual, anything that *requires* a complex explanation, seems to come with the territory these days, according to most of the teaching guidebooks. In *The Craft of Teaching*, Kenneth Eble says that "cheating is natural, common, and greatly affected by the situation in which individuals are placed" (165). Joseph Lowman, in *Mastering the Techniques of Teaching*, opines that "though cheating among college students cannot be justified or condoned, the motivations that lead to it are too universal and understandable to allow instructors to treat perpetrators harshly" (207). McKeachie looks at the literature on teaching and notes, with what seems like a tone of resignation, that "studies of cheating behavior over several decades invariably find that a majority of students report that they have cheated at some time" (113). And while we might find it surprising to think that graduate students would "cheat" on their dissertations, studies have shown that cheating and plagiarism persist in graduate schools of all kinds, particularly in business schools. A 2006 report based on surveys of 32 graduate schools in the United States and Canada found that "56 percent of graduate business students had cheated, compared with 47 percent of graduate students in non-business programs" (Mangan, A44). What I find alarming about this statistic is not the higher number of cheaters in business schools (undergraduate business majors also have higher cheating rates than those in other programs), but the fact that 47 percent of graduate students in general report having cheated within the past year!

So, in other words, the chances are pretty good that you will encounter instances of cheating and/or plagiarism in your first year of teaching, and you will be surprised, disappointed, angry, and confused about how to respond. I'll try to guide you through this minefield, one of the toughest areas for a teacher to negotiate, by considering three aspects of violations to academic hon-

esty: the demographics and mechanics of cheating and plagiarism; prevention; and response.

Demographics and Mechanics

WHO CHEATS?

For the past two decades, Donald McCabe, a professor of Management and Global Business at Rutgers University, has been
conducting surveys about the extent of cheating by students of
all levels in higher education. The results of his first survey, produced in 1990, led to the founding of the Center for Academic Integrity, a research and advocacy organization that sponsors and
catalogues studies on cheating, and that promotes efforts to prevent and reduce the problem. The Center is now lodged within
the Kenan Institute for Ethics at Duke University, and regularly
produces new information and survey results on cheating and
plagiarism. McCabe alone claims to have surveyed over 100,000
college students in the United States and Canada, at more than
140 institutions, over the past fifteen years. Much of the research
and results are available online, at the website listed in the Resources section below.

At the time of this writing, McCabe's latest research, produced
in 2005, reported the following statistics, which I'll cite directly
from the Center's summary of the research:

- On most campuses, 70% of students admit to some cheating. Close to one-quarter of the participating students admitted to serious test cheating in the past year, and half admitted to one or more instances of serious cheating on
  written assignments.
- Internet plagiarism is a growing concern on all campuses as
  students struggle to understand what constitutes acceptable
  use of the Internet. In the absence of clear direction from

faculty, most students have concluded that "cut & paste" plagiarism—using a sentence or two (or more) from different sources on the Internet and weaving this information together into a paper without appropriate citation—is not a serious issue. While 10% of students admitted to engaging in such behavior in 1999, almost 40% admit to doing so in the Assessment Project surveys. A majority of students (77%) believe such cheating is not a very serious issue.

• Longitudinal comparisons show significant increases in serious test/examination cheating and unpermitted student collaboration. For example, the number of students self-reporting instances of unpermitted collaboration at nine medium to large state universities increased from 11% in a 1963 survey to 49% in 1993. This trend seems to be continuing: between 1990 and 1995, instances of unpermitted collaboration at 31 small to medium schools increased from 30% to 38%. (Center for Academic Integrity)

All of this (depressing) information leads us to a very simple answer to our question. Who cheats? Everyone cheats!

That flip response doesn't take into account the fact that levels of cheating vary across different kinds of institutions, different majors and programs, and different levels of education. But the sheer numbers of cheating students, if we can trust the research, definitely suggest that cheating is happening in every kind of class, and by every kind of student. Ask around a bit among the more experienced faculty in your department, and I bet you'll find confirmation of this. I've had plenty of slow and lazy students cheat in my classes, but I've also discovered plagiarized papers from some of the smartest and seemingly nicest students I've had.

So don't assume that, because you are not seeing it, students are not cheating or plagiarizing in your classes. The odds are pretty overwhelmingly against that prospect.

HOW DO THEY CHEAT?

The trajectory of the mechanics of cheating is captured nicely in the transition from 1978's *Animal House* to 2004's *Old School*— in other words, from rooting through the garbage in search of the mimeographed exam to using technology to radio the exam questions to helpers who can look up the answers and wire(less) them back to your hidden earpiece. A more academic perspective comes from a report of a museum exhibit in Russia which chronicled the arts of cheating—logarithms written on a pair of panties; jeans skirts outfitted with seventy pockets designed to hold small scrolls of paper; a new generation of tiny earpieces, invisible to the casual observer, that can receive messages from cell phones (MacWilliams).

Obviously, the mechanics of cheating will vary depending upon the sort of assignment you are giving. In quizzes and exams, students can use old-fashioned methods such as writing down formulas or facts on their bodies, their clothes, their pencils, their books or notebooks, their desks, and anywhere else that will accept ink or graphite and be visible to them during the exam. Any electronic device that a student might carry these days will be equipped with a memory function which they can use to store information, and then keep on their lap during an exam for discreet reviewing. Cell phones, PDAs, iPods, calculators—all of them carry the potential to aid cheating. Cheating on written assignments tends to come with less variation these days—students cut and paste material from the Internet, or they download entire papers from the enterprising websites that sell essays on every subject imaginable. Students with money can submit an assignment to some Internet sites and have a scholar-for-hire produce a paper tailored directly to what they need. In order not to draw too much attention to themselves, students can even request lower-quality papers which would be more in line with the quality of their overall work in the course—you can order an A essay, in other words, but you can also order a C essay if you prefer. Of course, it's still possible for students to cheat by going into the library and finding books and articles that aren't available online—but any student who goes to all that trouble, it seems to me, deserves to get away with it. At least they're in the library.

Cheating in this respect seems to me a bit like downloading music for free, with the faculty playing the role of the recording industry. Students find ways to cheat, just as they find ways to download music, and every strategy we devise to foil a new cheating method will only inspire creative students to find new ways to fool us. Between the time I am writing this and the time the book appears, some new methods of cheating or plagiarizing will doubtless have appeared on the map, followed a year later by a technique to foil that method.

The question I am not considering in much detail here is *why* students cheat, in part because the reasons seem obvious enough to me, and in part because mostly it doesn't matter. Students cheat because they're lazy, because they messed up and forgot about a test or an assignment, or because some tragedy or unforeseen circumstance prevented them from studying or getting their work done, and cheating is their last resort to save their scholarship, or preserve their GPA, and so on. Whatever the reason, the action is a breach of academic honesty, and your role as a new faculty member is not to analyze the culture of cheating in the United States but to figure out how to prevent it and respond to it when it happens. Some consideration of why students cheat, though, will be relevant for the prevention strategies you should use, so let's turn to those now.

Prevention

To get to one of the reasons why students cheat, put yourself in the position of a student taking two different kinds of courses: in one of them, her grade depends entirely upon her performance on a midterm and a final exam; in the other, her grade depends on several exams, two papers, an oral presentation, multiple quizzes and in-class writing opportunities, and her participation in the course. In the first course, cheating is not only easier to accomplish—because you only have to orchestrate it twice during the semester—but it has a much larger payoff, since successful cheating on one exam helps secure a high grade for 50 percent of your coursework. In the second course, figuring out how to cheat on all of those assignments would probably add up to more work than it would be just to do the assignments, and each instance of cheating, with all of its attendant anxiety and risks, has a much smaller payoff. In other words, the fewer assignments you have, and the more grade pressure you place on each of those assignments, the more you tempt students into cheating.

The prevention solution here should be obvious, and it falls in line with the recommendations I have made in other places in the book: give students lots of opportunities to do well in your course by giving a wide range of grade-bearing assignments, testing their skills and knowledge multiple times and in multiple ways. This reduces the rewards of cheating on any single assignment, and—even if students do get away with cheating or plagiarizing on an assignment, and don't get caught—ensures that they are still doing plenty of legitimate work for your course. It has the additional pedagogical benefit of offering students multiple chances to succeed, and rewards students who learn in different kinds of ways. Two high-pressure tests might not accurately reflect the intelligence and effort of a student with strong test anxiety, whereas a test, a paper, and an oral presentation will ensure that she has been given a fairer shake in the course.

Even in large classes, where lots of papers or oral presentations might not be an option, you can still vary the kinds and frequency of exams or shorter assignments that you give in order to reduce pressure on the major testing times (midterm and final). Give weekly short-answer quizzes that will add up to a full test grade, or vary the format of your exams from one to the next—multiple choice or short answers or identifications or longer essays.

The second prevention method definitely applies more to smaller classes. McKeachie argues that "students are not as likely to cheat in situations in which they are known as in situations in which they are anonymous members of a crowd" (117), and this makes good sense to me. It's much easier to lie to a stranger than it is to someone you know, after all, and if you have no personal relationship with your students, they will have less compunction about seeing you as one element of a system they are trying to beat. As much as possible, then, try to develop a relationship with your students—not necessarily personal ones, as I discussed in the last chapter, but intellectual relationships grounded in your common interest in the course. And at the very minimum, your relationship with the students should be based on a shared knowledge of one another's names, which means that—at least in classes of thirty or fewer—you should make a deliberate effort to learn every student's name.

I tell my students to give me three weeks to learn their names, and I work hard at doing so. I take roll for the first two weeks, at the beginning of class; every time I collect or return an assignment, I take an extra few minutes to check off the names as I go; whenever a student speaks in class, I ask them to say their name.

And almost without fail, I get at least one positive comment on student evaluations at the end of the semester about the fact that I knew every student's name. Even in large classes, where you have no hope of learning all the names, you can learn a dozen or two, simply by working to remember the names of students who speak in class or visit you in office hours. Mary McKinney, who runs the *Successful Academic* website, has a great article with all kinds of other tips for learning students' names (the article is available online; see the Resources section).

A third prevention strategy, especially for papers, is to design assignments that are difficult or impossible to plagiarize—at least in one piece. If you give students an assignment to write a five-page essay analyzing the title character of Herman Melville's story "Bartleby the Scrivener," you are joining a long list of faculty members who have trotted out that pedestrian topic over the past century. You can be sure that term papers on the Internet abound on that subject, and that potential plagiarists will be able to pick and choose from many samples. If, on the other hand, you give students the assignment to analyze how accurately the actions of the story's title character are reflected in Crispin Glover's portrayal of Bartleby in the modernized film version released in 2001, then you are offering to your students an assignment that should challenge them intellectually and remove the temptation to pull an entire paper from the Internet. Some plagiarism may still be possible, even in a unique assignment like this one—for instance, they might rely on a character analysis of Bartleby pulled from Sparknotes, and then simply add their own thoughts on the film. But such an assignment will at least prevent the kind of wholesale plagiarism of an entire essay that precludes any intellectual work on the part of the students.

Conceiving and designing unique assignments may take a little extra thought, and a little extra work, but it has benefits beyond simply preventing plagiarism or cheating. Such assignments can help both you and the students see the course material in new ways, and will relieve some of the mind-numbing boredom you might feel if you had to grade thirty general essays on "Bartleby" every semester for the next thirty years. In a similar vein, your unique assignments and exams should go into a cycle, with each one making its appearance every few years, so that students can't simply pass along their ideas or papers to fellow fraternity members. Test and paper banks are common features in fraternities and dorms (my neighbor, who attended a business college, has described for me the massive file cabinet in which his fraternity stored a well-organized archive of papers and tests for re-circulation), so asking the same kinds of questions or giving the same assignments every year will encourage students to rely on the wisdom and experience of their older peers, rather than on the gray matter in their heads. Designing unique assignments and exams, and varying them from year to year, can be one of the most effective methods you have of preventing cheating and plagiarism.

You should also make sure, as I noted in Chapter 6, that students understand the rationale behind your unique assignments, and the benefits they will receive from completing them. When students can see the connection between the assignment and the learning objectives of the course—and they have bought into those learning objectives—they are less likely to see assignments as hoops that they have to jump through, and hence less likely to get whatever help they can to boost them through those hoops.

Fourth, you need to be present and alert during your exams. You will be tempted, as we all are, to use exam time to grade, or to prepare for another class, or simply to rest your brain and stare out the window for forty-five minutes. You may also feel embarrassed about moving around the room, as if you suspected students of cheating; you want to treat them like adults and assume they don't cheat. I understand that completely, but we have already established that plenty of adults cheat, and you need to take reasonable steps to prevent that from happening in your classroom. You can certainly allow yourself to do some work during an exam, but you should remain attentive, with your eyes on the class whenever possible, and every five or ten minutes you should get up and stroll up and down the aisles. You don't need to stalk down the aisles like a member of the Gestapo seeking wrongdoers; nonverbal communication can send strong signals here, so you should move around the room as if you are looking to provide help and answer questions. In large classes that may be more anonymous than you would like, write on the board, before the students arrive, any additional instructions you might have to prevent temptation—having students sit in every other chair, or clear the memories on their calculators, or put away all electronic devices. Talk with your department colleagues about measures they take to ensure that students remain honest during an exam; you might discover additional problems you need to watch out for, or strategies that work well on your campus.

Fifth, many colleges and universities have begun to partner with plagiarism prevention businesses such as Turnitin.com. This website, founded by a graduate student in neurobiology back in the late nineties, only works if you have students turn in their papers electronically. You then submit those papers electronically to the company's database, which takes two steps: it creates what it calls a "digital fingerprint" of each essay, and compares that fingerprint to what it finds on the Web; it then stores that fingerprint so that it can be compared with future submissions. The first step goes beyond what you would be able to accomplish yourself just by Googling a portion of a student's paper, because

Turnitin.com has access to the many sites that sell student term papers, which you could only access by paying for it. The second step prevents students from recycling work from one year to the next, since it would catch a replica of a paper that was turned in a second time, even years later.

Turnitin.com has spawned considerable controversy, regarding both its effectiveness and its legality. The legal issues concern whether students' right to privacy or intellectual property issues come into play when their work is stored by this database and used for commercial purposes (the company is a for-profit enterprise). On a more practical level, what you receive back after submitting a student's paper is a report on the percentage of the student's writing which matches other writing on the Internet, with a list of matching phrases and sentences. But seeing a few matching phrases in such a report does not necessarily indicate plagiarism: we all say things all the time that others have said before us, after all. So instructors have to be careful not to jump to quick conclusions on the basis of these reports; we still need to do some analyzing and thinking before determining whether a student should be confronted with a charge of plagiarism. However—and here's why I'm considering this issue under the section on prevention—if your university does subscribe to such a site, or has any other mechanisms in place to detect plagiarism or cheating, make sure that all of your students are aware of them. You don't have to get into too much detail—doing so will only inspire efforts to foil the system—but if you give them the basic information about such cheating and plagiarism prevention mechanisms, and let them know that you will make full use of them, this may be enough to keep students on the straight and narrow path.

Finally, make sure you are absolutely clear with students on what constitutes cheating and plagiarism in your courses. In courses that involve students doing substantial amounts of writing for a grade, spend fifteen or twenty minutes in class explaining what plagiarism looks like. Students often won't have a very clear idea of what kinds of paraphrasing are acceptable and what kinds are not, and will almost certainly be fuzzy on what kinds of information require source citation and what kinds are part of general public knowledge. For courses that require extensive research papers, spend part of a class walking them through the reference and citation protocols in your discipline (at many institutions you can turn your class over to a reference librarian for an hour to handle this). They should then have a better idea of what it means to cheat, but even so you should clarify for them exactly what you allow and don't allow on homework assignments, quizzes, and exams.

Response to Cheating

But no matter how clear you may be, and how many steps you take to prevent plagiarism and cheating, you will eventually encounter them. What then? Play the benevolent pedagogue, or the disciplinarian master? Forgive and forget, or punish severely? The teaching guidebooks are pretty divided here, which suggests how vexing a question this is—Barbara Gross Davis recommends immediate disciplinary action (301), while McKeachie favors a response only in the most extreme situations. The few recommendations I will make here chart a middle course, and are designed both to address the offense and to protect you.

First, make absolutely sure that the student has indeed cheated or plagiarized. No student keeps her eyes completely focused on her desk during an entire exam, and sometimes students make legitimate mistakes when they are writing papers, such as copying sentences from a source onto notecards or a laptop and then forgetting that they are direct quotations when they copy them again into their papers. So give students the benefit of the doubt until you believe your evidence is incontrovertible. Such evidence would include printed copies of a website from which a student has lifted multiple sentences or paragraphs, or a visible notecard or banned cell phone during an exam, or anything else that you could use as concrete evidence when you confront a student. A brazen and creative student can always find ways to explain away anomalies that might point to cheating, but that aren't supported by very concrete evidence.

Not having incontrovertible evidence doesn't mean that you should not deal with the question, however. The numbers on this vary, but I've seen estimates that between 20 and 40 percent of faculty members ignore signs of student cheating in their classes (Gross Davis cites the 20 percent figure, for example)—and of course it makes perfect sense that faculty who ignore cheaters, and become known for this on campus, are more likely to attract cheaters in future classes. In cases where you don't have incontrovertible evidence, question rather than accuse. If a D student turns in an A paper that you have not been able to find a source for, call him into your office and ask him about his ideas, his writing process, and his sudden improvement. If the student has cheated, a conversation like this will make it clear enough that you know, and—while it won't address the issue of this particular paper, unless he confesses—it should prevent him from trying it in the future.

When you do have incontrovertible evidence, I recommend two courses of action.

First, do not get angry or take it personally. The student cheated for his or her own reasons, not in order to convey any particular message to or about you. I know from experience that it can be hard not to see it that way—the first thing I always want to ask of a cheating student, in my most biting and sarcastic tone, is "Do you think I'm an idiot?" Believe me, they think a lot less about you than you might imagine, in this and every other respect in life. So your confrontation with the student should be as dispassionate as possible. This might prove difficult in the face of a student who is sobbing or angry, but you have to keep yourself composed if you want to remain focused, as you should, on what happens next.

Second, as to what will happen next, I'm with Joseph Lowman on this one: "Be sure to follow your school's procedures; do not take justice into your own hands—even with the student's complicity—and arrange a private sentence such as a lower grade or an F" (208). The school's procedures will usually be spelled out in written form, either in a separate publication on academic honesty or in the student handbook or a faculty policy guide. Those procedures might include referring the student to a particular office on campus, or having students sign a settlement form, or some other specific measure. Protect yourself, and the student, by sticking with the established procedures. This may seem unduly harsh, to both you and the student, especially when you are feeling sympathetic toward a student who is sobbing and repentant in your office. In such cases you might be sorely tempted either to overlook the incident, or to arrange a private sentence.

So keep this prospect in mind: If you decide to give a student a second chance by allowing him to redo the assignment without penalty, or to take a lower grade as a punishment for the infraction, you might turn out to be one of forty instructors—one for each class the student takes in his college career—who give this student a "second" chance. I know I have been stressing the importance of giving students the benefit of the doubt wherever possible, and I continue to recommend that, since you still have the rest of the semester to spend with a cheating student. Don't characterize cheating students as evil people, and grade them accordingly for the rest of the semester. Assume they made a terrible mistake, and treat their subsequent work as objectively as possible. But that generous assumption doesn't change what your response should be to the cheating—drunk driving, after all, might be a terrible mistake, but it still deserves a legal response. If the college's procedures for responding to cheating involve referring the student to a central office, or documenting it somehow, take those steps. Only if you do this can the students who don't deserve your generous assumption—that is, the students who really are attempting to cheat their way through college—be discovered and punished appropriately. Following the established procedures also protects you against charges of dealing with students unevenly, favoring some students over others, or skirting college policies.

When I started writing this chapter, I envisioned it as a quick primer on cheating and the response to it—one of the shorter chapters in the book. But it has expanded to nearly the length of the other chapters, and this reflects the fact that while you may only have to deal with a few instances of cheating or plagiarism in your first year, you will find these incidents the most awful and vexing moments of your academic career. Here more than anywhere else, I would emphasize the importance of consulting your peers and your department chair for information on the campus culture and practices, and following the official policies that your institution has in place. Discovering academic dishonesty will be awful, but inevitable, so do some thinking about it in advance, and rely on the wisdom of those who have gone before you.

To circle back for a moment to the first chapter of the book, remember that you can and should use the syllabus, and the opening days of the semester, to set and explain your course policies on academic dishonesty. If you have included a statement of these policies on the syllabus, and you should, then you have an easy opening to talk about it with students—to explain what constitutes academic dishonesty in the kind of work they will do for you in the coming weeks, and to describe the penalties in scary and excruciating detail.

In the best-case scenario, no one will cheat in your first semester, and you will have wasted a paragraph's worth of space on your syllabus, and five or ten minutes of classroom time.

But don't count on the best-case scenario.

Resources

The Center for Academic Integrity. "CAI Research." June 2005. *http://www.academicintegrity.org/cai_research.asp*, January 24, 2007.

The statistics from Don McCabe's most recent surveys on undergraduate cheating are contained in this summary page.

Eble, Kenneth. *The Craft of Teaching*, 2nd ed. San Francisco: Jossey-Bass, 1988.

See the chapter entitled "Cheating, Confrontations, and Other Situations," pp. 164–180.

Gross Davis, Barbara. *Tools for Teaching.* San Francisco: Jossey-Bass, 1995.

Lang, James. "Dealing with Plagiarists." *The Chronicle of Higher Education,* May 14, 2002. *http://chronicle.com/jobs/news/2002/05/2002051401c/careers.html*, January 24, 2007.

This column appeared only in the online edition of the magazine, and remains available online. It details my experiences in dealing with plagiarists in my first few years, and the thinking that brought me to the response policy I recommend above.

Lowman, Joseph. *Mastering the Techniques of Teaching.* San Francisco: Jossey-Bass, 1984.
Lowman covers cheating in the chapter on tests and grading, pp. 207–208.

MacWilliams, Bryon. "The Art of Cheating." *The Chronicle of Higher Education,* 52.4 (September 16, 2005): A46.
The article on the Russian museum exhibition on the technology of cheating, complete with cheat-sheet panties.

Mangan, Katherine. "Survey Finds Widespread Cheating in MBA Programs." *The Chronicle of Higher Education,* 53.6 (September 29, 2006): A44.
Some statistics on cheating in MBA programs.

McKeachie, Wilbert, and Marilla Svinicki. *McKeachie's Teaching Tips: Strategies, Research, and Theory for College and University Teachers,* 12th ed. Boston: Houghton Mifflin, 2006.
Academic dishonesty is covered in "What to Do About Cheating?" (pp. 113–122).

McKinney, Mary. "What's Your Name Again?" *Inside Higher Ed,* February 13, 2006. *http://www.insidehighered.com/workplace/2006/02/13/mckinney,* January 24, 2007.
A great collection of ideas for learning students' names, and reducing some of that sense of anonymity in the classroom.

Thompson, Michael. "Hidden in Plain Sight." *The Chronicle of Higher Education,* 52.15 (December 2, 2005): B5.
The confessional article from a doctoral student on his plagiarism.

Finding a Balance Outside
the Classroom

If you're teaching for the first time in the fall semester, as most new teachers will be doing, and you are in week 10, you're just a few weeks away from Thanksgiving break. You are probably looking forward to that break tremendously, not only for the few days of blessed relief you will get from your classroom responsibilities, but also for the opportunity it will give you to take care of some of the life tasks you've been neglecting over the past two months. While your friends in the corporate world anticipate a Thanksgiving break of eating, drinking, and watching football or traveling or shopping, you are planning to grade a stack of papers, clean the house, and maybe get the oil changed or schedule a dentist appointment. Lucky you!

You'll be doing all of this because you will find your first semester of teaching an all-consuming one, especially if you are on the tenure track and are doing this full time. But even if you are only teaching one or two courses, easing into teaching as a graduate student or an adjunct, you will still find that concerns and ideas about teaching bully their way into your brain and muscle everything else out during that first semester. Teaching is public speaking, after all, and public speaking—no matter how many times you do it—requires preparation and energy, and for most of us it produces anxiety. The fact that you are speaking in public multiple times each week has an amazing ability to keep your attention focused on your teaching responsibilities, and can push into the background the tasks that don't generate such anxiety—reading an article for your dissertation, or getting the oil changed, or going out to dinner with your significant other—or that don't have such constant deadlines (e.g., prep for Monday's class, grade those quizzes for Tuesday, write an assignment sheet for Wednesday, and so on). Robert Boice, who has spent the last couple of decades conducting a long-term study of how new faculty members acclimate to their roles and responsibilities, echoes all of this in one clear conclusion that he has drawn from his research: "In my 20 years of observations, far and away the most suffering for new faculty occurred in relation to classroom teaching" (12).

Even a stunningly brilliant guidebook like this one won't keep you from suffering a little in your first semester of college teaching, or from resenting the way it has taken over your life. You can take some comfort from the fact that with each semester of teaching, the other parts of your life slowly work their way back into your brain, and you can mostly return to the sort of life that you led before you started teaching. During my first year on the tenure track, I was speaking with a colleague a few years my senior about the fact that course preparation seemed to drain away every spare minute I had.

"One hour," he said to me. "I allot one hour to prepare for each class I teach, and when the hour's up, I'm done prepping for that class."

I was flabbergasted at this, and embarrassed by the number of hours I seemed to spend preparing for each of my classes—was I a complete idiot? I'm open to that possibility, but the explanation was mainly that I was in my first year and he was in his third, and you won't believe how much of a difference those two extra years of teaching experience can make.

So how do you overcome this problem in your first semester, and keep intact those parts of your life that don't relate to teaching? If you can figure out a good answer to this question, it's your turn to write a book about teaching. The best advice I can give you is to prepare in advance, taking care of as many life tasks as you can before the semester starts, and abandoning any ambitious plans you have for research or writing during your first semester of teaching. You should not abandon those plans altogether, especially if you are on a tenure track at a research institution, but set modest goals for yourself, and be prepared to fulfill fewer of them than you would like (more on this later).

I don't want to leave you completely twisting in the wind on this topic, so I will give you the few tips I have gathered on managing the different components of your academic life, the full spectrum of it, in your first year. Of course, graduate students will face a completely different set of challenges outside the classroom than full-time faculty will—and neither of these groups will confront some of the special obstacles faced by adjuncts or post-docs. I will focus here on the few areas that have some relevance to all these groups of new teachers.

Teaching: Moderating Prep Time

The major problem with teaching, in terms of managing your life, will be preparation time. Of course it also takes time to grade, and to hold classes, but those time periods have clearer boundaries than the time you will have to set aside for preparing for class. Especially when you are anxious about what will happen in your classroom, the time you spend preparing can expand to fill any space you allow for it. Boice describes one faculty member, a participant in Boice's studies to determine what traits and behaviors enable new faculty to succeed in their first year (and what traits lead them to failure), who was spending thirty hours a week preparing for two undergraduate survey courses; this faculty member was convinced that if he had even more time to prepare, he could do a still better job of teaching (57). John P. Murray, another researcher who has studied how new faculty adjust to their roles, quotes a new faculty member from his study who reported devoting fifty hours a week to preparation time (8)..Obviously, devoting this many hours a week to your preparation time is a guarantee that you will have less time than you need for your other academic responsibilities—including both service and writing—not to mention everything else you need to do to survive and live a normal life.

Rather than recommending the advice of my slightly senior colleague who mandated a maximum of one hour's preparation time, usually just before class, I'm going to follow Boice's recommendations for moderating class preparation time, an approach he calls "nihil nimus," a Latin maxim meaning "nothing to excess" (the complement of my father's old dictum, "everything in moderation"). Boice argues that many new faculty members make the mistake of seeking large chunks of uninterrupted time in their schedule to prepare for their classes, and then find themselves frustrated for one of two reasons: they can't find such large chunks of time, especially in their first year on the tenure track, or they sit down at the outset of one of those chunks and find themselves unable to accomplish much, and end up wasting the precious time that they do have. He reports that successful new faculty members, by contrast, have different habits for class preparation: they practice what he calls *active waiting,* which has three components. First, they make preliminary notes on a class's preparation well in advance of the actual class, if only in

brief, separate intervals of time. Second, they begin the preparation process before they might feel ready to—before they have
read that one last article, in other words, or formulated a full idea
in their mind. Finally, they prepare for the class in short, regular
sessions over a longer period of time, rather than waiting and
doing all preparations in one chunk right before class. All this
might suggest that your mind may be occupied with the preparations for a single class period for a longer stretch of days than it
would be if you prepared in a single session, and that would be
true. But Boice's recommendations suggest that preparations can
be brewing in the back of your mind while you are accomplishing other tasks, and that you can put together a successful lesson
plan in a handful of brief sessions, over the course of a few days,
that might amount to only an hour or two of concentrated working time.

Boice reports many other working habits of successful new
faculty in his book, and makes recommendations along these
lines in the areas of research and service as well (he spends a lot
of time encouraging his readers to slow down and wait—I've
never had anyone tell me to stop and breathe quite so much as he
does). I didn't know about his study or recommendations during
my first year on the tenure track, and I prepared for class more
as his unsuccessful faculty members did than his quick starters.
But over the few years following my initial year, I began practicing his habits as a sheer survival strategy, since I was teaching
three or four classes a semester as well as spending parts of the
week at home with my pre-school-aged children. I simply never
had large, uninterrupted blocks of time, so the only way I could
prepare for courses—or write, or fulfill service obligations that
required homework away from meetings—was by stuffing my
preparation time into the small chunks of time that opened and
closed quickly all throughout my day. I can thus add my own

personal experience to the results of Boice's study, and can say that I have become significantly more efficient and productive in my teaching preparation using his methods than I was when I was constantly searching for what I thought were ideal working conditions—big, quiet, uninterrupted blocks of time.

What is the difference between these two approaches to course preparation in practical terms? Let's say you are teaching a lecture course on Monday at 11:00 A.M., a survey in your field that requires you to present information or ideas or theories for at least part of the time—but, of course, following the recommendations of this book, you also try to include an interactive component in each class period. The students will have reading to do for Monday's class, reading that you have done before but probably need to review before class. You finish your work week on Friday in the early afternoon, but you haven't done the reading yet. You have the weekend ahead of you, so you'll do your course prep then. Friday night your brain is too fried to work; Saturday the kitchen sink gets clogged and you spend the day trying to clean it out; and on Sunday a friend invites you to a museum in nearby Big City, and you can't turn down an opportunity like that. All through your time "relaxing," though, you have a low-grade anxiety about Monday's lecture in your mind. Sunday night you do the reading for the course, and Monday morning you arrive in your office at 8:00 A.M., ready to prep. But of course you have thirty e-mails to go through, and two students actually visit you in your office hours, so the closer you get to class time, the pressure you feel to get your ideas down makes it increasingly difficult to concentrate. You end up writing a mediocre lecture and just leaving time for questions at the end. That's the pattern of Boice's unsuccessful new faculty member.

A more Boice-like strategy might look like this. For fifteen minutes before you leave on Friday, you look back at your syllabus and remind yourself what you are addressing on Monday, and how it fits into the course. You open a file for Monday's lecture on your computer and write down the three main issues you need to address, just a sentence or two on each issue. On Saturday, in between attempts to snake out the drain pipe in the kitchen sink, you hop onto the computer every once in a while and add two more issues you remember you need to cover. You get an idea for an interesting exercise at the end and note that down as well. At the museum you see an exhibit that illustrates perfectly one of your five main points; when you get home you find the online version and throw the link into your file for use in the lecture. Now that you have a rough structure in place for your lecture, the reading you do on Sunday night is far more productive—you highlight in the text, as you go, where the important quotes and facts will fit into your lecture. Monday morning, when you arrive, entails simply running the train down the tracks you have already laid, putting all the pieces in place and getting it into final form—work you can do between answering e-mails and talking with students.

Two points in particular about these contrasting preparation styles stand out for me. First, the slow and gradual preparation process allows more time for real-life examples or interesting illustrations to find their way into your teaching. If you sit down for an hour before class and rack your brain in search of real-life examples for five concepts, you're going to have trouble. But if you have those five concepts in mind three days in advance, just living your life for the next three days will bring you at least a few of them—and they will be better, and more thoroughly thought out, than the ones you come up with in a one-hour cram session. Second, while it may seem like the Boice preparation style has the negative effect of having your courses in the back of your mind all the time, it's better than the alternative—that is, doing nothing about your course and having anxiety in the back of your mind all weekend about Monday's lecture. Especially in your first year, you will feel anxiety about the vast majority of your classes—so it's better to replace that anxiety with thoughts about preparation, and get your work done at the same time. I still allow myself at least an hour before every scheduled class to finish my preparations, but these days I've become so efficient at back-of-the-mind preparation that frequently I can tidy up the lesson plan in ten or fifteen minutes, and then have the remaining time to address the administrative tasks I'm usually trying to avoid, or to walk down the hallway and chat with a colleague about the Red Sox.

This style of working, of course, may not match well with your personality—I know plenty of people, mostly students but including some colleagues, who claim to work better under pressure with deadlines looming. My personal take on that line is that pressure and deadlines certainly can help people produce a great first draft of a paper or a lecture—but that having a few more days to reflect on it always leads to a better paper or lecture. Whether you follow Boice's recommended preparation style or not, the larger point here is that you have to find ways to limit your preparation time. A rough guideline for the maximum preparation time you should allow yourself, as I've mentioned earlier, is two hours for every hour you spend in the classroom. It's a little harder to set such clear boundaries for preparation time if you are using the slow and gradual preparation approach, since preparation time will be scattered through your days, but the productive nature of that approach should keep you easily within that limit.

Researching and Writing: Finding Gaps

Unsurprisingly, Boice recommends the exact same strategy for researching and writing as he does for teaching preparation—

and here too I think he's right on the mark. However, I'm going to step away from his text and rely instead on an essay that Jay Parini published in *The Chronicle of Higher Education* in April of 2005, entitled "The Considerable Satisfaction of Two Pages a Day." Parini has been teaching at the college level for the past three decades, and has also been an incredibly productive writer. His name graces the bindings of dozens of books, including volumes of poetry, novels, biographies, and many anthologies which he has edited or had a hand in editing. He writes regularly about education and the writing life for the *Chronicle,* and has even written a book about teaching. With such immense writerly productivity in so many different areas, it's difficult to imagine that Parini could not make a good living from his writing alone, but he has written in more than one place about his need for an academic schedule to keep him motivated and working.

So how does he get it all done? The title of his essay gives it away: Parini makes a commitment to writing two pages of text a day, in whatever genre he happens to be working on. Writing two pages a day, as he points out, produces a very long book every year. He doesn't hold himself with complete rigidity to this schedule: "I'm not neurotic about it—sometimes I don't feel like writing at all. But I aim for two [pages], and I usually get two" (B5). He does his writing at a local diner in the mornings, he explains—a luxury of time that you may not be able to afford in your first year, especially when you have papers or exams that need returning, or a class that needs some final prepping, a few mornings per week. Parini cites as his exemplar a scholar and professor who mentored him in his academic life, and who likewise was immensely productive while carrying a huge load of university responsibilities. Parini asked him once for the secret of his productivity, and the man replied (as if quoting from Boice): "I've learned how to use the odd gaps of 20 minutes or so that occur at various points in the day" (B5). Outside of his morning routine, Parini goes on to explain, he has learned to use these spaces as well.

When I tell people that most of my writing has been produced in the same way, I sometimes get a dismissive reaction from faculty whose work requires more hard research and data collecting and analysis than mine. My first two books—both written in my first four years on the tenure track—were memoirs, after all, creative efforts that didn't require much conventional research. For scholarship, some people will tell me, they need those large blocks of time to review their notes, plan things out, and gear up and get ready to write—or, for scientists and social scientists, time in the lab or in the field. There may be some truth to this, although I think it's worth noting that I wrote a scholarly dissertation on the Parini plan, and that Parini himself has produced several biographies in this way, work which obviously does require conventional research. Still, I would offer two responses to this objection.

First, in your first year of full-time teaching (or even if you are just teaching a couple of classes as an adjunct or graduate student), *you will not have large blocks of uninterrupted time during the semester.* You just won't. You may get large blocks of uninterrupted time over your breaks, but you will probably find that you want to do other things with those particular blocks of time—like sleep, or read trashy novels, or catch up on all the episodes of *Lost* that you've missed, or reacquaint yourself with your spouse and your children. Every new faculty member I have known, since I have been on the tenure track, has told me about their ambitious plans to get research and writing done during their breaks; and without fail, their responses to my post-break question about how their research went come out as sheepish excuses for why they didn't get nearly as much done as they had hoped.

The faculty in Murray's study express these hopes: "I hope to write 2 articles during the summer," one says; "100% of my time is teaching," another laments, "in the summer I hope to do research" (13). As Murray goes on to point out, though, new faculty who learn to put teaching and scholarship together from the very start are more likely to succeed in their profession than those who pin their hopes on future breaks.

I think you'll find that the multi-stage process of producing a work of scholarship—digging for material or working in the lab, reviewing literature, taking notes and making outlines, drafting and revising—lends itself to small chunks of time as much as creative writing does. Your 15-minute chunk of time after lunch on a Tuesday might consist only of reading an article you know will be important, or of copying down the quotes that you know will work for a chapter into a new document. Even if you insist that the drafting of a scholarly work requires large chunks of time, and that you want to wait for break, you can still make an effort to do as much of the preparatory work as possible during the pockets of time that you might find throughout the week for writing. Every new teacher in higher education will be laboring under the obligation to write something—essays for courses, a dissertation, articles or books to improve your job or tenure prospects—and this approach to research and writing, articulated most eloquently by Parini (and presented with more research support in Boice and Murray), can help if you can train yourself to work this way. Set the bar pretty low for your first semester of teaching, but then keep raising it a little in subsequent semesters until you find the right balance.

Serving: Focusing Your Obligations

Service obligations, more than anything else, depend upon your situation (tenure track, adjunct, graduate student); still, everyone

will have some kind of service obligation, or at least could benefit from engaging in some service activity. Service requirements
almost always come as a surprise to new faculty, and hence may
stir up resentment at this unexpected drain on your time. When I
was writing my memoir about my first year on the tenure track,
and went back and reviewed my calendar to discover how much
time I spent in meetings and lectures in my first semester, I
counted more than two dozen events which I was obliged or
strongly encouraged to attend, the lengths of which ranged from
an hour to half-day affairs. This doesn't even count the amount
of time I might have had to spend preparing for meetings, following up on tasks that grew out of those meetings, or attending to
other service elements like writing letters of recommendation or
advising students on course selection. The service requirements
for tenure-track faculty will always be heavier than for graduate
students and adjuncts, and—especially at colleges which do not
have strong expectations for research in the tenure process—will
count toward one's tenure case. Service for graduate students
and adjuncts takes place on a more voluntary basis, although
here as well new teachers are sometimes "volunteered" by department chairs or senior faculty.

The advice I have here applies to all new teachers, no matter
what their position. For some schools to which they might apply
for faculty positions, graduate students will benefit from having
performed some service activity. The graduate student conference you helped to organize won't necessarily count for much if
you are applying to an Ivy League institution, but it will count in
your favor if you are applying for a job at a community college or
a small liberal arts college that emphasizes teaching and service for new faculty. Hiring committees in those institutions will
want to know that you have an understanding of, and interest in,
the college or university that exists outside of your classroom
and library carrel. The most difficult challenge that most ad-

juncts face is the fact that they are not always made to feel welcome as full faculty members. Volunteering for a service activity
or two can go a long way toward helping adjuncts be included in
a department, and toward getting to know the other faculty—
thus helping to break some of the sense of isolation that many
adjuncts feel even within the departments in which they are
teaching.

For all these types of new teachers, then, I recommend a simple strategy for your first year of teaching: find one service opportunity and make it your own—stamp your name on it, do it
well, and then use it to ward off other requests that you get for
service work. That one opportunity might be undertaking a difficult committee assignment, or serving as adviser for a student
publication or event (such as a colloquium), or even jumping in
and proposing an event or initiative that you bring to your new
position. If you have kept your eyes open in graduate school, you
will be familiar with the range of possible academic activities
and events that go on outside the classroom; think about what
kinds of events or programs don't yet exist on your new campus,
and propose developing one of them to your departmental chair
or dean. You will rarely have a request to give yourself more
work turned down, and you can take such an initiative and use it
to make connections and establish your presence on campus. A
graduate student or an adjunct in particular can make an impact
by proposing and developing a new event or series or idea, or
even by helping out with a long-standing committee or program,
and the full-time faculty will usually be grateful for your work.

If you are new on the tenure track, you probably won't be able
to avoid other requests to serve on committees, even if you have
proposed a new idea—committees are formed at every level of
the university, from the department to the entire faculty, so there
are enough of them that everyone gets tapped on a regular basis.

Nose around a little and find out how often different committees meet, what kinds of work they do, and what time commitments they require. Senior faculty will have served on many committees, and—assuming you have found a senior faculty member you can trust—they can give you a realistic assessment of the work that different committees require. Once you've scouted around a bit, agree to be placed on a committee that isn't too burdensome. If you are serving on one committee, and simultaneously working on something new for the department or the institution, you should use those two commitments to beg off any other requests you receive for more service work. No experienced faculty members in their right mind would fault a new faculty member, who was committed to two clearly defined service obligations, for asking politely if she could avoid making any other commitments for the time being. Be diplomatic about it, but meet new requests with an explanation of the commitments you have already made, and ask if it would be possible for you to help out next year instead (between your first and second year, practice your skills at weaseling out of things).

Surviving Academic Politics

Finally, you will need to practice your survival skills in your first year of teaching, which means figuring out how to negotiate your way through encounters with the department chair, possibly a dean, your colleagues, a review of your teaching, and various other challenging situations and people. You will have to do all of this in an environment which does not regularly present opportunities for either formal or informal discussions of how things are going for you. As much as I would have loathed the idea of some kind of new faculty support or therapy group in my first year, in retrospect I can see that it might not have been such a bad thing. Academic work is a business we mostly practice alone, despite meetings and classes—you will often feel plenty alone even while you are teaching—and therefore the opportunities to compare your experiences with those of others, and to pick up information that will help you survive the psychological challenges of your first year, can be difficult to come by.

I'm not a therapist, and I don't normally recommend things like breathing exercises to people, so I'll limit myself here to two suggestions.

First, you should focus your energies in this realm, in your first semester, on gathering information. Christopher Lucas and John Murry's useful book, *New Faculty: A Practical Guide for Academic Beginners,* offers these four questions as ones to which you should seek answers during your first year of teaching, especially if you are on the tenure track:

1. Formal organizational charts aside, where does real power and authority reside within the department or division as well as within the college or university? Who are the power brokers and how do they influence decision-making?
2. What expectations of you are held by your newly acquired colleagues? What are the actual norms (both formal and informal) with which you will be expected to comply?
3. Which academic policies and procedures are held to be most important or authoritative?
4. What does the immediate academic unit most value with regard to teaching, scholarship, and service? (11)

These are sensible questions, and if you can figure out answers to them, you will be much better prepared to bow down to those who merit bowing, and to ignore or befriend those who don't.

The way to find answers to these questions is to spend your first year with your head down and your mouth shut. Attend the meetings, ask questions if you must, but mostly you should just listen and absorb. Do not take sides in disputes, or do anything other than offer a sympathetic ear to anyone who complains to you about anything, or tries to influence your opinion of other people. There are many sides to every story, so don't commit yourself to one side of any story in your first year. Listen as much as possible, and hold off on decisions about whom to trust and whom to mistrust until at least your second or third year in a department. Smile at everyone, make small talk, and be noncommittal about any substantive departmental or personnel issues. Whatever the issue may be, you're "still thinking about it."

Second, form some kind of social network with other new faculty, even if that only means meeting a colleague for coffee once a week to commiserate. You will probably have an orientation session with your fellow new hires if you are on the tenure track, so that's an opportunity to introduce yourself to others, and to lay the groundwork for friendly e-mail exchanges or an invitation to meet for lunch. Graduate students frequently will be sharing offices, and often will take classes together, so the opportunities for discussion are built into your environment. Adjuncts will have the hardest time meeting others. The two most social places in an academic department are the copy machine and the coffeepot, so learn to love coffee and maybe get in the habit of sending chain letters to all of your friends, so you have plenty of excuses to go to the copy machine. Some departments and campuses will have an adjunct group or network already in place to address concerns and provide social opportunities; if so, use that network to find opportunities to meet with others.

In those meetings, whether they take place over coffee or red wine, with fellow graduate students or a new tenure-tracker in your department, you will carry on a long-standing tradition, taking part in an activity that has sustained the souls of teachers since the beginning of time: complaining about your students. That dialogue will see you through the first half-hour of conversation, and then the talk should turn to what you have been doing in the classroom that works, and doesn't work, and what you're thinking about trying, and why it will work or won't work, and so on. I have found that fifteen minutes of talking about teaching with a colleague usually proves far more productive for course preparation than an hour of staring at my computer screen, so seek out opportunities to talk with others who are in the same boat as you; the time spent thinking out loud about your first experiences as a teacher should pay you back in the end. You'll find, too, that each of you has heard slightly different things about your colleagues and about the department, and comparing notes on all of that will help you start to form a fuller picture of your work environment than you could piece together on your own.

I realize you may be objecting at this point that you're not really a social kind of person, that you don't make new friends easily, that you prefer working with your mice or sitting quietly and reading poems to talking with people you don't know. To which I can truthfully reply that I am right there with you. But in most academic environments, judgments about your career are made by your colleagues—as in departmental votes on your tenure case, for example—so you have to learn, at the very least, to seem like a normal and friendly human being, and to interact cordially with people who will be making decisions about your life, from your new colleagues to the senior faculty in your department and around the institution. So quit your whining, paste on a smile, and go make some small talk at the copy machine.

Resources

Boice, Robert. *Advice for New Faculty Members: Nihil Nimus.* Boston: Allyn and Bacon, 2000.
As this chapter indicates, I really like Boice's ideas, and they are supported by plenty of footwork he has done interviewing new faculty over a long career. That said, the book can be a little repetitive—you get the basic idea in the first chapter or two, and then he applies it to every aspect of academic life. So read the first couple of chapters, and then work out the rest for yourself.

Lang, James. *Life on the Tenure Track: Lessons from the First Year.* Baltimore: Johns Hopkins University Press, 2004.
Much of the advice in this chapter grew out of the experiences of my own first year, which are chronicled in this book.

Lucas, Christopher J., and John Murry. *New Faculty: A Practical Guide for Academic Beginners.* New York: Palgrave Macmillan, 2002.
This guidebook gives generally sound advice for new faculty.

Murray, John P. "New Faculty's Perceptions of the Academic Work Life." Annual Meeting of the Association for the Study of Higher Education, Sacramento, Calif., November 16, 2000. *ERIC.* EBSCO. Assumption College Library, Worcester, Mass. December 14, 2006.
Results of surveys that Murray conducted of new faculty and their experiences on the tenure track.

Parini, Jay. "The Considerable Satisfaction of Two Pages a Day." *The Chronicle of Higher Education,* 51.31 (April 8, 2005): B5.
Parini's thoughts on this topic are also contained in his book, *The Art of Teaching.*

Re-Energizing the Classroom

You are skidding along the downward slope at this point, as you head into the last third of the semester, and that's the really excellent news. By now you might be starting to envision how the semester will wind up, and how you will organize those final five weeks in order to accomplish all the goals you have set for the semester. You may be heading to your disciplinary conference over the winter break, and you have been making those plans, and thinking about taking long naps and reading for pleasure during the break (both are activities I would recommend highly). It's all good.

All except for one thing. By this point in the semester, most of us begin to feel as if we are going through the motions in the classroom, trotting out the same old teaching techniques every day. Our students are overwhelmed with the approaching end of the semester—when they will have a major assignment or exam in every one of their five courses—and may appear listless and exhausted in class, their eyes glazing over a few minutes after you open your mouth. I always get the feeling, about this time in the semester, that whenever I announce the plan for the day, the students are regarding me with cool skepticism, and thinking to themselves: "Is this all you got, dude?" And my response would usually have to be: "Yeah, it's all I got."

If you have been following the recommendations of this book, you have been varying your teaching techniques all through the semester, and so the students have seen you lecture, and hold discussions, and work with groups, and maybe use some other interesting classroom format that you dreamed up before the semester started and tried out a few times. But by this point in the semester, you have trotted out everything you can think of pedagogically, and you don't have enough gas in the tank to keep on top of your other obligations and spend hours dreaming up brilliant and inspirational new teaching strategies. Frankly, you're not even sure the stuff you have been doing thus far has been working. Duffy and Jones describe this point in the semester, which they call the doldrums, like this: "As the initial high energies [of the semester] are taxed, a vague feeling of discontent surfaces in the classroom environment. Professors can begin to doubt the effectiveness of their teaching, and students can become overwhelmed, questioning the applicability of the course" (36). Everyone goes through this dull period in the semester; the chatter at the copy machine will be as listless as the students' responses in your classroom, or will consist primarily of complaints about students, the teaching load, the department chair, or life in general.

I'm not sure it's possible to prevent these doldrums from making their appearance during a semester—a college course is like a marathon, and every marathon runner will hit periods of exhaustion during the race. But you can prepare yourself in advance for their arrival, both psychologically and pedagogically; the latter will be the focus of this chapter. Psychologically, the only preparation I can offer is the knowledge that this period will come, that it's normal, and that it comes to an end eventually. As the close of the semester looms, you'll find that your energies revive, not unlike the way students' attention revives as you approach the end of a lecture. But don't let the fallow periods make you doubt your calling as a teacher, or the efficacy of what you have been doing; if you have those feelings, keep them at bay with the promise that you'll revisit them at the end of the semester, when you can catch your breath—and then you'll probably find that they have dissipated.

Pedagogically, the best method for busting out of the doldrums is to experiment a little in the classroom. Try something completely different, something that you're not sure will work, but that will surprise the students, and get them to think about the course and its subject matter in a new way. Experimentation doesn't have to entail a ton of advance planning; it might be one-off or maybe two-off classroom sessions, as opposed to thinking about how to restructure the course entirely. I have two or three experiments that I like to use every semester, ones to which students always seem to respond well, and which I am usually excited to introduce into the classroom each year. But I hold them off for as long as possible, knowing that I'll need them at about this time in the semester to revitalize flagging classroom energy.

Of course, dreaming up experimental teaching techniques is much easier said than done. The whole point about this period of the semester is that you're drained, so you won't be inclined to innovative thinking. You have to lay the groundwork for the implementation of experimental teaching strategies before and all through the semester, by keeping yourself informed and fresh as both a teacher and a learner. I've thus divided this chapter into two parts: the first section consists of five simple experimental strategies that faculty in most disciplines could try out at this point in the semester; the second describes a few activities to help you remain fresh as a teacher, and to stay informed and prepared to develop new teaching strategies when you need them most.

You may look at some of the experimental teaching strategies described below and see them as less serious or content-focused than you would like, and that might be true. But we have seen already that while a discussion or small-group activity might introduce students to less new content than a lecture, it can still provide an essential opportunity for students to think and write and talk their way through their ideas about that content. Similarly, although these experiments might not offer course content or develop thinking skills in conventional ways, they can perform the invaluable function of revitalizing students' interest and attention in whatever content or thinking skills you have left to teach in the remainder of the semester. One or two such experimental classes, followed by three or four traditional classes taught to revitalized students, may accomplish far more than six classes of mechanical and listless teaching—and little learning—during the low period of the semester.

Five Experiments

POSTERS

I'll start with the experiment that I reserve for my mid-semester doldrums: asking students to work in small groups to map out a text or set of ideas on a posterboard. The precise nature of the strategy depends upon the course I am teaching, but in a literature course I usually will try it when we are reading a novel, hopefully one that is long and complicated and could stand some clarifying. I might ask students to create a visual representation of the major plot points of the novel; or, in a novel whose plot doesn't need this kind of scrutiny, I might ask them to create a graph or list or chart that compares and contrasts the novel's major characters; at other times I have asked them to draw connections between images and image-systems in a novel or poem, or to do the same thing with a work's major and minor themes. I have kept all the posters that my students have constructed over the years, and the range of visual representations they have developed is astonishing. Many of them add an extra dash of creativity to their posters, adorning them with graphics and cartoons and crude drawings of scenes and characters. As much as anything, those drawings convince me of the value of the technique as a doldrums-buster; the students were enjoying themselves while they worked on the challenge I had presented to them. They were also thinking, however; the innovative approaches to novels which I have seen students develop in subsequent paper assignments, and which they have told me stemmed from the poster session, have fully convinced me of that.

Practically, the only real advance planning you need here is to get to the bookstore before class and pick up enough posterboards and markers for the class (I usually have them work in groups of three or four), or ask your department secretary if such supplies are available in the office somewhere. You'll need to think about what you want the students to represent on the posters, of course, which really could be anything. The idea is not so much that they have to draw things as that they have to construct a visual representation of relationships among things— people, books, ideas, places, time periods, arguments, theories, problems, strategies for completing an assignment or paper, and so on. Even a posterboard with a line drawn down the center, dividing the space into two columns for a comparison list, will do the trick. The posters force the students to see the material in a new way, and often can prove revealing to the instructor, as they have for me. Most of the students will find the instructions for this project disconcerting at first, since the assignment will be an unfamiliar one. It helps, therefore, to think about one or two ways in which they might organize their posterboard, and to put an example up on the board while you are giving the instructions. But don't limit them, or give them too much help; they are usually slow to start, but eventually—the light bulb moment—they catch on and throw themselves into the project. When that happens, the energy level in the classroom is as high as it is all semester.

My formal lesson plan always allows time for the students to show off their posterboards and explain them at the end of the hour, but it turns out that we almost never have time for this show and tell. This used to bother me, but I've realized now that what matters in this exercise is the process, not the product. Sometimes I will let them work to the end and then ask them to bring the posterboards in to the next class session and set them around the room for everyone to view for a few minutes before class starts. The more I do this exercise, the more I downplay the final result. The strongest insights or ideas that they gain will come from the creation of their diagram; anything they get from viewing the work of others is a nice bonus.

FIELD TRIPS

The best part about teaching students over eighteen is that you won't need thirty bag lunches, juice boxes, and permission slips from Mom and Dad for this one. Getting everyone out of the classroom and to some site or event that relates to the course material usually takes two class periods—one for the trip (or as missed-class compensation for a trip that takes place outside of the regular classroom hours), and one for a discussion of the trip afterwards. But such trips are usually worth the effort, as they can help students see how the content and thinking skills you are teaching in the course operate in the world outside the classroom. Visible reminders of the relevance of the course to that world are a sure means to (re)capture student interest.

Of course, field trips at this educational level usually go beyond the scope of trips to the local museum—unless you are an art teacher or a historian, in which case expeditions to see the local art or history museum, and to talk (for instance) about how historical societies and museums help determine what counts as the past, might do nicely. But you have to plan creatively here— which you can do by thinking about how and where your disciplinary theories and subject matter operate in the world. A political scientist might attend a city council meeting with her students; a Spanish teacher might visit the local Hispanic Heritage center; a chemist could arrange for a tour of a local manufacturing plant. You might not see such opportunities until you have spent a year or two in the community, and learned about the existence of such visitable places, so keep an eye out in your first semester or two, or ask around your department. Of course, you may not even need to leave campus for field trips. An environmental biologist at my college takes students into the wooded places on campus; I have taken students in my creative nonfiction writing class outside to write about various locales on campus; a theologian might lead a visit to the campus chapel or religious center; a civil engineer could lead a walking campus tour with a focus on the layout of the roads and walkways. In addition, you will find your college's general program schedule jampacked with lectures, readings, performances, and exhibitions by visiting and local and even student talent; find a way to incorporate one of these into your course schedule, and build content around it.

In terms of logistics, you do have to be careful about transporting students off campus. The institution may have vans you can borrow for such events, but I have always found it safer and easier to require students to find their own transportation, with some encouragement from me to carpool whenever possible. Still, check with your department chair, or your campus counsel (every college or university has an in-house lawyer), to see whether you should have the students sign a release form for an off-campus event. You will also inevitably find that one or two students cannot attend anything you schedule outside of the normal classroom hour. In this case, try to offer an alternative for them—visiting a site on their own, or attending a comparable lecture or event—in order to ensure that the entire class has this shared experience of getting out of the classroom to see your discipline in action.

INKSHEDDING

The third technique, inkshedding, is one that a *Chronicle of Higher Education* reader e-mailed me about in the fall of 2006, and I wrote about it in the October column of that year, which addressed the subject matter of this chapter—shaking things up during the mid-semester doldrums. This technique provides a method for generating ideas in a discussion class where the discussions may have begun to flag, or where one or two students have been dominating the discussion, letting everyone else sit back and relax. Inkshedding was first developed by writing teachers Russ Hunt and Jim Reither in the 1980s. You can find all kinds of information about it at Hunt's website, listed in the Resources below. Of course, as with any popular teaching technique, many different practices now fall under the name of inkshedding, as instructors have personalized it and made it their own.

The version suggested to me by my reader, Dan Cleary, who teaches English at Lorain County Community College, works like this. Dan begins that day's class by asking students to spend 5 minutes writing down their thoughts on the main discussion question or issue for the day. That writing should be what composition teachers call "freewriting"—that is, the student writes whatever comes to mind, without anyone making judgments about it or corrections to it. Freewriting's function is to help generate thoughts and ideas, so it's an excellent starting place for discussions of any kind. When the students have finished their 5 minutes of freewriting, they pass their notebooks to another student. Everyone reads the new notebook in front of them and then spends 5 minutes freewriting in response to the first student's thoughts. That process continues through several iterations, until—after 20 or 25 minutes—the students have engaged in an extended dialogue with one another, all on paper, and are ready to start talking about their ideas out loud.

As Dan points out, that technique "encourages everyone, even the shy students, to participate in the class 'discussion.'" Moreover, the written process helps to spark the verbal discussion: "I've never had a dead-end discussion after an exercise like this," Dan told me. "In fact, students often laugh or jeer or cringe or applaud while reading and listening to the texts produced from inkshedding. That'll keep them interested and engaged!" I like best about this technique the fact that everyone takes part in the exercise, even if they do so only on paper. However, you can ensure everyone's participation in the oral conversation simply by asking the shyer students to read aloud one of the statements in a notebook, not even necessarily one of their own. This technique could work equally well in small or large classes; how you process it afterwards might vary according to course size, but the writing and exchanging of notebooks will work in any course.

TRIALS

In the classroom, as in real life, you can always get people's attention by putting somebody famous on trial. Conducting mock trials in the classroom is the fourth experiment I have both read about and tried, one that can be adopted—with some creative thinking—in just about any discipline. When I conducted a trial in my classroom, I put the main character of Albert Camus's *The Stranger* on trial, and simply divided up the classroom into prosecutors and defendants; I played the judge. The students were lawyers for his appeal, and were expected to argue either to overturn his conviction or to uphold it. A novel featuring a character's tangle with the legal system presents an obvious opportunity for this experiment, but I have mostly heard about historians putting famous figures on trial in the classroom; I first learned of this technique from a history professor at Northwestern, Edward Muir, who had used trials in his undergraduate classes.

Putting famous historical figures on trial doesn't require much planning—you just have to dream up the charges, and then determine the roles that you will have students play in the classroom. My trial did not give a voice to the defendant, but that can be an easy role for the faculty member to assume, since your familiarity with the material means that you can respond to students' questions more knowledgeably than anyone else. You obviously want to have prosecutors, lawyers for the defense, and a judge or jury; you can have teams for each of these roles, or a combination of teams and some individuals working on their own. All of this requires some logistical thinking, and might take up two or three classes; if you play the defendant, and have two small-group teams to prosecute and defend, and then leave everyone else to the jury, you are committing the students to roles that require different levels of activity at different times. The prosecutors and defense might need a class or two in advance to prepare their work, while the jury might need a second class to debate their verdict. But you can organize the trial in many different ways, depending upon the size of the class; you can also draw a written assignment from it, in which students might deliver their verdict and offer an appropriate sentence if they have found the defendant guilty.

You don't have to teach history or literature to adopt this technique in your classroom, though. Philosophers have plenty of famous figures to put on trial, or to retry—Socrates is the most obvious example, but trying Eichmann through the lens of Hannah Arendt might prove equally interesting. A trial of any seminal or influential thinker or figure in a discipline could help students understand how that discipline has evolved over time, and how standards of evidence and inquiry change. Theologians might try God on various charges; economists could try Karl Marx; psychologists Sigmund Freud, and so on. You don't even have to limit yourself to trying individuals; you might put a theory or idea on trial, one that has a controversial place in your field, that practitioners of your discipline are debating in academic journals, and that you can make accessible to students. In any of these cases, the trial can be used to reinforce the importance of using evidence in arguments, of framing and answering good questions, or of exploring how we make judgments in cases in which reasonable claims compete; in general, the trial will impel students to see the figure or issue through a new lens, and will involve everyone in the classroom in some way.

CASE STUDIES

This technique will seem like nothing new to my colleagues in business and law departments and a few other select fields, but you can always shake things up with a case study. Case studies present to students a real-life problem scenario—one that may or may not have actually happened—which they learn about, explore, and recommend actions to resolve. Ideally, students use the knowledge and thinking skills developed in the course to resolve or make recommendations about the case. Harvard Business School is famous for its use of case studies, which have been used there as a teaching method since the early part of the twentieth century. The initial impetus for their development was the simple fact that there were no textbooks at that time to teach business studies, so the faculty wrote up descriptions of real business scenarios for students to study. In addition to the many other business programs and courses that now rely on case study teaching, the disciplines of law and education also frequently rely on case studies these days. The simplest method for working with a case is to write up the scenario (no more than a couple of pages of text), hand it out at the beginning of the class period, and then lead a discussion or arrange students in small groups to discuss the case and present their recommendations. The work listed below in the Resources provides plenty of excellent suggestions and information about how to write cases and conduct discussions of them.

As with trials, the fact that case studies are popular and fit well in one discipline does not mean they won't fit in other disciplines as well. Duffy and Jones provide a nice set of examples of how case studies might work well in other disciplines:

> For a Spanish class mired in the doldrums, a case depicting a bumbling traveler in Madrid confronting new customs and trying to settle into a hotel would certainly highlight the need to learn the ways of the country as well as its language. For a calculus class that is tearing its collective hair out trying to understand integration over a surface, a case that portrays a hypothetical but typical student working out a similar problem might enable the whole class to learn the correct method. For an ethics class, a case that describes three reactions to a cry for help might initiate a heated discussion on responsibility. (191)

I especially like the idea of introducing a case that involves developing a lesson plan for teaching other students about the subject matter—you could always put students in the position of a teacher trying to come up with creative methods to teach students in high school or elementary school about the issue on the table. You will doubtless discover this semester that teaching helps you learn and see your own discipline in new and deeper ways, so this technique transfers some of that experience to your students. You can also use it to talk frankly with them about the doldrums, and to ask their help in figuring out how to pull another class out of the doldrums—pulling yourself out of them in the meantime.

Three Strategies for Staying Fresh

BECOME A LEARNER AGAIN

You won't have time for this in your first semester or two of teaching, but once you have survived that first year, think about taking a course or lessons of some kind. You won't find any better way to gain fresh insights into teaching than to put yourself in the position of a student again, and to look with a more practiced and knowledgeable eye at what your instructor is doing. I first saw a faculty member do this when Ken Bain took an acting class with one of the outstanding teachers he wrote about in his study, during the time I was working with him at the Center for Teaching Excellence. I remember him preparing for his final speech, which was a monologue from a Tennessee Williams play, delivered frequently around the office in the days leading up to the end of the course. Duffy and Jones, as preparation for writing their book, sat in on each other's classes, and they write about the wealth of insights they gained from the experience (124–140).

In my first six years of college teaching, I took a drawing class at the local art museum, a scuba diving class, and piano lessons.

All three courses showed me something new about teaching, or reminded me about the importance of a teaching strategy or habit that I had been neglecting. Scuba diving, for example, reinforced for me the importance of devoting classroom time to practicing the skills I wanted the students to develop, rather than just spending class time doling out information. It was one thing for my scuba instructor to explain to me how to clear my diving mask when we were sitting in the classroom, where his instructions made sense; it was another thing entirely to get in the water and do it myself—I discovered that things were more complicated than I had envisioned, and that I needed some additional pointers. Ever since that course, I have devoted classroom time in my writing courses to letting students write in class, under my direction, rather than just talking to them about writing and then sending them home to complete writing assignments on their own.

Find something you have always wanted to learn about or do, preferably in an area completely different from the one you teach, and take a course during your first or second summer after teaching. Keep an eye on how the instructor runs the course, and note what works well and what doesn't. This experience not only provided me with concrete ideas for classroom strategies, but I think it also helped expand my brain and learn how to translate good teaching ideas from one discipline to another—how to take an interesting strategy for teaching drawing, in other words, and transform it for a class in which I was teaching the contemporary British novel. It flexed my creative pedagogical muscles in ways that nothing else I have experienced has done.

STAY CURRENT

You will always have far more to do than you can accomplish, and you never will catch up on the reading you should be doing for your own discipline. So asking you to stay current in the research on educational theory may sound like a bit much. But it doesn't require a ton of time and effort to keep yourself informed about new ideas and trends in education, or in the teaching of your discipline in particular. For starters, try these three simple things.

1. Almost every academic discipline has a journal or section of a journal devoted to writing about the teaching of that discipline, and some have multiple journals. You are probably acquainted with the major journals in your field, so you may know of these already; if not, ask others in your discipline, or the librarian for your discipline at your new institution (at most academic libraries, the disciplines are assigned in related groups to specific librarians who maintain the collections in those areas) if he knows the name of the journal in your field. Then either subscribe to it yourself or ask the library to subscribe to it, and catch up on its contents every summer. Most of these disciplinary journals have articles that focus on practical classroom strategies, so they can be a great source of ideas for innovative and experimental teaching methods.

2. For a more general overview of issues in academia, and their relation to teaching and the challenges you'll face as a new academic, consult the Career pages of the *Chronicle of Higher Education* (always available for free at *http://chronicle.com/jobs*) where you'll find regular columnists who weigh in on all aspects of academic life, as well as a constantly rotating list of essayists from all walks of academia who do the same thing. A second great online resource for graduate students and new faculty is the Tomorrow's Professor listserv, which sends out three messages a week during the academic year with excerpts

from new publications and research on teaching and academic life. You can see all previous postings, and subscribe, by visiting the website *[http://sll.stanford.edu/projects/tomprof/newtomprof/index.shtml]*.

3. Read one book on teaching per year. That's it—one book a year. Take it to the beach with you, and contemplate the classroom from the distance of the warm sun and the waves. I have provided a list of my own five favorite books about teaching and academic life in the closing chapter, so you're set for the next five years. By 2013, I expect you to be able to find your own teaching resources, so get moving.

BE NOSY

Find out what's going on in the classrooms of your colleagues, who should be one of the best sources for good new ideas about teaching throughout your career. I have a colleague whose ideas about teaching I always trust, and who frequently tries new techniques in her classroom. When I am stuck for a teaching strategy, I know that walking to her office and spending fifteen minutes talking to her about what I could do in my classroom will be more productive than two hours of staring at my computer screen and trying to brainstorm new techniques. Informal discussions about teaching happen in most departments in the hallway and around the copy and coffee machines, so it's not as if you will have to orchestrate such conversations. Just go into them willing to share what you're doing, and interested to hear what others are doing.

You can be nosy a little more formally in a couple of different ways. First, many campuses now have their own centers for teaching excellence, or for teaching and/or learning, or some other variation on those words and names. These centers will have numerous functions, but most of them host discussions about teaching among faculty, or promote lectures or workshops that faculty can attend. Even on my campus, which does not have such a center, a group of us host a twice-yearly colloquium on teaching for anyone who's interested, and we just pick a topic and discuss it together. Find space in your schedule for one event like this per semester. Even if the declared topic or speaker at such an event doesn't seem of immediate interest to you, give it a try anyway; my experience at these events has been that just sitting with my colleagues and talking about teaching, even if only in the Q&A period or open discussion after the workshop, always proves enlightening and productive for me.

Second, see if you can arrange with a colleague—either a new faculty member like yourself or another junior member in your department—to exchange a few classroom visits. Talking about teaching with your colleagues can be wonderful, but nothing beats sitting in on someone else's classroom and seeing how they conduct class, especially if they have invited you on a day when they are trying something interesting. The reverse will be true as well—you will benefit enormously from the reflections of an observer who has sat and watched you try something interesting in the classroom, especially if you and that observer can pledge brutal honesty to each other. The colleague with whom I consult frequently about teaching did this several times in her first years on the tenure track, sitting in on classes of mine and others in the department, and asking us to observe her classes. I gained as much from the experience as she did, and wished I had done more of it myself in my first year or two. Observing colleagues outside of your discipline can be equally enlightening, so don't limit yourself to searching for observation partners in your own department. Find a like-minded soul wherever you can on campus, someone who cares about teaching and wants to do it well, and propose that you sit in on one or two of each other's classes. One way or another, you'll get some new ideas out of the process.

Staying fresh is difficult, both throughout the semester and as the years of teaching pile up. But it matters.

I have a friend who has a great singing voice, and I have heard him sing the songs of other people many times. The first time I heard him sing a song that he had written himself, and that he clearly cared deeply about, was a real revelation—I felt a power in his voice that I had not heard before. He cared about that song, and it showed in his performance; I was really moved by it.

The same holds true for teaching. It's possible to go through the motions of a lesson plan very well, and for students to learn plenty even while you follow a mechanical script. But the real life and energy in a classroom come when you are excited about what you are doing, and the students know it. It will raise their energy level, which in turn will raise yours—and those will be the days that students will remember thirty years from now, and that will keep you coming back into the classroom every year.

Resources

Barnes, Louis B., et al., eds. *Teaching and the Case Method: Text, Cases, and Methods.* Cambridge, Mass.: Harvard Business School Press, 1994.

An excellent introduction to teaching through the case method, with examples from a variety of disciplines.

Duffy, Donna Killian, and Janet Wright Jones. "The Interim Weeks: Beating the Doldrums." In *Teaching Within the Rhythms of the Semester,* 159–198. San Francisco: Jossey-Bass, 1995.

This section of the book is dedicated to the middle weeks of the semester, and how to keep learning active and ongoing during that time frame.

Hunt, Russ. "What is Inkshedding?" *http://www.stthomasu.ca/ ~hunt/dialogic/whatshed.htm*, January 24, 2007.

Hunt's overview of the technique, with a clear explanation of its origins and how to employ it in the classroom.

Lang, James. "Becoming a Learner Again." *The Chronicle of Higher Education*, 51.33 (April 22, 2005): C1.

———— "Shaking Things Up." *The Chronicle of Higher Education*, 53.9 (November 11, 2006): C2.

Chronicle essays on some of the strategies discussed in this chapter.

— — — — — — — — — — • — — —

Common Problems

Q: You make it all sound so easy, Jim. Will I really be able to follow all of your suggestions and have the perfect first semester?

A: No, you won't. Students are human beings, and human beings never do what books tell you they are going to do. So in this chapter I'm offering an FAQ section on the most common problems you will find with your students, followed by advice on a handful of other common problems that occur in teaching for the first time.

Q: How do I handle rude student behavior in my classroom—talking, laughing, getting up and down during class?

A: "No experience of new faculty as teachers," writes Robert Boice, "is so dramatic and traumatizing as facing unruly, uninvolved students—especially in the large, introductory courses traditionally assigned to newcomers" (81). Undoubtedly true; equally troublesome, with the omnipresence of laptops and wireless-enabled classrooms, is the problem of students spending class time shopping for shoes online, rather than taking notes (see the following question).

Two major points here. First, rude student behavior often occurs because of what's happening at the front of the classroom. If students are talking and reading the student newspaper during the lecture, sending e-mails, or IMing their friends, your lectures may be boring. If students are chit-chatting with each other during the discussion, you may not be asking interesting questions. A well-taught class is the best preventive measure you can take to counter what Boice calls "student incivilities." His research on this issue suggests that newcomers face student incivilities much more frequently than highly rated teachers with years of classroom experience (81–98). Fortunately, you are doing the work right now to become a highly rated teacher; following the prescriptions of this book—and other preparatory work you do for your first semester—will be the best measure you can take against poor behavior.

Nonetheless, students, like the rest of the population, can sometimes just be rude idiots, so occasionally your best teaching efforts won't be enough to eliminate such behaviors. You won't always know about students surfing the Internet in class, but you will certainly know about noisy and rude students. When that happens, you can either shame such students by calling them on the behavior in front of their peers, or you can find ways to discuss the behavior with them in private. My non-confrontational personality, coupled with a dozen years of teaching and raising children, has convinced me that the latter route is the better one for correcting poor behavior. When identifiable students are acting uncivilly in your classroom (however you may define such activity), you can stop them after class and give them the standard lines you would expect—that such behavior makes it difficult for you and other students to concentrate, and so on. You can also ask them to come see you in your office, and discuss it there, if you think they require a more serious dressing-down. A third method that I have used is to append a P.S. to one of my final comments on their papers, addressing the behavior and asking them to improve it or to come see me in my office. Calling them on the behavior privately like this has always worked for me. If you try this and it doesn't have the desired effect, check with your department chair; seriously persistent and disruptive behavior should be observed by a senior faculty member or administrator so that you won't suffer for it in your teaching evaluations (and they may be able to intervene with the student).

Q: Students are bringing their laptops, cell phones, PDAs, and what-have-you to my classroom, and whenever I step out into the seats I can see that half of them are downloading music or text-messaging their friends. Some students have cell phones going off in class. What can I do about this?

A: This is probably the most annoying problem we will all face in the future, so it's best to consider it now and decide how you want to handle it. I think the solutions are different depending on the size of the class. In small classes, twenty to thirty or less, you need to have a strong physical presence in the classroom. You should be using interactive teaching methods in classes that size, of course, and such methods give you an opportunity to move out into the seats, work your way around the classroom, and let students know that at any given moment you may be standing behind them, seeing whatever they have on their desk or laptop. Don't isolate yourself in the front of the classroom; you should command the entire space of the room, and you need to make yourself felt at every desk. You don't need to be in constant motion, of course; students' awareness of your mobility will go a long way toward keeping them on task.

In larger lecture classrooms and auditoriums you can still do some of this, but the problems will be more difficult here. So you have two choices, and neither of them is ideal: learn to live with a certain amount of technological distraction, or ban the technologies that are disrupting your classroom. If you choose option one, it doesn't mean you should do nothing. At the very least, you should discuss the inappropriate use of technology in the classroom at the beginning of the semester, and perhaps even include on the syllabus a technology warning like the one cited by Michael Bugeja in a *Chronicle of Higher Education* essay on this subject:

> If your cellular phone is heard by the class you are responsible for completing one of two options: 1. Before the end of the class period you will sing a verse and chorus of any song of your choice; or, 2. You will lead the next class period through a 10-minute discussion on a topic to be determined by the end of the class. (To the extent that there are multiple individuals in violation, duets will be accepted.) (C1, C4)

Whether you use humor in such a warning or not, including an admonition on the syllabus gives you an excuse to discuss the use of technology with students in the classroom, and to help the conscientious (but perhaps clueless) students see how to comport themselves more appropriately.

However, if you are teaching in a large wireless-enabled classroom, facing a sea of laptops, and you are convinced that the vast majority of the students are not listening to your scintillating words, then don't hesitate to ban laptops, either outright or for specific parts of the class session. No student has a constitutional right to bring a laptop to class, so you have every right to forbid them (you might announce that you will make special provisions for students with disabilities, however). Don't feel bad about it; students have been taking notes with pencil and paper for many hundreds of years, and it won't kill them. A less stringent option would be to allow or encourage laptops for specific activities in class—for instance, asking students to join you in reviewing a website or program you have scouted for them in advance, or working with them on a program or problem, but then asking them to close the laptops for the 15-minute lecture module you have planned for the end of the class, when you will be summarizing the main idea of the day.

Remember—you are in charge. As Bugeja concludes at the end of his essay on inappropriate technology in the classroom, "Despite digital distractions, large classes, decreased budgets, and fewer tenured colleagues, professors still are responsible for turning students on to learning. To do so, we just may have to turn off the technology" (C4).

Q: Students are not coming to class, or they come late. Do I leave those choices up to them, since they are adults, or do I become an enforcer and start each class with a daily quiz?

A: An article on poor attendance in college and university courses, which appeared in the spring of 2007 on the website Insidehighered.com and provoked a massive outpouring of responses, offered a bleak picture of this issue. The article included the following statistics on attendance and tardiness patterns:

A 2005 survey of first-year undergraduate students by the Higher Education Research Institute at the University of California at Los Angeles showed that while a majority of college students spend 11 or more hours in class per week, 33 percent reported skipping class and 63 percent said they come to class late "occasionally" or "frequently." A similar survey showed that the proportion of students who report coming late to class has jumped from 48 percent in 1966 to

61 percent in 2006—evidence, one could argue, of a growing indifference to class in general.

At the risk of repeating myself, the first principle is to ensure that
you are creating a classroom experience which students could
not duplicate by copying someone else's lecture notes, or by listening to a recording of your lecture. Students, in other words,
should play a role in the classroom. If you are giving them a role to
play—through discussions, group work, in-class writing, problem-
solving, and so on—then you have every right to say that the success of the course depends upon the presence of the students,
and to require that presence. If you are standing in front of a po-
dium and lecturing for 50 minutes, then I'm with the tardy and
missing students on this one—why *should* they come to class,
when they can get the same material more efficiently, and in the
comfort of their dorm rooms, from other means?

As long as you are offering a class worth attending, which depends upon students for its success, then you should not hesitate
to drop the hammer on late and absent students. Take whatever
measures seem appropriate to you: locking the door at the start
of class, giving daily quizzes at the opening of class, calling tardy
students on the carpet as they walk in the door, penalizing students who miss more than three classes on their final grade. Consult the article on Insidehighered.com, and especially the responses that follow, for more ideas on combating this problem.

Q: I have trouble remembering the names of my own children;
the prospect of remembering the names of several sets of twenty
or thirty or forty undergraduates each year just seems impossible. Can I call on them as "red baseball cap" or "kid who plagiarized" or "crewcut" just to keep things simple for me?
A: I actually did know a teacher who managed this success-

fully. At the beginning of the semester he hit upon some aspect of a student's appearance or mannerisms, gave the student a nickname linked to it, and then referred to him or her in that manner in class. He pulled it off because he was eccentric and had a great sense of humor, and he didn't use offensive or embarrassing nicknames (no one was nicknamed "baldie" or anything like that). The potential ways in which this practice could go wrong are so numerous, though, that I really wouldn't recommend it.

Mary McKinney, a clinical psychologist who counsels academics on career issues, addressed this problem in an essay for the online academic news site Insidehighered.com, where she describes more than a dozen techniques for learning the names of students. Her list is worth consulting, and it's available online without charge (see the Resources list below for the reference). The one that I like best, number 12, may be the simplest. Every time a student asks a question or speaks in class, ask her for her name. Then repeat the name somehow in the answer—"Jane is asking an important question here"—and if that question or your response to it comes up in class again, associate it once again with her name: "You'll remember that Jane asked us this question last week." The more times you repeat the name, the more likely you will be to remember it. This technique has the bonus benefit of affirming the importance of students' contributions in your classroom, making visible to them how their ideas are woven into the fabric of the lectures and discussions. Classes of fifty or more obviously do not require you to learn everyone's name, but don't abandon names altogether. Learn any names that you can, but don't fret about not having comprehensive coverage.

Q: I have a student who flirts with me, or who asked me out for coffee, and I find him/her attractive, and we're only a few years apart in age. Can we date, either now or when the semester is over? Or does finding my students attractive make me a horrible person?

A: If you can make it through a career in teaching without ever feeling sexual attraction to a student, you should check to make sure you're not already dead, like Bruce Willis's character in *The Sixth Sense.* You have no reason to feel guilty about sexual attraction toward a student; we are sexual beings, and so are they, and they are young and like to wear skimpy clothes to attract their fellow students—and occasionally we might get snared in webs that were not intended for us. Sometimes, though, those webs *are* intended for us, and this makes the situation especially difficult.

Although you have no reason to feel guilty about sexual attraction to a student, you also should follow a clear policy on this: no sexual relationships with any student, including a graduate student, who is enrolled at an institution at which you are teaching. Not just enrolled in your class—enrolled in the college, even a few years after you have taught that student. Is such a relationship ethically wrong? I believe it is, for a variety of reasons, but I know thoughtful people who disagree, and my recommendation here is not based on ethical concerns. It's very practical, and I have said it once before: as a graduate student, adjunct, or tenure-track faculty member, *you are vulnerable.* Do not do anything that will jeopardize your career—and sleeping with students, however far removed they may be from your classroom, will jeopardize your career. You may not see anything wrong with sleeping with a graduating senior, but plenty of your colleagues might, and those colleagues will make decisions about your career. You will be amazed at how quickly word of a sexual relationship between a student and a teacher can spread around campus, and a rumor like that one has the potential to follow you for the remainder of your career. So steer very clear of acting on any sexual impulses you have for your students; sublimate those feelings into wholesome activities like painting Civil War figurines or learning to play the recorder.

Q: What special teaching secrets do I need to know for teaching labs or online courses?

A: The sources I consulted about teaching in these special situations all relied on the same basic information and ideas about teaching and learning that I have been describing throughout this book. This means that while you certainly may have to manage technical parts of these teaching situations differently than you would a large lecture or a discussion course, the basic principles remain the same. In other words, you still need to orchestrate these kinds of classes according to the same theories about student learning, about designing and responding to assignments, and so on, that operate in more conventional classroom situations.

In some ways, both of these special teaching situations provide more opportunities for one-on-one (though not necessarily face-to-face) interaction with the instructor, and hence may prove to be more effective than other kinds of classes. That said, the technical parameters are indeed different, but you will probably be sufficiently familiar with those from your student days—since no one will be teaching labs who has not spent lots of hours as a student in the lab—to get you started. Beyond that, you will have to think creatively about how to translate the fundamentals of good teaching into these situations. For more concrete help in these technical areas, and links to other resources, begin with McKeachie's chapters on these teaching situations, listed in the Resources below. More specifically, online teachers can consult Ko and Rossen, while scientists who will be teaching in labs should consult Rick Reis's book, which covers not only teaching but many of the specific elements that new faculty in the sciences will confront during their academic careers.

Q: I tend to get stage fright with public speaking, and so I am massively nervous about the first day of class. I'm afraid my hands will shake, or I'll faint, or my heart will explode, or something terrible like that, and the students will lose all respect for me.

A: I had these kinds of nerves going into my first interview on a morning news program, after my first book came out, and what really helped me was a technique I recommend to everyone: spend the evening before your first day watching the comedy *What About Bob?* in which Bill Murray plays a man paralyzed by every fear you can imagine. Watching him "baby step" his way into self-confidence by the end of the movie did wonders for my own confidence.

If, however, this doesn't seem like an adequate strategy for you, the best thing you can do is to ease your way into the first class, so that the moment of initial exposure to the students is a muted or more gradual one. For months before the class begins you will be building up in your mind to that moment when the students are sitting before you, rows of unfamiliar faces, and you open your mouth to begin the long adventure of the semester. The prospect of that moment is what terrifies you. Therefore, prepare to eliminate that moment. Get to class early and dissipate the unfamiliarity of the students by walking around and handing out the syllabus, greeting the students by name. Or begin the class simply by handing out the information sheets, and asking each student to fill one out. You may even begin with a group activity, like the exercise recommended by Michael Gennert that involves having students work in groups to read the syllabus and ask questions about it. The ten to fifteen minutes that this exercise will buy you, or the time that students spend filling out information sheets, will enable you to settle more easily into your first day of teaching and will tone down your anxiety considerably.

Q: You keep telling me to consult my department chair about this or that, but I've discovered that my chair is insane / out to get me / incompetent / a potential serial killer. I've learned this from a colleague / all of my colleagues / my amateur sleuthing, the techniques for which I remembered from reading *Encyclopedia Brown* mysteries as a kid.

A: The possible causes of and responses to this situation are endlessly variable, so following any advice I might give here could actually make the situation worse. Just remember the following general principles:

1. If your own observations and/or a chorus of your colleagues agree that the chair is a problem, remember this: You have no power. Unless your chair is doing something illegal, or borderline illegal (such as inappropriate sexual comments or subtle harassment), you won't be able to do much to stop him or her, and you have to remain on the chair's good side or you will end up teaching all 8:00 A.M. classes in a windowless basement. You also will have a hard time getting tenure. Fortunately, chairs come and go (in my department, we elect or reelect them every three years), so patience and martyrdom are your best bets. For advice and consultation, you can sometimes find a reliable chair-substitute in a senior faculty member who has held the position of chair in the past. Walk around the hallways looking sad and pathetic, and a former chair might take

pity on you. As Jay Parini mentions in *The Art of Teaching*, if you can establish a relationship with an emeritus faculty member, they can prove excellent mentors as well— folks who have long institutional memory, and plenty of wisdom, but who will not sit in judgment on your tenure case (96–104).

2. One person complaining about another person, including a faculty member who complains about the chair, does not tell you anything you can trust about either of them. For all you know, the complainer is the insane serial killer, and the chair is handling this person the best way she knows how. So be careful of becoming the person to whom a disgruntled faculty member likes to vent, whether it's about the chair or anyone else. Smile and nod, but don't express an opinion about anything until you figure out what's really going on. Anyone who button-holes you continuously to complain about other faculty members, or about anything at all, should be avoided as much as possible (this holds true in life as well).

3. If you get into a situation in which it seems as if the entire department is against you, and no one is treating you fairly, and you find that you have been in this situation before . . . well, I'm going to be the one to be honest with you here. The problem, my friend, may be you. Consider a major personality overhaul.

Q: Any final advice for me, Jim?

A: Hand lotion. Nothing dries out your hands like chalk, especially during the wintertime. Keep some lotion in your desk, and apply it liberally. My department assistant would be very grateful, I'm sure, if I followed this advice myself and stopped borrowing hers all the time.

Q: Do these ten questions really cover all of the problems I might have in the classroom?

A: Yes. OK, no. But rather than continuing to fish for you, I am going to teach you to fish on your own. An excellent resource for getting and giving advice on just about any teaching question you can imagine is the Forum section of the online version of *The Chronicle of Higher Education,* which you can find at *http://chronicle.com/forums.* Look in particular at the thread "In the Classroom," but you will find advice and discussion about teaching in lots of places. This particular forum has its share of idiots, like every place in the world, but many thoughtful and interesting people post messages seeking and dispensing advice on the boards, and you will find a thread there—or you can start one of your own—on every vexing problem that you are likely to encounter in and out of the classroom.

Resources

Boice, Robert. *Advice for New Faculty Members: Nihil Nimus.* Boston: Allyn and Bacon, 2000.

See especially chapter 8, "Moderate Student Incivilities," for Boice's research on this issue and his advice on how to prevent and respond to incivilities.

Bugeja, Michael J. "Distractions in the Wireless Classroom." *The Chronicle of Higher Education,* 53.21 (January 26, 2007): C1. *http://chronicle.com/jobs/news/2007/01/2007012601c/careers.html,* January 29, 2007.

An interesting article about the problem of students' use of the Internet in wireless classrooms, with a few suggestions for how to combat this. Available online.

Ko, Susan, and Steve Rossen. *Teaching Online: A Practical Guide,* 2nd ed. Boston: Houghton Mifflin, 2003.

A comprehensive guide to online teaching.

McKeachie, Wilbert, and Marilla Svinicki. *McKeachie's Teaching Tips: Strategies, Research, and Theory for College and University Teachers,* 12th ed. Boston: Houghton Mifflin, 2006.

See the following chapters: "Laboratory Instruction: Ensuring an Active Learning Experience" (266–277), and "Teaching by Distance Education" (288–297).

McKinney, Mary. "What's Your Name Again?" *Inside Higher Ed,* February 13, 2006. *http://www.insidehighered.com/workplace/2006/02/13/mckinney,* January 3, 2007.

McKinney's article is followed by an interesting discussion among readers about the importance of learning names, and offering other techniques for doing so.

Parini, Jay. *The Art of Teaching.* New York: Oxford University Press, 2005.

Parini's book contains a very wise argument about the respect we should give to our emeritus/a faculty members.

Powers, Elia. "The Elephant Not in the Room." *Insidehighered .com,* May 1, 2007. *http://www.insidehighered.com/news/2007/05/01/absent.*

This piece is about absenteeism and tardiness, with a long following thread of debate and advice.

Reis, Richard. *Tomorrow's Professor: Preparing for Careers in Science and Engineering.* New York: Wiley-IEEE Press, 1997.

A good preparatory guide for new faculty in the sciences. Reis went on to write a column for the *Chronicle of Higher Education* on this same topic for a few years, and then founded the Tomorrow's Professor listserv.

Student Ratings and Evaluations

The thirteenth week of the semester is the best teaching week of the year: Thanksgiving holiday week. Most colleges and universities will shutter up the campus on Tuesday or Wednesday afternoon of this week, and allow everyone a brief respite before the sprint to the finish line of the semester. Be forewarned that many students will want to make that respite less brief, and will skip the last day of classes that week or simply beg off the entire week altogether. You shouldn't feel obliged to accommodate those students, although I sometimes reward the diligent students who are with me that week with a shorter class period or a real piece-of-cake writing exercise. But while I wouldn't recommend scheduling a major exam in a 4:00 class on the Wednesday before Thanksgiving, I also wouldn't recommend just canceling class or bowing to the students' desire for a longer break. When classes are scheduled, you should hold classes.

But it remains a short week in any case, so this gives you time to look ahead to the end of the semester, toward that terrible and yet intriguing moment when the tables will be turned and the students will have the opportunity to sit in judgment upon you: the biannual ritual of students evaluating their teachers.

To backtrack a moment, one of the most maddening and anxiety-

producing aspects of your first semester of teaching will be that
you receive little or no formal feedback on how well you are doing. You might have a visit from your department chair, and she
might meet with you afterwards to talk about what she saw in
your classroom, and how you can improve, but that (if it happens
at all) might be all you get. Of course, if students are walking into
class, leaving on their headphones, and glaring at you with mur-
derous eyes through the entire fifty minutes, this will give you
an indication that things aren't going as well as they might. But
such obvious signs of discontent, or of contentment, won't happen very often. Mostly you will look at the students every day,
who are mostly attentive, and you will wonder whether they are
learning anything, and if so, whether it has anything to do with
your teaching. In jobs in other kinds of businesses, new employees will receive regular performance reviews to get them on
track; in academia, we prefer to let our new employees flounder
around on their own for as long as possible—the ones that survive, we figure, have what it takes to be a teacher.

This is sad and stupid, but (mostly) true. So, unless you seek
out additional feedback on your own (more on this below), the
first real and extensive feedback you'll get on your efforts during
your first semester will come from the students, in the form of
end-of-semester rating forms that students will fill out in the final
week or two of classes. Most such forms consist of two parts—a
section of questions to which students respond with numbers
(i.e., students will rate your effectiveness as a teacher, in multiple categories, on a scale of 1 to 5), and another section of open-
ended questions to which students will write their responses
(i.e., "Would you recommend this course to another student?").
Generally you will receive, then, a report that presents to you the
raw numbers from the first section, and a transcript of the students' comments in response to each question. All of it will be

anonymous—you won't know which students made which comments or gave you which numbers, a step taken to prevent you from retaliating against the students for negative comments by changing their grades (or influencing your view of them if they should take future courses with you). And the information will arrive after the semester has concluded—in some cases, you won't get it until weeks or months after you have started your second semester, depending on the efficiency of your institution in processing the results of the student forms. Many institutions are now moving this entire process online, which obviously streamlines it, but you still won't get any feedback before you have turned in your final grades.

These student rating forms have been around for many decades now—the first rating forms were used at the University of Washington more than eighty years ago, according to researcher James Kulik—and are just about universal in American colleges and universities today. They have gained such importance in part because colleges and universities have increasingly been required, in recent years, to document their efforts at *assessment*— an academic buzz word that refers to the process of determining what and how much students are learning in an institution. Pressure for assessment comes from accrediting agencies—regional bodies that certify that a college or university has the power to grant degrees. That's why, whatever your dreams for quick financial success, you can't just hang out a shingle on your house with the words "Jimbo's University for Learnin'!" painted on it, and start handing out degrees. Degrees from non-accredited institutions—like the online institutions that you probably receive e-mails from several times a week—aren't worth the paper they're not printed on. All of this might seem like more than you need to know at the moment, but it's worth keeping words like *assessment* and *accreditation* in your mind, because when you hear those words being thrown around at a department meeting—especially if you're on the tenure track—run for cover. As important and laudable as these processes are, they always translate into more work for faculty, and that's the last thing you need this first semester.

Pressing forward to more practical matters, this chapter has two purposes: to dispel many of the myths that surround student rating forms and their use, and to encourage you to seek feedback on your teaching from your students on a more regular basis, rather than waiting until after the course has ended.

Myths first. No area of teaching in higher education fuels more myths, untruths, hasty generalizations from small samples, anger, and criticism than the student rating forms. The strong emotions come from the fact that most institutions use those forms as an important part of their evaluation of your teaching, so if students are dumping on your teaching, it has a professional impact. The fear of being dumped on, and the anger that faculty members feel when it happens to them, has led to a whole set of common beliefs about and criticisms of the process of having students evaluate our teaching, the most persistent of which include the following:

1. Students are not competent to evaluate their teachers. What do they know about organic chemistry, after all, except what you have told them? So how are they capable of determining whether you have taught them well?
2. Students only give high ratings to teachers who are flashy performers, or who tell lots of jokes, or who have style but not necessarily substance. They can't tell the difference between good teaching and entertainment.
3. Students give high ratings to teachers who give students little work and are easy graders, and punish teachers who give higher workloads and fair grades.

4. Teaching is an art, which can't be measured with numbers or judged the way you would judge a salesperson's profit margin.
5. Students will only recognize the importance of what I'm teaching, and hence my brilliance as a teacher, after they have graduated and are out in working world—at which time they will also recognize the pandering idiocy of my colleagues who receive high ratings from their students.

Doubtless because of the emotions they inspire, the myths that surround them, and their importance in the evaluation of faculty for hiring and promotion and tenure, student ratings have been the subject of an incredible amount of research—more than two thousand books and articles and counting at the time of this writing. Myths about the forms stem in part from faculty members' resentment and fears about their teaching, but also from a handful of these studies that have produced anomalous results supporting these myths. What you should remember, though, is this: the vast majority of studies on student ratings have concluded that well-designed rating forms provide a reliable measure of student learning and teaching effectiveness when those results are compared with other measures of learning and teaching effectiveness—including students' performance on course work and external exams, interviews with students, alumni surveys, and the judgments of trained classroom observers. I'm going to be very blunt here: in my experience, faculty who complain most vociferously about the validity of student ratings, and seize upon the anomalous studies in support of their complaints, are usually faculty who deserve the low ratings they get.

I want to provide a quick explanation to dispel the five myths listed above, and then I'll move into the more practical matters of how you can use the ratings form to improve your teaching, and how you can supplement the forms with ratings taken at earlier points in the semester, and with additional resources to help improve your teaching. I'm relying on three overviews of the research on student ratings to dispel the common myths, all written by higher education researchers who have excellent and reliable track records: Ken Bain's white paper on the use of student ratings to improve teaching, William Cashin's survey of empirical studies that have been done on student ratings (both Bain's and Cashin's articles are available online—see the Resources list below), and James Kulik's review of the major conclusions we can draw from the empirical research.

1. *Students' inability to rate good teaching.* This myth is based on a common-sense partial truth—namely, that students don't have the qualifications to make sophisticated judgments about the effectiveness of different teaching methods. True enough. But an effectively designed form should not be asking them for such sophisticated judgments (see Bain for more information on what makes a form effective). Instead, the forms should ask them how much they learned in the course, what you did that helped them learn, and what you did (or did not do) that didn't help them learn. And the research overwhelmingly supports the conclusion that students are very accurate judges of how much they learned in a course, when you compare their scores on exams with their ratings. As Kulik puts it, very simply, "Students generally give high ratings to teachers from whom they learn most, and they generally give low ratings to teachers from whom they learn least" (12).

2. *Style versus substance.* This myth stems from a famous and widely reported study in which researchers had an actor pose as a professor, named Dr. Fox, and give an entertain-

ing but nonsensical lecture; afterwards, the students rated him very highly. This study was widely publicized because it confirmed the hopes that many faculty had that student ratings were a sham. Multiple reviews of the study, however, have demonstrated serious methodological problems with it. More important, though, is the fact that no question on the rating form in this experiment asked whether the students in Dr. Fox's class *learned* anything of substance. If you don't ask important questions, the answers the students give won't tell you anything— and the researchers in this study did not ask the most important question of all. Again, a well-designed rating form will identify teachers who are helping their students learn, whatever style of teaching they may use.

3. *High ratings for easy teachers.* It's easy enough to dispel this one. William Cashin's research on student ratings addresses all of the possible variables that might influence students' perceptions of both course and teacher, from the gender and age and enthusiasm of the instructor to perceptions of the workload in the course. Cashin reports that, indeed, a correlation does exist between the amount of work students are assigned and the ratings they give— but the correlation is the *opposite* of what this myth suggests. In other words, Cashin explains, "students give *higher* ratings in difficult courses where they have to work hard" (7). The correlation is very small, and thus perhaps not significant, but it's enough to demonstrate the falseness of this myth. An equally small correlation does exist between the grades student expect to receive and course ratings—higher ratings when students report that they expect their final grades in the course will be good ones. So again, here the myth may rest on a plank of truth. But the

correlation is too small (between .10 and .30) for it to provide a very solid foundation. And, as Cashin points out,
students who have been well taught, and have learned a
lot in the class, would expect to earn good grades and
would rate the course highly. So even a more significant
correlation would not necessarily prove this myth.

4. *Teaching is an art.* There is an element of truth here as
well, since many styles and strategies of teaching can be
used to achieve the same ends, and a teacher exercises art-
fulness in selecting methods and applying them in the
classroom, just as a sculptor has the choice to work with a
variety of different materials to realize a particular artistic
conception. However, student ratings of teaching should
focus primarily on how well the teacher has helped the
student learn, and all of this research I am citing definitely
tells us that we can measure this—we can give students
an exam on the first day of the course, for example, and
then one on the last day, and measure their learning between those two time periods. A well-designed form can
help us understand what the teacher has done to advance
the student's learning, and what other factors might have
come into play. Unfortunately, not all forms are well designed. A form at one institution where I taught, for example, asked whether I started and ended class on time. I can
see why administrators might want an answer to that
question, but it tells me nothing whatsoever about the effectiveness of my teaching, or about student learning in
my classroom. Because the forms will be used by administrators to make judgments about your teaching, you can't
afford to ignore the results of any question just because it
doesn't tell you anything helpful about your teaching.
However, when it comes to reviewing your results and

trying to use them to improve your teaching, focus on the questions that matter.

5. *Students see my brilliance only in retrospect.* This one is just plain false. Kulik reports a study in which the researchers compared end-of-term ratings for courses taken by 1,400 students over a three-year period with ratings that these same students filled out over a four-year period following the completion of the course. The correlation between the two sets of ratings was extremely high (.83), suggesting that few students were changing their minds after a few years had passed. Other studies have compared alumni ratings of teachers with current student ratings of those same teachers, and found that "current students give favorable ratings to teachers whom alumni remember fondly and poor marks to teachers whom alumni remember unfavorably" (14). If they hate you now, in other words, they're going to hate you in twenty years.

Student rating forms are not perfect measures of student learning or of your teaching by any means. They provide one perspective only, and students clearly are *not* competent to rate some aspects of your teaching—your mastery of disciplinary content, for example. But good questions on student rating forms can yield valid and useful information, so don't fall prey to the myths you have heard or may yet hear, and dismiss the forms as a popularity contest or as meaningless.

Practically, what can you do both to ensure that you receive good ratings, and to use them to improve your own teaching?

The following sections describe three steps you can take to help your ratings in your first semester of teaching, all of which will take a little additional time and effort, but which should prove worthwhile.

Know Thy Forms

First, ask your department chair for a copy of the rating forms at the beginning of the semester. If you know in advance the kinds of questions that will be asked about your teaching, you can take deliberate steps to address those issues in your teaching. Although student rating forms should not endorse any particular strategy of teaching—that is, the form should not lead students to believe that any one particular teaching strategy is the best one—many of them unfortunately do. For example, if a form asks whether you use group work in the classroom, that form is implying that the use of group work is a good thing. This may not be true for every teacher and classroom, so that question really shouldn't appear on a valid form. If it does, however, it tells you two things: that your department or institution wants its instructors to use group work in the classroom, and that you had better use some groups this semester. An advance look at the form will help you identify particular teaching strategies that you need to practice or avoid in order to receive strong ratings.

Seek Earlier Feedback

You do not have to wait until the end of the semester to seek feedback from your students on your teaching. Many instructors collect feedback from their students at the semester's midpoint, or at a variety of points along the way, both to determine how well students are understanding the material or developing the desired skills and to see what they might do differently in order to improve student learning in the course. Of course, assignments and exams will let you know how well students are learning, but it would be far more beneficial to the students if you could identify problem areas *before* their graded assignments were due, so that you could help them perform better on the assignments. If you realize, from a spate of wrong answers on a final exam question, that the students have missed a major element of the course, it's too late to do anything about it.

I'll offer here three simple methods you can use to collect feedback from students along the way. The first two of these come from Thomas Angelo and K. Patricia Cross's book called *Classroom Assessment Techniques*, a massive compendium of methods for assessing what's happening in your classroom, and gathering information from your students about your teaching and the students' learning. The best and most widely cited of these techniques are the two simplest: the Minute Paper and the Muddiest Point.

1. "To use the Minute Paper," the authors explain, "an instructor stops class two or three minutes early and asks students to respond briefly to some variation on the following two questions: 'What was the most important thing you learned during this class?' and 'What important question remains unanswered?' Students then write their responses on index cards or half-sheets of scrap paper . . . and hand them in." This technique, as Angelo and Cross point out, provides "manageable amounts of timely and useful feedback for a minimal investment of time and energy" (148). Both questions will provide you with useful information at the end of a lecture or discussion. If every student mentions as the most important thing she learned some trivial but entertaining point from your lecture, you know you need to revisit the main idea; if a significant number of students have an unanswered question that was covered during the lecture, you know you need to review. You can also use their unanswered question to help

you decide how to begin or structure the following class period. In any case, the students' responses to these questions will take just a few minutes to read, and will help you see whether the ideas or concepts or skills you are teaching correspond with what the students are learning.

2. The Muddiest Point technique is a truncated variation of the Minute Paper; students are asked to respond—again, in just a minute or two at the end of class—to the question "What was the muddiest point in today's _____?" Fill in the blank space with "lecture," "discussion," "reading," or whatever else you are teaching. Again, the students' responses will make for quick reading on your part, and will help direct your teaching in the next session. What I really like about this technique is that the response process has a learning component to it, as Angelo and Cross point out: "Learners must quickly identify what they do not understand and articulate those muddy points . . . even though the technique is extremely simple to administer, responding to it requires some higher-order thinking" (154).

The third method you can use to gather feedback from students, more specifically about your teaching—with an eye to improvement—is to take 10 or 15 minutes at the end of a class in the middle of the semester and administer a survey with some version of these two questions: "What classroom activities or assignments have been most effective in helping you learn this semester, and why?" and "What classroom activities or assignments have been least effective in helping you learn this semester, and why?" The students respond in writing, with a paragraph for each question—15 minutes tops. They can keep their responses anonymous, but this shouldn't be necessary, since you are not asking them to make judgments about you or the course—only about their own learning. You should pay most attention to the teaching methods or assignments that are mentioned by multiple students as being positive or negative. If only a small percentage of the students complain about group work, don't let that deter you from further group work. Nothing you do will please everybody. But if a majority of the students cite group work as the least effective part of the course, consider talking with them further about how you might alter the group work so that it would work better for them—or just let group work go for this semester and rethink your strategies for next time.

A key to getting helpful and honest answers from such a survey is to write these questions carefully so that you are not asking students to make judgments about you or the course. The questions have to be phrased in such a way that they ask students to comment on what has worked for them, so the response just becomes a description of their personal experience—and you should reiterate this to them in your oral explanation of the surveys before they fill them out. If the wording of the question implies a judgment about you—for example, "What teaching methods have been the most effective this semester?"—you will get a bunch of responses like this: "They've all been great! It's a great class! You're the best!" Students will usually jump on an easy opportunity to suck up, especially when you still have power over their grades. So you should explain carefully, both in writing and in class, that you are interested in seeing what you can do for the rest of the semester that will help everyone learn as much as possible in the final weeks, and this will only work if they give honest responses about their experiences in the course thus far. Such an explanation should result in feedback that you can use to make modifications that will ultimately improve your end-of-semester student ratings, not to mention improving the course.

As a slightly Machiavellian aside, you can use the opportunity of administering such a survey to give a little speech to the students about how you much you care about their learning, that you want the course to be the best possible experience for them, that you value their input and feedback on how the course is going, and so on. Such a talk, combined with an actual effort to get their ideas, will give the students a more favorable impression of you for the remainder of the semester than they might have had otherwise, and should contribute to better ratings at the end of the semester, even if you make no changes whatsoever to the course. However, I highly recommend that you discuss the results of the survey with them in the following class, and find at least one or two small ways to make modifications to the course in order to show them not only that you wanted their responses, but that you actually listened to what they had to say. You may also find that students are uncertain about the purpose of a particular assignment or activity, and you can use a discussion of the survey results to help them see how the parts of the course support each other and cohere. Do the surveys in good faith, and the Machiavellian aspects should prove to be a bonus—whenever I have conducted a survey like this, I have always received information that helped me change the course for the better.

Many new instructors will find an additional resource on campus to help them get early feedback from their students: the Center for Teaching, or Teaching and Learning, or Teaching and Learning and Technology, or Teaching Excellence, or some other variation of these terms. These centers work with graduate students and faculty to initiate and sustain dialogues about teaching on campus, to fund research on teaching and learning, and to help individual teachers work on their teaching. They welcome the opportunity to work with new faculty, and they almost always offer a variety of services that can help you get feedback on your teaching, both from the trained experts who work in the centers and from your students. They might offer videotaping services, or send an observer to visit your class and provide feedback, or have methods for getting more extensive feedback from your students than you might be able to obtain on your own. So consider contacting the appropriate center on your campus—not all campuses will have one—and asking them to help provide you feedback on your teaching before the end of the term.

Classroom Transparency

Be transparent in your teaching. Take the time to inform students why you are doing what you are doing in the classroom— the reasons behind a specific classroom activity, or assignment, or exam. Make sure they understand how the major activities and assignments tie into the learning objectives of the course, and will ultimately help them become wiser, or more skilled, or better human beings. Unless they know these things, students might complain that certain activities or assignments are pointless. Don't give them reasons to make that complaint.

To get back to the forms themselves, which you will probably be asked to distribute in the final week or two of the semester: the important thing to remember is that you will get information from students about your teaching, and you should take it seriously. You should supplement your institution's efforts to collect their impressions with your own efforts to do so, and you should let the information you receive help you become a better teacher, both in this semester and the next. Ignore the gripes you might hear from your colleagues about this process—if you don't believe me, consult the articles listed below on the subject, and see for yourself what the data tells us about student ratings of our teaching.

As a final note for this chapter, I'll say a word or two about how to respond to the ratings you'll ultimately receive at the course's end. Every set of rating forms is bound to include one person who says you are the worst teacher ever, one person who says you are the best teacher ever, a few who complain that you assign too much work, and a series of conflicting comments—for instance, two people who say the discussions were life-changing, and three who say they were boring. That's standard stuff, and you should try not to worry about any criticisms or comments that come from one individual form, especially hurtful ones. It will be hard to do this—we all tend to focus on the negative comments, no matter how many positive ones there are to offset them. But do pay attention to comments that come from several or more students, or comments that confirm suspicions you already have about the course. In other words, if you felt you needed to organize your lectures more effectively, and two people mention that same thing on their forms, you should make improving organization in your lectures a priority for next semester. If more than a handful of people make the same complaint about anything, that too probably deserves work or reconsideration for next semester.

But I would strongly recommend that you take one final step to help you respond effectively to your forms—request a meeting with your department chair to review your ratings together, and discuss how you can improve. Don't feel that you have to hide poor ratings from your chair—she will be getting copies of them in any case, as will some dean somewhere on campus. Speaking to your chair about your ratings will accomplish three things. First, she can identify for you kinds of comments that might be typical of students at your institution—if all instructors receive complaints about the workload, for example, she will know that, and can tell you safely to ignore those comments. Second, your chair may be able to offer you help and advice on improving in those areas in which you need help with your teaching. I say "may" because, unfortunately, becoming a chair does not necessarily mean that person is an expert teacher—so you may get good advice, and you may not.

But you should still schedule the meeting, for the third and most important reason, in which we slip back into Machiavellian mode for a minute. No one assumes that you will walk into your first semester in the classroom as a stellar teacher, and earn uniformly positive ratings. We all know that it takes time to learn to teach well. So what your chair, or dean, or evaluation committee want to see from you in your first few years of teaching—if you want to stick around—is that you are working to improve. As Robert Boice says, "By no means, in my experience, does a committee of evaluators of new faculty expect great teaching out of the gate; instead, they look for evidence of systematic work at improvement and of reasonable acceptance from students" (59). So when it comes time to write a self-evaluation for things like promotion and tenure, this will be one topic you might be asked to address: how has your teaching improved and developed since your hire, or since your last application for promotion? Meeting with your chair—or with the coordinator or director of the teaching center on your campus, if you have one—starts you off on the right track in this regard, showing the powers that be how eager you are to improve your teaching, and to learn from your mistakes (even if it's not true).

Resources

Angelo, Thomas A., and K. Patricia Cross. *Classroom Assessment Techniques: A Handbook for College Teachers,* 2nd ed. San Francisco: Jossey-Bass, 1993.

A big book, with lots of methods for gathering information

from your students about how a course is going, or for assessing their learning at any point in the semester.

Bain, Ken. "Evaluation of Teaching Using Student Ratings." 1996. *http://www.montclair.edu/center/white.html,* January 29, 2007.

Some of the material in this essay appears in Bain's book as well, but this is the most comprehensive presentation of his research on student ratings that I know. In addition to discussing some of the common myths and realities of student ratings, this article identifies questions on a rating form that will yield valid results.

Boice, Robert. *Advice for New Faculty Members: Nihil Nimus.* Boston: Allyn and Bacon, 2000.

See my comment on Boice in Chapter 10.

Cashin, William E. "Student Ratings of Teaching: A Summary of the Research." *IDEA Paper* 20 (September 1998): 1–6. *http://www.idea.ksu.edu/resources/index.html,* January 29, 2007.

The website given above will take you to the index; click on issue number 20 for Cashin's very clear and comprehensive overview.

Kulik, James. "Student Ratings: Validity, Utility, and Controversy." *New Directions for Institutional Research,* 27.5 (Spring 2001): 9–25.

A good statement of the conclusions we can draw from the research.

Last Days of Class

As the end of every semester approaches, I always have this vision that my students and I will spend our last day of class reminiscing about what a terrific course we had and sharing war stories. We'll have some lattes, chuckle over the time I tripped on the overhead projector cord, and then the students will give me a hug or a pat on the back on the way out, promising to IM me or inviting me to become one of their MySpace friends.

What usually happens instead is that they fill out the student rating forms, I review the final exam for them or answer questions about the final paper assignment, and then I stand behind my desk watching them leave class 20 minutes after they arrived. Some of them wave goodbye or thank me, but mostly we are all just too tired at that point to do much beyond being grateful that it's almost over.

Despite the advice I am about to give you now, and the advance plans you might make for the last day of the semester, you will be sorely tempted to do as I have done (more times than I would care to admit) when you get to that final day—take care of administrative business and get out of there as quickly as possible. You'll be tired, you'll have tons of work to do, and you'll just want to go back to your office and sit down and think about absolutely nothing for a little while.

However—and I have to say this to you, even if I have not always followed my own advice—the final days of a course can be a fruitful time to help students process what they have learned and reinforce the most important ideas or skills which they have (you hope) acquired in their time with you. Moreover, since you may be handing out the course evaluations on the final day of the semester, coupling that administrative task with an inspired pedagogical exercise can put students in a positive frame of mind when they are filling out the rating forms.

Inspired pedagogy, on this final day, will compete with the administrative tasks, though, which do need taking care of. So this chapter, which really concerns the last couple of days of the semester, will address the main things you need to accomplish during the endgame, concluding with two simple pedagogical exercises you can use to finish your first semester with a strong focus on student learning.

Student Rating Forms

The first semester I used student rating forms, I waited until the end of the very last class and handed them out in the final fifteen minutes. I said my goodbyes and left the classroom, expecting that the students would now provide their careful evaluations of my teaching. As I walked out of the building and turned down the pathway to my office, I couldn't resist one final look back—and saw, to my amazement and eventual anger, a student from my class sauntering out of the building thirty seconds after I had exited. Although he was a freshman, he was smart enough to know that evaluations were anonymous, and hence, for him, optional.

I never made the same mistake again, and you shouldn't either. Although the passing out of rating forms may seem like a pretty straightforward task, you should follow these three guidelines:

1. Administer the forms during the beginning or midpoint of the final class. Most institutions ask that you leave the room while the students fill out the forms, so designate a student to come out and get you when the forms have been collected. If you do them near the end, leave a final piece of business to take care of once they have completed the forms (such as handing back work).
2. Don't hand back any graded work until the evaluations have been completed. If you have graded work to hand back that day, save it until the end of the class. A student who receives a low grade on a paper you have just handed back might allow that grade to influence his written comments.
3. Many students don't know what the forms are used for, or whether they mean anything. Before you distribute them, spend a minute or two explaining that you value the students' input on your teaching, and intend to use it to make changes for future courses. As with the midterm evaluations, a simple speech like this can help put the students in a constructive frame of mind rather than a purely critical one. Give them the feeling that they have the power to help you, and that you really want their feedback.

Review for Final Exam or Assignment

If the students have a final paper or large assignment, you have presumably given this to them some time back. If you are administering a final exam, the last class period may provide an opportunity to review for that exam—though you might leave review sessions to teaching assistants if you are teaching a larger course, or you might decide to hold a review session at some separate time and date, as many of my colleagues do. Review sessions held outside of the normal classroom hours are usually optional, and are often driven by students' concerns and questions. You might prepare a brief explanation of the format of the exam, for example, and then remind them of the major topics and units of the course, but then let them ask questions or clarify issues that remain unclear to them. A written handout or study guide can be very helpful for the students as well; in my composition and creative writing courses I will provide a two-page handout on the final day that reminds them about all the writing techniques we have discussed in class that semester. I ask them to review the list and check their final paper against it. You might also provide the students with tips on how to study most effectively for the exam—whether they should reread the text(s), review their notes, memorize anything, do practice problems, or anything else.

Some faculty members use quiz-show formats or games to review for the final exam, which seems fine, although I've never tried it. Consult the article by Bryan Gibson in the Resources list for an example of how you might do this. Ultimately, how you review will depend upon the kind of course you teach, so there will be a lot of variation. I can give you one general principle to follow, though. Think about your final exam as providing an opportunity for students to show you what they can do—to synthesize what they have learned, filter it through their own brains, and present it to you anew. Your final exam should be an opportunity for them to reinforce their learning. It is *not,* and should not become, a hurdle they have to jump over, or an obstacle they have to negotiate. In other words, do not construct a final exam, or conduct a review session, as if you are the keeper of secrets, and their job is to crack your spy codes. You should not be trying to trick them, to show them how little they know, to lower their grades, or to become like the bridge keeper in *Monty Python and the Holy Grail* who requires people to answer three questions before they can cross, or else they are catapulted into the gorge. The final exam should be the students' final learning experience in the course, and any review session that you conduct should help prepare them to succeed on it.

One last question concerning the assignment or exam you will give at the end of the semester: should it be cumulative? If you believe that the material you teach is only important enough for students to retain for a few weeks or a month, and then they are free to forget it for the rest of their lives, then don't make it cumulative. If you believe that what you teach matters beyond the confines of the three months you spend with them, then make it cumulative.

In other words, make it cumulative.

Final-Day Pedagogy

A surprisingly small amount of literature exists on the final day of class, which I only discovered when I went looking for resources to supplement this chapter. One of my favorites was a short essay by an environmental scientist who concludes his 400-student course for non-majors with a series of rituals designed to express the emotions of acceptance, gratitude, integrity, and hope. In the closing moments of the class, the professor states his hope for each of the previous versions of the class he has taught—for example, "May they do good work in the world"—and rings a bell after he names each class. Then he asks the students to express their hopes for the world, and rings his bell one final time to send them out into the world.

I am trying very hard to avoid making fun of this article, because I believe completely in the writer's conviction that it is "important . . . to create space for the exploration of feelings during the final class meeting of the semester. After all, this meeting marks the end of a long journey that has usually called forth considerable exertion from both teacher and student" (Uhl, 165). Moreover, judging from his description of his final classes, he makes this creative stratagem for his final class work.

However, I would have a very hard time pulling this off— I mean, I don't even own a bell—and I suspect you need a lot more confidence in your teaching than you will have, after fifteen weeks in the classroom, to get students to stand up in front of 400 peers and express their deepest hopes for the world. So I'm going to recommend that for this semester you keep your bells on the jester hat you're saving for your next Halloween party and revisit this exercise in the future. For now, I'll stick with recommending two very practical exercises you can undertake in the final class of the semester; neither of them requires much advance planning, and both will help focus that final class on learning.

First, you can hark back to the very first day of the semester, and return to the students the information sheets that they filled out way back then. This technique will only work if you had the students answer on that first day not only basic informational questions, but one or two substantive questions designed to get their initial impressions of the subject matter. If they did respond to one or two such questions from their uninformed initial perspective, they might find it interesting and surprising to look back at those initial impressions and compare them with what they now know about the course content. Hopefully, they will realize from this comparison that your combined work throughout the semester really has helped them learn something new and substantial. To reinforce that, ask the students to write a half-page or one-page in-class essay on how their understanding or perspective has changed from what they wrote on that first day. Depending on how much time you have, you can ask a few of them to share what they have written with the class, and you can collect them at the end for a quiz grade, or just for your own edification. It can be difficult for students to step back, while they are drowning in theories and definitions and textbooks and new ideas, and notice how much they are accomplishing in a course; a final exercise like this one will help them achieve that longer view.

You can do an easy variation on this exercise if you didn't do the initial student information sheets, or if you did them but they are crammed into the pocket of the airline seat on the plane you took to visit your relatives at Thanksgiving (where they may be residing with a set of quizzes I left in just such a place). Simply ask the students, again for a quiz grade or for your own edification, to write a paragraph describing the most important thing they learned during the semester. This is a low-pressure task, but it does require some thinking, since the students have to reflect on everything they have learned and determine which idea or skill or piece of information seems most important to them. You can follow up this exercise using one of the small-group or discussion techniques you should be familiar with by now. In a small class, of twenty or less, you might ask everyone to give their responses briefly aloud; in any size class, you could put students in groups and ask the groups to compare their answers to see if they can agree upon the most important thing the class has learned.

A second pedagogical strategy you might try during the last class period, if you are giving a final exam, is to ask the class to help you construct some questions for the exam. I recommend designing the format of the exam (along the lines discussed in

Chapter 6, drawing up sections and questions that will test and reinforce the learning objectives of the course) before you conduct such a class, and then designating a specific section in which students might help you write some of the questions. For example, if you have an exam which contains three parts—say, multiple choice, short definitions, and essays—you could ask them to write some essay questions, one of which you will choose and put on the exam. Remember, though, that students will be less experienced at designing assignments than you are, so you will need to give them some help. If you want the essay questions to test their abilities both to articulate major concepts and to compare and contrast the concepts from the different units of the course, you will have to explain that, and perhaps even explain what skills or knowledge each part of the exam is designed to test, so they don't duplicate work from elsewhere on the exam (this seems to me like good practice in any event—they should be as informed as possible about the format and purpose of the exam). Or, if one section of the exam will require them to write short definitions for ten out of the twenty terms you covered in the course, ask them to make a list of the three or five or ten terms that have seemed most important to them, with an explanation for their selections. In any case, you should incorporate their work somehow into the exam, so that this doesn't seem like mere busy work; either use one of their questions or ideas, or modify it to fit in with whatever else you are doing. In terms of the structure of this exercise, follow the same procedures you have been using throughout the semester: the students might write a question or two on their own, and then work in groups to propose a set number of questions, or they might go straight to the groups. This exercise definitely deserves discussion, though, since their questions will help you see what has seemed important to them, and you can use the discussion to affirm their perceptions or push them in a different direction (if necessary) before the exam.

- - - - - - - -

And that, my friends, is it. Sometimes I have the energy to give my students a rousing farewell speech, urging them to keep reading and to train their newly honed interpretive skills on the world around them, and sometimes I just say so long and thanks for all the fish, and I'll see them at the final exam, or whenever they turn in their final papers. In either case, I walk slowly back to my office, with tremendous feelings of relief, and sit in the recliner I bought from the Salvation Army in my first year on the tenure track and wonder why, in my thirty-seven years on this planet, I haven't made it to Iceland yet.

In Wayne Booth's *The Vocation of a Teacher,* he asks a question that I'm sure many of us have wondered about: "Why, if I claim to love teaching so much, am I so relieved when it's *over?*"

Amen to that.

You will be very glad it's over, but don't let that make you question your vocation. We're all glad when it's over.

Resources

Booth, Wayne. *The Vocation of a Teacher: Rhetorical Occasions, 1967–1988.* Chicago: University of Chicago Press, 1991.

English professor and literary theorist Wayne Booth philosophizes on teaching and education.

Gibson, Bryan. "Research Methods Jeopardy: A Tool for Involving Students and Organizing the Study Session." *Teaching of Psychology,* 18.3 (1991): 176–177.

An interesting way to conduct a final review session.

Lang, James. "Finishing Strong." *The Chronicle of Higher Education,* 53.9 (December 1, 2006): C2.

A review of some ideas for the final day of the semester.

Uhl, Christopher. "The Last Class." *College Teaching,* 53.4 (2005): 165–166.

This is the article about bell-ringing to commemorate the last day of class.

Teachers as People

You will have noticed—because you're smart!—that I have cheated a bit with the structure here at the end because I had you saying goodbye at the end of the fourteenth week, and you probably will have at least a half of a fifteenth week, if not a full one. But I wanted to reserve this last chapter for a more philosophical issue, one that steps back a little from practical classroom advice but will still engage you during your first months of teaching.

Hark back with me for a moment to that first college class of mine, in my T-shirt and cut-off khakis, teaching composition at 8:30 A.M. to seven sleepy undergraduates. I mocked my choice of dress earlier in the book (for good reason), but of course I chose those clothes deliberately. I wanted to convey to the students that I was a regular guy, just like them, and that while we both were forced by the system into this unequal power relationship, I also lived on campus (my apartment was so small that I could cook while sitting on my bed) and ripped up my khaki pants just like they did.

Eventually I realized that this wasn't really true, and that in fact people weren't ripping up their khakis anymore, and I gravitated toward a more authoritarian attitude in the classroom—one that conveyed that, despite my baby-faced looks, I was in charge around here. Over the next several years, and even into my first year or two on the tenure track, I was still sorting out the person I wanted to be in and around my classroom—wondering how tough I should be as a grader or classroom manager, how I should deal with students I saw around campus, how much of my personal life should be visible to them when I wanted to give examples from real life of abstract concepts. In all of this I was trying to settle on my teaching persona—the person I wanted to be with my students, one that was related to, but distinct from, my persona as a father, or husband, or friend.

It seems to me in retrospect that I wasted lots of time and energy thinking about this issue, but I'm still close enough to it to know that it will occupy some of your time and energy as well, probably a good bit of it in your first semester of teaching. To sound a note from T. S. Eliot's "The Love Song of J. Alfred Prufrock," we prepare a face to meet the faces we greet each day, and the face you prepare for your students will differ from the face you prepare for your spouse or your morning coffees with your best friend. That's not a good or a bad thing. To borrow a popular phrase that I really can't stand, it is what it is.

Jay Parini's *The Art of Teaching,* an autobiographical meditation on three decades of college teaching, offers the most eloquent discussion of this issue I have seen thus far; he compares the construction of a teaching persona to that of finding a writing voice:

> Teachers, like writers, also need to invent and cultivate a voice, one that serves their personal needs as well as the material at hand, one that feels authentic. It should also take into account the nature of the students who are being addressed, their background in the subject and their dispo-

sition as a class, which is not always easy to gauge. It takes
a good deal of time, as well as experimentation, to find this
voice, in teaching as in writing. (58)

Parini's descriptions of his own efforts to find an authentic voice
mirror mine in some ways, and probably will be familiar to many
of us—shuttling between early efforts to be just one of the gang
and subsequent attempts to adopt a more authoritative persona.

What kind of teaching persona you construct probably depends a lot on why you are teaching in the first place. If you are
in the classroom as a necessary evil that enables you to pursue
your research and get paid for it, you are likely to keep your persona an impersonal one; if you are here because you love inspiring young minds, your persona may be a warmer and more open
one. Your persona will also depend on your personality in general, of course—if you are the guy who was in the car behind me
this morning and honked because I didn't turn right on red at an
intersection with a clearly posted "No right turn on red" sign,
eventually your impatient nature will come out in the classroom.

But the part I always wondered most about, and wondered in
secret, was to what extent I should reveal myself, or at least the
other parts of myself, to my students. When I was teaching a
poem about having children, was it OK for me to mention that I
had shared the poet's experience? If I saw something in an episode of *The Simpsons* that related to the course, would it compromise my authority as a teacher if I revealed that I was a devoted
viewer of a cartoon? In other words, how much of my real personality, and my real life, belonged in my teaching persona? You'll
wonder about it, too.

So I'm going to give you two pieces of information on this
subject, neither of which has any real practical consequences—
which is why this chapter is so short, and comes at the end.

First, this issue will become less pressing as each semester of teaching goes by. What eventually happens is that your teaching persona becomes less and less separate from yourself, as you become more comfortable in the classroom. Parker Palmer argues, in *The Courage to Teach,* that successful teaching comes only when we are willing to teach from our inner selves; Elaine Showalter, in *Teaching Literature,* offers a similar distinction between the teaching persona and the true self, and suggests that the classroom deserves as much of our true self as possible. I'll confess to a little bit of discomfort and skepticism about the idea that we have a "true self" buried within us somewhere that we need to carry into the classroom and hold forth in all its shining glory. I prefer to think about it in a different way: the more experience I have as a teacher, the more I am willing to allow other parts of my life, or other faces in my life—father, husband, musician, and so on—to form part of my teaching persona. And I agree with Palmer and Showalter in the sense that as my teaching persona has accepted more of those other parts of me, it has become a more comfortable and effective one.

Over time, you'll fall into a comfort level that determines what you reveal and don't reveal to your students, and then staying on that level will become second nature to you. You're thinking about this issue now because your teaching persona is a new one for you. Whenever we are preparing a face for the first time, we fret over it, whether it is the face we present to potential new in-laws, or our dissertation committee, or a new faculty orientation session. Your teaching face elicits extra fretting at first because the face is one that you may be wearing for the next forty years, and because anywhere from a handful to many hundreds of students will be staring at it for an hour two or three times a week.

So I could tell you just to relax and be yourself, but that won't help you one bit. Just hang on—this one gets better with time.

The second piece of information may help you relax a tiny bit, however, and it comes in the form of a story.

One of the priests I wrote about in the chapter on lecturing, the one who practices the more casual lecture style, told me this story one evening after dinner and drinks at a neighbor's house. In this story he was new to teaching himself, in the seminary, and one of his service responsibilities was to make himself available as a spiritual director—a mentor, in other words—to any seminarian who requested him. As a new teacher, one who wanted to impress his superiors, he wanted to be as welcoming as possible to potential mentees, so he set up a table outside his office with a sign-up sheet for the seminarians—the only faculty member, he noticed, to do so. Weeks went by, and no signatures appeared. He became deeply concerned, afraid that he was teaching so poorly that he had scared all the seminarians away. Finally, sick with worry, he went to the head of the seminary and confessed his concerns, asking why no one had selected him as spiritual director. He laid bare his fears that the seminarians were all talking about what a terrible teacher and priest he was. The seminary head then pointed out to him that the seminarians had been told they were not allowed to select their spiritual directors until a specific date—and that date had not yet arrived.

The seminary head then said something to the priest that he never forgot, and that is worth keeping in mind during your first years of college teaching:

"Just when you think everyone's thinking about you," he said, "it usually turns out that nobody's thinking about you at all."

This humbling bit of wisdom seems to me true in many respects in life, but for our purposes I can assure you of its truth in relation to your students. I'm telling you this not only to help you think more calmly about your teaching persona, but also to comfort you when you make your first real classroom gaffe: tripping over the projector cord, or teaching a class session with your fly open, or belching aloud unexpectedly, or any of the other mishaps that you probably have had a few nightmares about by now (and if you haven't yet, they're coming). In the moment of their happening, such events certainly may provoke your students to laughter, or curiosity, or embarrassment on your behalf. But within thirty minutes of leaving your classroom, as the students become absorbed in someone else's lecture, or are planning their weekend or complaining about the dining hall food with their roommates, you are long gone from their brains. You are one of four or five teachers they have, and one of a myriad of authority figures and adults in their lives—you get a few hours per week in their brains, if you're lucky, when you're standing in front of them. Beyond that, you may not even register when they pass you on campus. I can't tell you how many student advisees I've had, weeks into the semester, who aren't able to tell me the names of the professors they have in their current courses. Scary, but true.

All the agonizing you might do over your teaching persona, then—or over anything else that happens in your classroom that might reflect on your personality—doesn't amount to much in the minds of your students. Let this perspective liberate you as much as it can, when it comes to thinking about your teaching persona, and—I can't seem to help saying it, even though it seems so simplistic—just be yourself.

Resources

Duffy, Donna Killian, and Janet Wright Jones. "Exploring Teaching Styles." In *Teaching within the Rhythms of the Semester*, 1–26. San Francisco: Jossey-Bass, 1995.

Here is a very sensible quote from this chapter of Duffy and Jones's book: "The issue is not to name the [different] styles and then to determine in the abstract which style is the most effective, but rather to become aware of one's own personal style and then to discern ways in which to enhance the effectiveness of that style" (12).

Parini, Jay. *The Art of Teaching*. New York: Oxford University Press, 2005.

More a reflective look at a life of teaching than a practical guidebook, Parini's book is a worthy read nonetheless, especially on the subject of the teaching persona.

Parker, Palmer. *The Courage to Teach*. San Francisco: Jossey-Bass, 1998.

Palmer's work has inspired and renewed lots of teachers whose love of the vocation may have been sagging. Again, this book is light on practical advice, but heavy on inspiration. Despite some new-agey sentiments and language, it's hard to resist Palmer's passion for our calling.

Showalter, Elaine. *Teaching Literature*. London: Blackwell, 2003.

This is an excellent guide, both theoretical and practical, but obviously limited in scope to those who teach literature.

Top Ten Resources

Start with these ten resources for further reading and investigation on teaching in higher education. The first five items are books, placed in the order in which I think they will best help you as a new teacher—i.e., begin with Bain, and move from his work through to Palmer. The same holds true for the next five resources—all websites or periodicals, ordered according to my estimation of their usefulness for new faculty.

1. Bain, Ken. *What the Best College Teachers Do.* Cambridge, Mass.: Harvard University Press, 2004.
2. McKeachie, Wilbert, and Marilla Svinicki. *McKeachie's Teaching Tips: Strategies, Research, and Theory for College and University Teachers,* 12th ed. Boston: Houghton Mifflin, 2006.
3. Gross Davis, Barbara. *Tools for Teaching.* San Francisco: Jossey-Bass, 1993.
4. Duffy, Donna Killian, and Janet Wright Jones. *Teaching within the Rhythms of the Semester.* San Francisco: Jossey-Bass, 1995.
5. Palmer, Parker. *The Courage to Teach.* San Francisco: Jossey-Bass, 1998.

6. The *Careers* pages of *The Chronicle of Higher Education,* available online at *http://chronicle.com/jobs.* Three to five new essays on academic life appear on these pages per week, including my monthly column on teaching, for which I welcome readers' ideas and comments.

7. The Tomorrow's Professor listserv and archive; you can read all previous postings, and subscribe to the listserv, here: *http://sll.stanford.edu/projects/tomprof/newtomprof/index.shtml.*

8. The Center for Teaching Excellence / for Teaching and Learning, or some other variation of those terms, on your campus. If you have one, they will usually have a website with links to other resources, and a library of books and articles on teaching.

9. *College Teaching,* a journal from Heldref publications, contains practical suggestions as well as articles on the state of teaching in higher education.

10. *The National Teaching and Learning Forum,* available in print and online, also mixes the very practical and more reflective aspects of teaching. Visit *http://www.ntlf.com.*

Appendix A
Appendix B
Index

APPENDIX A

- -

A Sample Syllabus

English 375 – Spring 2006   Professor Jim Lang
Contemporary British Novel   Office Address:
MW 2:30–3:45   Office Phone:
                                  Home Phone:
                                  Office Hours: M: 3:45–5:15;
                                  TU/TH 1:30–3:30; W: 9–12,
                                  3:45–5:15
                                  e-mail:

Course Overview

In this course we will read British novels written from the end of
World War II to the present, and analyze four prominent trends
in the fiction of this period. We will begin with two novels that
explore the origins of—and remedy for—evil and violence in the
human condition (*Lord of the Flies* and *The Collector*). British
writers in the decades immediately following the Second World
War were especially interested in this issue, as they struggled to
reconcile traditional notions of what it means to be a human being with the horrors of the war, the experience of the Blitz, and
the events of the Holocaust, as well as with an upsurge of youth
culture and violence in the 1950s and 60s. Next we will consider

an experimental novel by B. S. Johnson, which challenges the boundaries and definition of the traditional novel. Like writers in many countries from the 1950s through the 70s, numerous British writers of this period played with the fictional form. We will move from Johnson to two novels that raise theological questions, and discuss the place of religion in contemporary life (*The End of the Affair* and *Oranges Are Not the Only Fruit*). These works reflect a common intellectual pursuit for British writers and intellectuals in the postwar period: searching for meaning in an increasingly secular world, and wondering whether religion has anything left to offer us in the second half of the twentieth century. Finally, we will close with two works that explore the changing face of contemporary England, one focusing on the role of women and immigrants in an increasingly culturally diverse England (*Brick Lane*), and one on England's complicated relationship with its history and traditions (*England, England*).

All of the novelists we will read are asking fundamental and still-relevant questions about contemporary life: What makes human beings commit acts of violence against one another? How do we find meaning in an increasingly secular world? How are our traditional societies and cultures changing? Throughout the quarter we will keep these fundamental questions at the forefront of our inquiry. We will also ask more specific questions about the social context of postwar Britain. We will look at art, film, and television from the period, and read historical background material. Each student, finally, will work with another student to prepare an oral report on some aspect of contemporary British culture.

Texts

William Golding, *Lord of the Flies*
John Fowles, *The Collector*

B. S. Johnson, *Christie Malry's Own Double-Entry*
Graham Greene, *The End of the Affair*
Jeanette Winterson, *Oranges Are Not the Only Fruit*
Monica Ali, *Brick Lane*
Julian Barnes, *England, England*

Course Promises

This course makes a set of promises to you (assuming you fulfill the expectations below). By the end of the semester, you should be able:

1. To identify and describe in writing four prominent trends in postwar British fiction, and understand the relationship of those trends to postwar British society and culture.
2. To develop your skills in reading analytically and writing formal academic essays.
3. To research, prepare, and deliver an oral report that provides valuable information to your colleagues, and that sparks and holds their interest.
4. To understand and describe literary works as modes of social inquiry—akin to works of philosophy, sociology, history, etc.—which arise from and attempt to account for specific historical contexts and circumstances.

Course Expectations

This course will only fulfill these promises if you promise the following in return:

1. **To attend class.** This course will rely largely on discussion. For this format to succeed, you must be present and on time. You will receive points for participation and at-

tendance in this course. You may miss two classes without penalty. Beginning with your third absence, you will lose 25 points from your final grade total for each subsequent absence. If you miss more than five classes, **you will fail the course.**

2. **To read the assigned materials.** The literature and background material we read will provide us with the common ground upon which we will base our conversations. Without that common ground, our conversations will lose some of their richness. We will have weekly in-class writing exercises to ensure that you are keeping up with the reading, and to help stimulate class discussion.

3. **To be attentive and participate in class.** Participation does not simply mean speaking aloud in class, although that is essential. Students should participate by actively following the discussion, and by contributing to our quarter-long conversation through the insights they present in their papers and projects.

4. **To complete the required assignments in a timely fashion.** The assignments provide you with both informal and formal opportunities to articulate your responses to the issues we'll be discussing. You will get the most out of the course if you turn in your work on time. **Extensions require one full day's advance approval from me.**

Assignments and Evaluations

We will have weekly writing exercises in class, which are designed both to ensure that you are keeping up with the reading, and to stimulate discussion on that day. At least once a week, I will pose a question about the reading at the beginning of class, and ask you to write a paragraph or two in response. These exercises will be graded on a 10-point scale.

You will take a mid-term exam which will ask you to apply the historical background material you will have read to the first four novels of the course, and to draw connections between those four novels.

You will write one brief and one longer analysis of a single novel. The second of these analyses must include the use of one critical source.

You and a partner will research and offer a presentation, during the last week of the semester, on some cultural product of contemporary Britain: a television show, musical group, film, building or architectural trend, or other artistic production.

You will write one final paper, which will be a comparative analysis of two or more novels. This paper will incorporate your independent research on the novel or its cultural and historical contexts, and will require you to use the research and documentation skills that you should have developed in Approaches to Reading and Interpretation.

Weekly Writing Exercises: 150 points
Oral Presentations: 100 points
Mid-Term Exam: 100 points
Brief Analysis Paper: 100 points
Longer Analysis paper: 150 points
Final Paper: 300 points (Annotated Bibliography: 50 points;
    Paper: 250 points)
Attendance and Participation: 100 points

Presentation Topics on Postwar British Culture
Ealing Studios (Film)
Merchant-Ivory (Film)
28 Days Later and *Shaun of the Dead* (Film)
Monty Python (TV Comedy)

Fawlty Towers (TV Comedy)
Ricky Gervais and Stephen Merchant (*The Office* and *Extras*) (TV Comedy)
Coronation Street (TV Soap Opera)
The Kumars at No. 42 St. (TV Comedy)
Gilbert and George (Art)
Francis Bacon and Lucien Freud (Art)
The Reconstruction of the Globe (Architecture)
Prince Charles and Architecture (Architecture)
The Royal Festival Hall (Architecture)
Sex Pistols and Spice Girls (Music)
The Clash and Big Audio Dynamite, I and II (Music)
Football and Manchester United (Sports)

Academic Dishonesty

I expect that all work you produce for the course will be your own. If you plagiarize any material from outside sources for your written work or presentations in this course, or on the final exam, **IT WILL RESULT IN A FAILURE OF THE ENTIRE COURSE.** There are no exceptions to this, and no second chances.

ADA Statement

Assumption College provides accommodations for any student with documented disabilities. If you have a disability and believe you require accommodations, please contact the Dean of Studies Office at 7846 or visit Alumni 026. Please also see your instructor early in the semester so we can make any necessary arrangements.

Weekly Schedule

Week 1
W 1/20: Introduction to Course; Introduction to
Postwar Britain

Week 2
M 1/25: *Lord of the Flies* (Chaps. 1–6); Supplemental Reading:
Critchfield, Bergonzi, Sinfield
W 1/27 *Lord of the Flies* (Chaps. 7–12); Supplemental Reading:
Christopher

Week 3
M 1/30 *The Collector* (3–120)
W 2/1 *The Collector* (123–200)

Week 4
M 2/6 *The Collector* (201–305)
W 2/8 *Double-Entry* (Foreword, Chaps. 1–9)

Week 5
M 2/13 *Double-Entry* (Chaps. 10–finish)
W 2/15 NO CLASS
**Brief analysis paper due on Thursday, 2/16 by 3:00 pm
in my office.**

Week 6
M 2/20 *Affair* (Books 1–2)
W 2/22 *Affair* (Books 3–4)

Week 7
M 2/27 *Affair* (Book 5)
W 3/1 **Mid-Term Exam**

Week 8
Spring Break: NO CLASSES

Week 9
M 3/13 *Oranges* (Genesis, Exodus, Leviticus)
W 3/15 *Oranges* (Numbers, Deuteronomy, Joshua)

Week 10
M 3/20 *Oranges* (Judges, Ruth)
W 3/22 *Brick Lane* (Chaps. 1–4)
Week 11
M 3/27 *Brick Lane* (Chaps. 5–9)
W 3/29 *Brick Lane* (Chaps. 10–13)
Week 12
M 4/3 *Brick Lane* (Chaps. 14–16)
W 4/5 *Brick Lane* (Chaps. 17–21)
Longer analysis paper due on Friday by 3:00 pm in my office.
Week 13
M 4/10 *England, England* (3–89)
W 4/12 *England, England* (89–163)
Week 14
M 4/17 EASTER: NO CLASS
W 4/19 *England, England* (163–175)
Annotated Bibliographies Due
Week 15
M 4/24 Presentations on Contemporary British Culture
W 4/26 Presentations on Contemporary British Culture
Week 16
M 5/1 Final Questions; Course Evaluations
No final exam. The final paper will be due during or before the regularly scheduled final exam period for the course.

Student Participation Evaluation Form

SPA 140.01 Introduction to Literature in Spanish
Professor Maryanne L. Leone
Assumption College

Evaluation of my class participation   **Name:** _____

Participation will be evaluated in three aspects: Preparation for Class, Group Interaction, and Whole Class Interaction. You may earn 10 points in each category, for a maximum total of 30 points per week.

Criteria	Points
Preparation for Class	
I read carefully, look up unfamiliar vocabulary, and make annotations in my text. I review my notes from prior classes and make connections. I develop my own ideas about the text.	10
I read the texts, look up unfamiliar vocabulary, and prepare activities.	9
I read the texts.	8
I did not read all of the required texts.	6

Criteria	Points
Interaction: Group Work	
I am engaged and take a leadership role every day.	10
I am usually engaged and contribute as much as others.	8.5
I am interested, but I contribute more passively than actively.	7
I sometimes get off topic and/or I do not contribute as much as others.	6
Interaction: Whole Class Work	
I contribute my *own* ideas and respond to my peers *and* the instructor's comments on a daily basis.	10
I participate and listen to the instructor and others on most days.	8.5
I participate occasionally, but I am interested.	7
I do not usually participate in class discussions.	6

Date	Preparation	Group Work	Class Work	Total	Your Comments	Instructor's Comments
22–26 enero						
29 enero–2 feb.						
5–7 feb.						
12–16 feb.						
19–23 feb.						
26 feb.–2 mar.						
12–16 mar.						
19–23 mar.						
26–30 mar.						
2–4 abr.						
11–13 abr.						
16–20 abr.						
23–27 abr.						

Index